# Bound to Love
### a memoir of grit and gratitude

## Skye Blaine

*Bound to Love* is a work of nonfiction. Most names have been changed.

Copyright © 2016 Skye Blaine

All rights reserved. No part of this publication may be reproduced or transmitted in any form or by any means, electronic, mechanical, magnetic, photographic including photocopying, recording or by any information storage and retrieval system, without prior written permission of the publisher. No patent liability is assumed with respect to the use of the information contained herein. Although every precaution has been taken in the preparation of this book, the publisher and author assume no responsibility for errors or omissions. Neither is any liability assumed for damages resulting from the use of the information contained herein.

First printing: October 2015

ISBN: 978-0-9779483-5-2

Author's websites and contact information:
    www.skyeblaine.com
    www.theheartofthematter-dailyreminders.org
    skye@skyeblaine.com

Published by:
    Berkana Publications
    Sebastopol CA 95472
    USA

Book layout and cover design by Berkana Publications

Printed in the United States of America

To Boudewijn, my partner and husband of twenty-six years, who has demonstrated patience, generosity, and kindness throughout this process. I began the memoir in 1992 and quickly discovered I knew nothing about writing. A long learning process ensued, culminating in my earning an MFA in creative writing in 2003. I'm not sure he believed the book would ever get finished! Still, he supported me at every turn, and has read the manuscript more times than anyone should have to.

And to Thom, my bright, complicated, precious son. I'm still asking for miracles.

# Acknowledgements

Back cover blurbs: Kathleen LaMar and Lynette Chandler

Katie Watts: for her encouragement and final, thorough edit

Diane Nelson: for her professional eye on the cover

Patricia Evans: who intuited the title during lunch at a writing conference

My beta readers: Jennifer Anderman, Brian Lowe, Maya Balenz, Barbara Green, Maria Krahn, Lynn Woodward, Miriam Louisa Simons, and Hawk

The Sebastopol Friday Memoir Group and its fearless leader, Steve Boga

Big Rig critique group in Sonoma County, CA: Patrice Garrett, Marie Judson-Rosier, Laura McHale Holland

Antioch MFA writing program mentors: Brian Bouldrey, Susan Taylor Chehak

Robert Hill Long, who encouraged me to go to graduate school

Patty Hyatt for the first, formal edit, and for her friendship

The Harpies critique group in Eugene, Oregon: Patty Hyatt, Kris Landon, Candy Davis, Karen Keady

Elizabeth Lyon, my first writing teacher

WriteLab: an online writing/critiquing program which is no longer available, but provided a solid base on which to build

And my dear son Thom: without him, there would be no book

I'm sure I've missed some kind soul who assisted me along the way. Contact me, and in the next printing, I'll happily make the correction.

∞

Memory is both fragile and humbling; the people in this memoir probably remember events differently.

I have undergone rigorous self-examination to recall and recount what took place decades ago.

To honor privacy most names have been changed.

## Chapter One

I did not get the child I dreamed of—the physically perfect child, the model child of every parent's dream. As a mother, to write these words makes me a heretic—mothers aren't supposed to feel this way, and if we do, we certainly aren't encouraged to voice it. It's a secret that mothers keep. I only recently had this conversation with my son, Thom; it took me thirty-plus years to admit these feelings even to myself. It's good that Thom is blessed with a wicked sense of humor, because he chuckled and said, "M-M-Mom, I-I didn't get what I wanted either."

He got a body that has given him struggle, pain, and disappointment. I noticed recently that my son's hairline has receded a bit at the temples, and was stunned afresh that four decades have passed since his birth. Those years often seemed like the highest mountain range, impossible to traverse with the skills I had in the face of the powerful challenges that confronted us. I scrambled to discover what new expertise was required, and to pocket it as fast as I could. I worried whether my faith in a positive outcome would be robust enough to sustain me; and if it were not, I doubted we could thrive on the strength of our bond alone.

Forty-one years ago, in May 1974, alone and single, I lay on my waterbed in a sunlit home I had rented in Mill Valley, California. Even renting was uncertain, but I plunked down the hard-earned cash anyway. My hands cupped my domed belly. I whispered, "Please, let my child be healthy." Although I could not have named who I whispered to, I can still taste the intention, the yearning—perhaps even desperation—behind those words. My future as an unwed mother loomed, overwhelming. To have any hope of succeeding, I needed each step to unfold easily, beginning with a sturdy baby.

"Please let my child be healthy"—I invented this, my first conscious, spoken prayer. Prayers weren't welcome in my family; in fact, they were implicitly forbidden. No child would have dared, not in the face of my implacably atheist father, nor my mother who always stood in support of him. They were an unmovable pole in our lives. My parents talked in kindly but patronizing tones behind their church-going friends' backs. They saw their faith as weakness.

In hindsight, for a prayer to be driven from my lips, my intuition must have already known that my unborn child—a child with whom I have formed such a strong bond—would grapple with confounding challenges to his body and his spirit. When I surrendered to the monumental task of parenting him, I shouldered his obstacles as my own.

This is how, as a mother, I wrestled with the unique difficulties of raising a disabled child, and how I birthed the strength, courage, and grit to meet those challenges.

## Home—January, 1974

"You can't bear children," the specialist had said eighteen months before.

"What?" I gawked at him; surely he didn't mean this—I had always assumed I would have kids one day. An empty space cracked open, new and raw, inside me.

"Endometriosis. It clogged the Fallopian tubes, caused those painful cysts you complain about." He stuffed his hands in his white jacket, and stared down at me, still straddled in the stirrups. "Zero chance of kids." Tight smile and raised eyebrows—he seemed pleased with his pronouncement.

His glance slid over the faded cutoffs and tie-dye T-shirt I had tossed on a chair in the corner, dismissed them as he had dismissed me. Even the rough way he had handled the exam conveyed his contempt. I didn't know why. Perhaps he saw me as an irresponsible hippie; in his eyes, I did not deserve to procreate. I pulled my feet free from the chill metal, rolled on my side away from his gaze that seared and blamed at the same time, and huddled on the hard vinyl table. I felt humiliated. Neutered. I yearned for a compassionate follow-up comment.

"Get dressed." He stalked out of the room.

For weeks I wandered through the tasks of my life in a daze. I didn't know how to grasp, or work with, this new picture of my life. Every woman I knew in my mother's generation had children. I hadn't considered an alternative. It had simply been a given that someday, I would marry and have a family.

The following summer, based on the finality of his "zero chance," I chucked my diaphragm and birth control pills into the trash.

A sharp nugget of a dream startled me awake; a baby's name, I knew that much—emblazoned heart-red on a banner chugging through the sky behind a one-motor plane. Even in the midst of the dream I knew a baby could not possibly be true.

Plane and banner sputtered by again, closer this time, then froze in midair in front of me. I awakened on my back muttering "not fair," flailing my head to rid images of motherhood dashed by that doctor a year and a half ago. Willing away the tendrils of the dream, I gulped frigid air. Where was I? I rolled my head toward the light and squinted at the glare. Snow. Not California. As the dream faded, reality returned. This was the guest bedroom in my parents' new home. Cincinnati in January.

I folded my arms over my chest to ease the grief of the impossible dream. Pulsing pain shocked me fully awake. My breasts felt hard, like—like what? Like a distended cow's udder, a cow long overdue for milking. Ignoring the cold, I shot into a sitting position and looked down at my chest. Even through my pajamas I saw the swollen outline of my breasts. I cupped my hands around them. Full. Tender. Throbbing. I turned and lifted the pillow, pressed my face into the cold fabric to stem a thick wave of nausea. Pregnant. I must be pregnant. Good God, no. Yes! Wry laughter spit out of me.

A visitor in my parents' home—twenty-nine years old, single, and pregnant. This wasn't how life was supposed to unfold, not in my family. I had heard my mother say "black sheep" about other people often enough to know I would pay a family price for believing the doctor's faulty pronouncement—still, I was gleeful he had been wrong. I preferred this unplanned-for outcome to the childless, barren plain he had predicted.

What a tangled mess. Somehow, I would have to find the courage to get us through. I rested my hands on my stomach, gazed out the window, contemplated the large, wet flakes that lazed toward the ground. Original grace could cause huge chaos.

## Birth Day—August 3, 1974

Events rolled like tumbleweeds in a rising wind. I finished my last day of bookkeeping at the Rainbow Bridge Bookstore on Friday, August 2, 1974 and drove home, looking forward to an empty calendar for five weeks—plenty of time to prepare for the birth of my child. That evening, my partner of one month, Ray, and I drove with a group of friends to a choir concert in San Francisco. Soon after intermission, waves of nausea rolled through me. I felt weighed down. Was I getting the stomach flu? I thought about leaving, but couldn't bear ruining the evening for my friends who had driven us. I shifted from side to side, trying to find any comfortable position. Shift. Breathe. Shift. Breathe.

"Your hand is so clammy," Ray whispered. "Are you okay?"

"I feel crummy," I said. "We need to go straight home after the concert. No stopping for a snack." Let the cramps be the Chinese take-out I ate for dinner, I thought. No more complications.

I clawed my way into bed around eleven-thirty and pulled the covers snug. Alternately I flushed hot and cold. When chills came, Ray snuggled close around me.

Around 3 a.m., as I trudged to the bathroom, water trickled down my leg. Startled, I turned on the light. When I looked closer, I saw pink streaks. Blood. Good Lord, I thought, I'm in labor. No. Not this! My sister had lost two babies in her eighth month, and now this baby was trying to come five weeks early. "Ray! Call Dr. McLean," I hollered. Sick at heart, I hugged the sink.

"Come to my office right now," my kindly obstetrician told him. "I'll check her there."

Perhaps it was the shock of seeing the blood. A crushing force overtook me and tried to expel my baby. I couldn't figure out what my body was doing. Certainly this must be the beginning of labor, not the end. Fright sliced through me like a hot sword, but my teeth chattered. "Get the car, will you? I'll throw on my robe."

Ray nodded and took off. I hobbled to the front door, supporting my belly with my hands and breathing with the contractions.

His face scrunched with worry, Ray drove me the excruciating mile to the office. Dr. McLean had barely begun the exam when another huge pushing contraction shook my frame.

"Do not push! Pant! You're fully dilated. Too late to stop this birth. Marin General, now!"

I blew out breaths and waited for the contraction to abate. "I'm not moving," I said, through gritted teeth. "Here! This baby will be born right here."

"Not with all the complications you've had. Follow me." He made a brief call ordering the admitting desk not to delay us. Ray drove at eighty miles an hour. Even while I panted, my mind whirled: my baby could die, just like my sister's had. No. Not that. Another prayer erupted in my mind. Please, make this okay.

Thank heavens it was pre-dawn—the streets were empty of traffic and no policeman clocked us. We squealed into the emergency room driveway where we abandoned the car. I was ushered into a wheelchair and whooshed directly to the delivery room. Thirty minutes later, with an ear-splitting wail of indignation, my baby rode out of my body on a gush of my blood.

The nurse handed Dr. McLean a sterile towel which he wrapped around my squalling infant. "A boy. Thomas, you said?" Before I could respond, a crash startled us. We turned to see the wheeled tray of instruments spin across the room, as an unconscious Ray sank to the floor. Dr. McLean barked, "Get him up!" to the nurse and grabbed surgical scissors. Instead of my newborn being settled into my arms, the cord that connected us was severed with an abrupt snip. To my dismay, the doctor plunked him into the bassinet. I had dreamed of holding my baby at birth, slippery and wet with my fluids, against my bare, warm skin. Now, I would never have that chance. Frustrated, I watched the team scramble to get Ray into a chair. All alone in the bassinet, Thomas squinted and blinked, a smear of my blood on the crown of his head. I caught the scent of iron in the room. I felt powerless. Yet mixed in, and confusing, love flushed through me for everyone in the room.

I turned away from the chaos around Ray and peered more closely at Thomas, at the thatch of dark hair that stuck up on his head as though it had been gelled. My son. The words tasted strange on my tongue, but they tugged at me, too. How wrinkled and helpless he seemed, and he was my full responsibility. I'm his mother, I thought. I'm supposed to know how to do this. But I didn't have a clue.

## Heartbreak—August 4, 1974

Standing at the window of my room at Marin General, I stared through the summer haze toward the rounded humps of Mt. Tamalpais. Pressing my palms down on the sun-warmed wood to steady myself, I waited for Ray to arrive. Before Thomas could be released, the hospital required our pediatrician to evaluate him. This was taking an awfully long time. Why hadn't the nurse brought him back to me?

I yearned for the familiar, I craved the known, but instead, my hands trembled with rushes of doubt that began in my belly and swarmed through my body.

Turning to gather Thomas's few belongings, I picked up an ivory and silver teething ring my mother had sent—it was three generations old, and had been mine as an infant—a yellow musical teddy bear, and a tiny, hand-me-down lapis-blue hooded robe patched like a wizard's cloak. I fingered the velvet and tried to picture dressing him in the robe, then cupped my deflated belly where he had been just one day before. The strangeness, the mystery.

A thin man with wiry black hair and a stethoscope slung around his neck strode into the room, introduced himself as Dr. Liebermann, and shook my hand.

"Where's my son?"

"It won't be long."

My belly cramped in response to his sober expression. Thomas's early birth had preempted our scheduled introductory appointment, so we took measure of each other for a long moment. Radiating vitality, he seemed intelligent and curious, and he looked directly at me. "Good and bad news both," he said.

My ears started to buzz.

"Thomas's heartbeat sounds off." He let his words hang, and kept his attention on my face. "Dr. Lindstow, the cardiologist, is examining him—he thinks Thomas has a hole between his ventricles."

The sunlit room took on a jaundiced light. My hand sprang to the metal frame of the bed, and I leaned against the bar for support. Oh God, I underwent surgery while I was pregnant to remove a huge ovarian cyst. Perhaps that had harmed Thomas. I couldn't seem to grab a full breath of air.

"Preemie heart sounds can normalize. Go ahead and take him home, but I want to see him in two days. Then I'll listen to his chest and we'll know one way or the other."

I pressed my fingers on my eyes to hold back tears. My body begged to fold into itself. One day, and I already cared so much. Dr. Liebermann stepped forward and wrapped his arms around me. I wept on his chest, soaking the front of his blue Oxford cloth shirt.

He waited until my sobs had quieted. "I know you're scared. Call me night or day. I'll sign his release papers now."

As he left the room, I collapsed into the vinyl armchair. I wanted my old life back, where my only responsibility was caring for myself. But that life was gone. A new crazy quilt lay in front of me, and I didn't understand how to piece it together.

Twenty minutes later, a nurse bustled into the room pushing a bassinet, cooed at the baby inside, and left. I nervously wiped my hands on my now-loose maternity jeans, tiptoed close, peered down at the bundled infant. His dark hair sprouted upward—cowlicks or just untamed, I couldn't tell which. He made little sucking sounds. With one finger, I stroked the black strands. He pressed his tiny lips together. I shook my head, amazed. He didn't look like me. I had the urge to glance at his wristband, but I had been fully awake at his birth; I had seen that hair. This *was* my baby. We were inextricably bound together. I had sung lullabies to him even before my belly swelled, well before he had kicked in response. My own blood kin. I could feel the weight of our future bending me to its will.

Gingerly, I reached into the bassinet for him—tried to cradle him properly against my shoulder and support his head—all without squeezing too hard. I breathed in the milky scent at the back of his neck. His legs shot straight out; he clearly didn't feel safe, so I eased him into the crook of my arm. His eyelids flew up, and he squinted at the light in the room. "It's okay," I whispered. "We'll be okay. We'll figure this out." We have to, one way or another, I thought. I had gotten pregnant; I had brought this on myself.

I laid Thomas down on the bed and carefully unwrapped the hospital baby blanket. The nurse had dressed him in a little white T-shirt and disposable diaper. When the cooler air of the room hit him, he squealed in shock and his arms startled open. Murmuring what I hoped were soothing sounds that would not communicate my uneasiness, I unbuttoned the collar of the velvet cloak and eased it over his head. He puckered his mouth, then opened it into a huge O and screamed in protest. I pulled my hands away from him. What had I done? I pressed on, trying to corral his arms into the sleeves of the cloak, without success. My hands got clammier. His screams turned into screeches.

The nurse stuck her head back in the room and smiled at me. "Need help?"

I nodded, and stepped back, wrapping my arms around my body to comfort myself in the face of all this unfamiliarity. As soon as the nurse took over, Thomas quieted. "They sense your nervousness, and then they get anxious, too." She slipped his arms easily into the sleeves. "You'll get the hang of it."

I had heard that at least six times in the last twenty-four hours, and wondered when, exactly, I would get the hang of it.

She smoothed the cloak over his feet, buttoned the collar, and set him in my arms. "There you go." She turned to leave, but then swung around at the door to add, "I think I saw your husband down the hall."

Ray was not my husband, but I didn't bother to straighten out the misunderstanding with a stranger. We had met when I was seven months pregnant, just four weeks before Thomas's premature birth. He had answered a rental ad for a room in our communal household. Over the phone, his voice had a lilt to it. I was immediately drawn to him.

"Do you have any other space, like a shed in the back? I'm a potter, and I'd love to set up my wheel," he said.

I thought for a moment. "We do, and no one is using it. That would be great. Why don't you come meet the roomies, see if we all hit it off?" I was interested in having Ray as a housemate; an artist would be a nice addition.

When he first walked in, I noticed how filled with light he seemed. He was about five feet ten, with clean, sun-bleached blond ringlets almost to his shoulders, and a friendly smile. He had just spent six months living in the country, meditating every day. He knew a lot about a wide variety of subjects, and told us he read voraciously. Everyone agreed Ray seemed like a good fit, and he moved in within a couple of days. The spark of friendship and connection flowered rapidly between us, and we became lovers. When I asked him to participate in the birth, he agreed.

Ray cracked open the door and peered in. He had pulled his abundant, soft curls back into a severe ponytail. I beckoned him into the room. "Do you want to hold Thomas?" I asked. He chewed his lip and nodded, so I set Thomas carefully into his arms. Ray immediately went stiff. "Rock him," I suggested.

They did not look like father and son. Ray tried out an awkward rocking motion.

"The pediatrician stopped by."

His eyebrows flew up as he glanced at me. "What did he say?"

"He had scary news."

His face dropped into a concerned frown, and he folded the edge of the blanket back so that he could see Thomas better.

"The doctor said he has a serious congenital defect in his heart." Again I could not hold back, and hot tears poured like a sudden squall.

Ray couldn't put an arm around me because he was holding Thomas, so he moved closer. "He's big enough, isn't he?"

I didn't understand what his size had to do with it. "He's under five pounds. Good-sized for a preemie, though."

"But he seems strong. This can't be."

I reached to take my son back. I needed him. "I hope you're right." But I doubted the doctor would have worried me if he were not confident in the diagnosis.

An orderly arrived with a wheelchair, and settled me in it—the required method to leave the hospital. The four of us made our way to the elevator. A well-coiffed woman in a silk suit rode down with us and turned to stare at Thomas several times. "You're not taking that baby home, are you?" she finally asked.

"Yes, I am," and added quickly, "His doctor just gave us permission." I snuggled Thomas closer, protecting him from her gaze. Ray didn't seem to notice—he was caught in the maze of his own thoughts.

"My heavens, that baby looks much too small to go home," she said.

I had been away from home less than a day, but as I walked down the hallway toward our two rooms, it felt unfamiliar, even foreign. I laid Thomas down. The changing area I had set up in a nook between the rooms wasn't at the right height—I had to hunch over, and the cream and baby powder were an uncomfortable reach. I hadn't grasped until this moment that my hand had to remain on him every second he lay on the table.

I tried to dress him again. Thomas's arms and legs flailed in four different directions. How had the nurse so skillfully completed this task? In my mind, I walked through the steps she had taken, mimicked her actions, and smiled when his tiny hands stuck out of their minuscule cuffs. The sky-blue stretch terry—a Dr. Denton-style sleeper and the only new piece of clothing he had—must have been designed for an eight-pound baby. He only filled up half of it. In consternation, I tied the legs of the sleeper, the excess fabric, into a knot.

I picked him up to soothe him. Screaming, he arched his back and almost leapt out of my arms. What a strong wail for such a little body! The books I read on early childhood development had drawn a very different picture. This baby had no plumpness and certainly wasn't mellow. I dropped into the rocking chair to nestle him close, hoping to soothe my raw nerves too. Much to my surprise, his screams subsided. I stared at my skinny boy with his shock of ebony hair. His large, wise eyes stared back. Then he raised his eyebrows, and rows of little lines creased his forehead. A ninety-year-old face appeared on my one-day-old infant. I blew out a long breath. He had survived so much already. Both of us had.

It had only been five months since I had undergone major surgery. By the time I was eight weeks pregnant, an ovarian cyst, catalyzed by the flush of hormones, grew to the size of a cantaloupe. Dr. McLean worried the cyst might burst in late pregnancy and threaten both my life and the life of my baby. Surgery was inevitable, he said, but he did suggest I wait until I was three months pregnant before having the cyst removed. By then, the basic organs of the fetus would be laid down, making the operation safer. I agreed.

In March, just prior to the surgery, Mom came out to stay so she could help me afterward. The day before I was to enter the hospital, I woke in a cold sweat, doubled over with stabbing abdominal pain. Dr. McLean hesitated to operate while I was so sick, but went ahead on my insistence. When he opened me up, he confronted a full-blown case of peritonitis, infection spread throughout my abdominal cavity. He removed both infected ovaries in order to save my life. Later, my mother reported his words after he came out of the operating room to speak with her: "Your daughter was a mess inside." It took two transfusions and massive intravenous antibiotics to stabilize me. The infection reoccurred a few weeks later, and I ended up in the hospital a second time. When it was all over, I was five and a half months pregnant and weighed only 105 pounds—a stick with a bump in front.

Now that Thomas was safely here—the only baby I could ever bear—I wondered if life would ever settle into a familiar, stable rhythm.

During our first day and a half at home, Thomas nursed, fussed, waved his arms, cooed and fussed some more. I grabbed sleep during his fitful naps. I had set up a little rocking bassinet by my waterbed, but no matter what I did to soothe him, night or day, he did not sleep longer than a couple of hours at a time. I had never experienced pervasive exhaustion; even all-nighters at college had not been like this. At first, Ray tried to help out in the early mornings. He tromped back to bed, awakening me, and thrust Thomas into my arms with more force than necessary. "Take him! I can't stop his crying." This was an abrupt change from his mellow attitude when he first moved in.

Night and day, Thomas seemed so vibrant and alert. Surely he would disprove the original diagnosis. But at my son's three-day checkup, Dr. Liebermann confirmed the cardiologist's suspicion. He explained the condition was called Tetralogy of Fallot—four structural malformations of the heart, including a pea-sized hole in the wall dividing the two lower ventricles. He passed me the stethoscope so I could hear the sound of my son's heartbeat. "Listen."

I pressed the stethoscope against his chest which was no larger than the palm of my hand. I closed my eyes to focus. The pea-sized hole I had been told about sounded gigantic. Where was the comforting lub-dub, lub-dub? I heard lub-swush, lub-swush instead, the wet sound of his blood sluicing through the hole. A hollow sensation opened in my chest. Neither my nurturing nor my love could cure this. A miracle could, perhaps the doctors could, but Thomas and I were outsiders in his cure. An imagined view of our future flattened in front of me. Unsure. Gray. I slowly passed the stethoscope to Ray, then crumpled my fist against my chest.

Ray's body went still as he focused on the sound for a few moments. When he looked up, we glanced at each other, then our gazes—in tandem—moved first to Thomas, then to the pediatrician. Dr. Liebermann picked up the telephone and made an appointment with the cardiologist in San Francisco for the next morning. I peeked at Ray again. My life had taken an abrupt, daunting turn. My life, not his. This might be too much; this might frighten him away. Then I would be completely alone with my threatened child. That thought terrified me as much as the serious nature of my son's diagnosis.

"By the way," Dr. Liebermann said, as I stood waiting to make the next appointment, "You should contact Crippled Children's Services."

"Crippled?" I echoed his word softly.

He shook his head. "They're changing the name. California Children's Services. Same initials—CCS." He jotted the name down on a prescription pad. "You'll face expensive cardiac procedures, and they can help with Thomas's medical bills. I'd go through their qualification process now." He touched my shoulder. "And I suggest you start giving blood. Ask your family, too. Get to know the Irwin Memorial Blood Bank."

"The blood bank." I must have looked stricken, because he stepped closer and caught my eye before he spoke again.

"It's hard to think about, but down the road, Thomas will probably require open heart surgery. Good to prepare ahead of time."

My heart thudded like hooves at the final turn on a race track. I wondered if I deserved this—I had smoked pot twice during the holidays before I realized I was pregnant. My mind kept repeating *This can't be happening.* Too much information, way too fast.

My feet felt like boulders as we headed toward the parking lot. Ray walked beside me, seemingly lost in his inner world. After two days, my reprieve—where I could pretend all would work out—had shattered into worry. Bewildered and weighed down by the unknown, I hugged my tiny son close to my body, felt his warmth, and sucked in his infant smell.

A day later, my sister Maggie arrived from Ohio to give me a much-needed hand. She offered to drive me to the blood bank. I wrestled my squalling child into a car seat—the smallest size I could find—but I still had to pad it with pillows so he wouldn't slip out. Neither

Ray nor I had the same blood type as Thomas, but we were told we could build up credits in the general fund.

"This is something you can do," Maggie said. "I imagine you're feeling darn powerless about now." Words sticking in my throat, I just nodded.

We found Irwin Memorial in San Rafael. Maggie helped me wriggle Thomas into the soft front pack, strapped him onto my body, and we entered the air-conditioned building. After I filled out the forms, the nurse wrapped the blood pressure cuff around my arm and puffed it up. As she watched the dial pulse downward, she slowly shook her head. "I'm afraid you can't donate."

"What do you mean?" I tried to keep my tone calm, but my fisted hands quivered as I spoke. I couldn't be locked out from this contribution.

"Your pressure is ninety over sixty—too low. You might faint if you donate. We can't take that risk."

"But I have to! For my son." I blinked my eyes fast to keep from tearing up.

The attendant glanced at my premature baby snuggled next to my chest, then peered closer. Finally she gave a slow nod. "Well," she said, pointing to a table in the corner. "Eat a cookie from the tray, drink a cup of coffee, and take a brisk walk. That might just do the trick. If you can get your pressure over 100—"

"Yes! Okay." Action I could take. It took two cups of their burned instant coffee, two stale chocolate chip cookies, and three stiff walks around the tree-lined block before my blood pressure rose enough for them to accept me.

Relieved at the nurse's change of heart, I gratefully handed Thomas over to Maggie, walked into the donation room, and lay down on a vinyl recliner. I'd better get used to this, I thought. As the nurse prepped my arm to put in the needle, I focused away from the pinching elastic and thought about the events that led me here.

Five months before, Mom had spent long days sitting by my bedside at Marin General Hospital after the surgery. When I was finally moved from isolation to a regular room, Thomas's biological father, Riccardo, came to visit. Mom had plumped my pillow; she sat reading near my bed with her hand on my arm—dressed, as she often was, in a tidy turquoise suit with a silk blouse, stockings, and demure heels. I had not expected Riccardo; we had never been a real couple, only involved for six weeks. He paced with his thumbs hooked into the pockets of his threadbare blue jeans. His dark eyes darted from corner to corner, avoiding both me and my mother. Mom never spoke to him. She acted as though he had never walked into the room.

Finally he eased closer and touched my foot. "You're okay, right?"

"Getting there."

He stared at me for a moment. "You look awful."

"Awful pale, you mean. I'll be okay. It'll take some time—I lost a lot of blood."

He nodded. "Take care of yourself." Then dipping his head toward my mother, he ducked out of the room. Mom rose out of the chair and squinted as she watched him lope down the corridor. I leaned forward to see as well. His wiry, walnut-brown, Afro-style hair bounced making him seem even taller than he was. She turned to me, hands on hips, eyebrows raised, and asked, "Before conceiving this child, did you give any thought at all to the gene pool?"

My face flushed hot. Even if she had known him, she would never see his proud stature or his bright mind; that would require looking past his hippie clothes and New Jersey accent. "You know this pregnancy was unplanned." I kept my tone even—we didn't raise voices in our family. "I was told I could never get pregnant." But shame swept through me at my own stupidity. I should not have trusted the doctor and thrown away my birth control pills. I had never intended to have a child with Riccardo; he was a rebound affair. My carelessness had brought me here. I rolled over and shut my eyes, too profoundly tired to say one more word.

I thought that day Mom had intentionally humiliated me. Now I understand she wanted to "knock some sense into me," force me to see I had chosen someone who was, in her eyes, "not our kind." She was desperate to hang on to what she felt sliding away—an appropriate daughter who would walk in polished pumps, wear white gloves, and keep up appearances at all costs. Of course she wanted that for me; she knew nothing else. She must have been terrified and troubled by the path she perceived I was taking. She needn't have worried about Riccardo being on that path with me; I never saw him again.

Thomas's rising peeps yanked my attention back to the blood bank. I glanced toward Maggie. She ambled around the waiting room, murmuring and rhythmically rocking Thomas. Back home, she was raising three children of her own; she could manage my baby just fine. In our mother's eyes, my sister had married "the right kind," a businessman who wore a suit and went to an office every day. But I knew that choosing a similar path to Mom's had not made Maggie's life any easier. It had not inoculated her life against difficulty.

I turned back to watch my blood drain into the bag, drop by hopeful, precious drop.

## Intercession—September 5, 1974

One morning, when Thomas was five weeks old, he seemed wan—almost translucent. The signs were subtle, but something was wrong. Just to make sure, I carried him to the window to peer at him in the natural morning light. His color really was washed out, and he didn't seem as alert. He had coughed a few times while I nursed him. This was new. I sighed; we seemed to end up at the doctor's every other day. I cuddled him close to my chest and searched for Ray, who was putting his tools away in the pottery shed.

"I can't point to anything; he just isn't right," I said.

"Could be your mama's intuition," Ray said, smoothing Thomas's cowlick. "I'm leaving for a class, but phone the doctor if you're worried."

I watched as he drove off. Sometimes he acted like Thomas's dad—concerned, involved—other times he seemed carefree, not feeling the worry I shouldered every moment. He had stroked Thomas in that fatherly way, smoothing his fuzzy hair. I didn't understand how he could just take off for school. Yet concerns for this baby's health had thrust us closer together than we might otherwise have been. Riccardo had walked away from this baby; I didn't know Ray well enough to grasp what he might do. Loneliness, confusion, and resentment gathered around me as I headed for the telephone.

Dr. Liebermann was out of town, but the nurse put me through to the physician on call, a woman I had never met. I let Dr. Smithe know about his heart anomalies, and described how different Thomas seemed from the day before.

"Bring him in right away," she said.

I grabbed a diaper and blanket in my free arm and headed for the car. Fifteen minutes later, the nurse ushered us into an examining room. I picked up the faint scent of diaper rash cream. It didn't comfort me. Dr. Smithe came in promptly and listened to Thomas's heart, moving the stethoscope from his back, to his side, to his chest, then returning to places where she had been before, attending ever more carefully. Her face seemed to grow more cautious as well. She queried me about his cough—what did it sound like, how often did it occur?

Finally she straightened up, re-snapped his sleeper, and handed him to me. "I'm afraid this is congestive heart failure," she said. "Quite serious. Life-threatening."

Profound fear and a dash of relief flashed through me—fear for my son and the treacherous time ahead, relief that my intuition had been right. Given enough time, maybe I could learn to be a competent, comfortable mother.

"I want him seen by a specialist today," she said. Even though Thomas had a routine appointment with the pediatric cardiologist the next morning, she called him to set up an immediate visit.

"You caught this early," she added, as she ushered us out. "Nice work."

"So this really is serious."

"Oh my, yes. I'm sure you're worried sick, but he will be in good hands."

I needed to be in good hands, too. Numb, I called Ray and went to pick him up. As soon as I saw him, I knew I couldn't trust him to drive the forty minutes to the city. I had seen him translate his own worries into rage at other drivers. I kept the wheel. My heart pounding, my body swirling with adrenalin, we rode in silence. My internal questions felt so huge I did not know how to broach them—questions not only about Thomas and his heart problems, but about our future as a couple. We had known each other only nine weeks. In the four weeks before Thomas was born it seemed premature to talk about Ray's role, and the month since his birth had been a wild ride of escalating bad news. We had never discussed whether Ray would actually parent this baby or not.

I was terrified that if I raised questions, the very magnitude of those questions would drive us apart. I avoided that outcome at all costs, afraid to shoulder all the responsibility for my son without a partner.

Thomas, exhausted from crying, and oblivious of the strain between the two people in the front seat, nodded off in his car seat.

Relieved that he had stopped squalling, I focused on getting us through traffic.

Moffitt Hospital crowns Parnassus Street. It is easy to find, but inside, the hallways are a maze. The ammonia from the freshly mopped floor made my nose smart. Before we could see the cardiologist, we were sent for an electrocardiogram on the second floor and a chest X-ray on the third. We wandered the warren of the hospital complex, shiny linoleum floors reflecting cool banks of fluorescent lights. I felt as if we wandered a hall of mirrors, and what was reflected back seemed impersonal, too sterile. I wondered how this spiritless place could heal anyone.

A young X-ray technician took Thomas from my arms. I was sure he wasn't old enough to be a parent himself. He directed us to sit on a wooden bench in the hallway. "He'll be fine," he said.

For the next forty minutes, I listened to my tiny son scream—first with indignation and rage, then abject terror, his howls ending in long, hiccupping quavers. I tapped on the door, but the technician called for me to stay outside. "You'll just make it worse," he said.

I wanted to fly into the room, but stood frozen, my head and fists pressed against the cool surface of the closed metal door. I wept and Ray paced; we were unable to console each other. Ray whirled and pounded the wall next to the bench, then hunched over, cupping his hands into his armpits. I was already battered by my son's screams; I couldn't deal with Ray's loss of control. I huddled on the bench, frightened. Finally, the technician returned Thomas to my arms, his face swollen and blotchy from crying, his breaths still coming in little infant shudders.

As I curled him to my breast, I snarled at the technician, "Show me what you did." He signaled me into the room, and I snuggled the blanket around Thomas as I rose to follow him. My baby had been stripped to his diaper and propped on a tiny plastic saddle. The attendants had stretched Thomas's arms above his head and tightened a form-fitting hard plastic tube around his chest and arms. He remained squeezed in that tube with his arms pinned above his head for the whole forty minutes. I could only imagine what that must have been like from his point of view: freedom of movement, warmth, nourishment, safety, all torn away—in their place, the chill of an air-conditioned room, imprisoned with all vital organs exposed, and no mother-love nearby. I was afraid that would alter his sense of personal safety forever.

"See?" The technician pointed proudly to the wall. "Cartoon characters to make the children feel more comfortable." I stared down at my five-week-old infant who did not know Bugs Bunny from the blood pressure rack hanging on the same wall. I shook my head and stalked away. My pulse thundered in my ears; I could only breathe shallow sips in my upper chest. My body had finally achieved attack readiness—too late. My first important test facing the medical establishment, and I had failed my son. I studied his face, puffy from crying. But what were the rules here? I did not understand how I could protect Thomas, and at the same time allow the medical world to diagnose his life-threatening problems and repair what they could.

We hiked the long shiny halls and boarded one of the crowded elevators back up to the fifth floor to see Dr. Lindstow. Stolid and serious, he placed Thomas on the papered table and probed his chest with his stethoscope for more than fifteen minutes.

"Sounds like a classic case of cardiac failure," he said, "but the next procedure will remove any doubt."

Earlier in the day, Dr. Smithe had talked about congestive heart failure, but I wondered what "classic" meant. Still shaken from the trauma of the chest X-ray, I listened to Dr. Lindstow explain the next test—invasive, he called it—which would be done in the "cath" lab. All I could think about was how small Thomas's heart must be. "Invasive" sounded huge.

"Why do you have to do this test?" I asked. "Isn't there a way to avoid it?" He told us heart catheterization provides invaluable information, but is tricky on infants. His team would open a vein in the right thigh, insert a catheter and thread it up into Thomas's heart. They would monitor pressures in the different heart chambers. X-ray video would follow injected dye as it circulated throughout his body. Thomas must remain awake; anesthetizing him would skew the results. This test had to be performed in a sterile environment, so I could not sit with him during the procedure.

"Won't it hurt?" I asked. The very thought of a tube passing up his tiny torso and into his even tinier heart made my own body cringe.

"Adults who undergo catheterization tell us it just feels weird," Dr. Lindstow said. "They say they feel pressure, that's all."

I didn't believe him. I rubbed my ice-cold fingers back and forth on my forehead, trying to absorb everything he'd said, but my brain had stopped processing.

Before the catheterization, the intern called us into a small room and went over the medical release point by point. "Your son could have permanent brain damage from this procedure. He could, in fact, die."

My own heart skipped a couple of beats, then thundered rapidly. Anger flushed hot through my body. My words snapped in the air. "So when I sign this document, the hospital protects itself from any liability, right?"

This intern was younger than I, but he already seemed to have lost his human touch. His eyelids twitched, his smooth, youthful face pulled down. For a moment he sat speechless. "Do you want this procedure done on your son?" he asked, bluntly. "Because if you do, you *have* to sign." He tapped the ballpoint on the table, impatient.

I peered at the release form he had shoved in front of me. I saw only blurry, meaningless text. I blinked hard until some of the words came into focus: "Stroke." "Death." Where was my instruction manual? I did not know how to be this kind of grownup.

I slowly penned my name, pressing hard to steady my shaking hand. Even so, my signature was unrecognizable. The intern glanced at Ray and offered him the pen.

"I'm not his father. I can't sign," Ray said, and gave a little shrug, his face twisted with confusion.

Loneliness swarmed over me, as it had many times in the last few weeks. My mind grabbed onto Riccardo. For a moment, I wondered if any of his relatives had heart anomalies. Now, since we were not in contact, I would never know. How had we so easily decided not to be together? This child needed a *family*.

Ray and I waited again, this time in a small room three sets of swinging doors away from the cath lab. The enormity of what I faced weighed me down; I leaned on my knees dangling my hands between them. I doubted my hands would ever be capable enough to cope with the mess we were in.

Dr. Lindstow padded into the waiting room two hours later. He still wore sterile green shoe covers. Sweat plastered his thinning hair to his scalp. The circles under his eyes had darkened, his shoulders were slumped. He rubbed the lines on his forehead, but he didn't look directly at me. When I noticed that dark smears stained his hospital greens, a rock lodged under my diaphragm. *Thomas's blood.* He seemed so shook up it was hard for me to grab a breath. Something bad had happened in there.

"Your child has quite a pair of lungs," he said, shaking his head, still focusing past me. "He appears to have tolerated the procedure, but the results confirmed my suspicions. He is definitely in cardiac failure."

Fear pooled in my chest. My arms felt so empty without Thomas. I needed to hold him close. "Where is he?" I asked.

"My assistant rushed him to the Pediatric Special Care Unit. He'll be there for at least a week." In the PSCU, he said, they could monitor his adjustment to the powerful heart stimulant digitalis—a product of the foxglove plant.

When Thomas reached twenty pounds, he would require open-heart surgery. I couldn't even think about what that meant. Not yet.

I grabbed each new edict the specialists provided, wanting to know enough, but not too much. I had to work to keep my faith and hope intact so I could cope with the next day, and the next, and the next.

This immense building with blue-tinged lights and distant people had—in an instant—become my new home. Ray and I trudged through the hospital labyrinth again, finding our way from the fifth floor to the PSCU on the second. I took the stairs; I wanted the fastest access to my son. You could die waiting for those elevators.

Over the next week, the cardiologist made minute adjustments to the dosage of medication to slow and strengthen my son's heartbeat. But Thomas faltered, struggling first against anemia, then pneumonia, and finally—scariest of all—tarry, black hospital diarrhea. I reeled at each new, devastating piece of information. His weight gain I was so proud of turned out to be only water retention from cardiac failure. My tiny, six-pound, skinny baby! Dr. Lindstow took him off breast milk; he said fasting would ease Thomas's digestive tract, and hopefully stop the diarrhea. Horrified, I watched the nurse stuff a latex nipple with cloth soaked in brandy—a "whiskey nipple," they called it.

"Wait!" I had avoided alcohol throughout my pregnancy. "You aren't really going to give him that?"

She stroked Thomas's lips with the nipple until he opened his mouth for it. "It will calm him," she said. "You don't want him to feel like he's starving, do you?"

Intuitively, I knew this path was wrong, but I could not think of how to respond—of course I didn't want him to feel as though he were starving. So, even though my heart was thudding, I remained quiet, wondering if down the road, this would come to haunt my son in some inexplicable way.

Although plenty of fluids were provided intravenously, for a full five days Thomas was not allowed to nurse. He just sucked away on the whiskey nipple they replenished on a regular basis. When he cried, he sounded fitful, desperate, and drugged. Drunk.

My breasts, swollen with milk, kept me awake at night as I lodged myself in the vinyl and metal chairs in the waiting room and tried to doze. I hung onto the belief that Thomas would pull through this cascade of worsening problems. I used the electric breast pump so I could freeze my milk, but the sucking action was so painful I opted for the hand pump instead, and developed instant empathy for cows. Stacks of four ounce bottles, each carefully dated and labeled "Thomas Blaine," built up in the freezer.

I stumbled from the special care unit out to the candy machines and back again, helpless to do anything but stand guard, a mother lion by my cub's side. A couple of times a day I joined five other mothers who huddled in the waiting room, chain-smoking Marlboros. I hadn't smoked in years, but with both the stress and companionship, I caved. One woman would buy, and hand them out to the others, a small kindness we could pass around.

"Kristin, how's Samantha today? I asked.

"I guess maybe a little better," she said, running her fingers through her stringy blond hair. "Hard to read those doctors. They're messing with her meds again. Do you think they really know what they are doing?"

"Probably not, but they're all we've got. We have to trust them," another mother said. Murmurs around the room.

We applauded each tiny improvement a baby made. We consoled whoever had received the most devastating news. Two days later, Samantha died, and Kristin never returned to the waiting room, not even to say goodbye. I watched her walk slowly down the hallway, each step taking her farther away from her daughter's body. I sat frozen in the chair for a long time.

Ray drove back and forth from Moffitt Hospital to Marin County, ferrying clothes and snacks while trying to keep his job afloat. One evening he even brought me some pot. I was tempted, but shook my head. I had avoided all drugs and alcohol from the moment I found out I was pregnant. Thomas would nurse again. I couldn't take any chances. Not now.

The diarrhea eventually cleared up and antibiotics knocked out the pneumonia. They allowed him to nurse again. In tiny increments, Thomas strengthened and adjusted to the digitalis. After ten arduous days, Dr. Lindstow released him from the hospital.

At home, Thomas was irritable and even harder to soothe. He often yanked away from my breast and howled. Had the hospital experience caused this? Before, he had cooed and kicked his legs in his bath. Now he screamed as though he felt threatened, or seared, by the warm water. When I tried tepid water, his reaction was still the same.

Night after night I slogged up and down the hallway trying to get him back to sleep, only to be awakened an hour later by his penetrating screeches. It seemed like we were connected by an overstretched rubber band—I woke up every time he stirred; he wailed if I tiptoed to the bathroom. Sometimes Ray walked him, but I could not sink back into sleep confident he could handle whatever arose—I was afraid he might lose control and shake Thomas.

This exhausting experience was nothing like I had expected. Wasn't parenting supposed to be rewarding, to cement a family together? Instead, I lay rigid, waiting for a frustrated Ray to thrust my howling baby back in my arms. Sometimes he jumped in like a full-fledged parent; other times he watched from the sidelines. I tried to understand, but his inability to be patient made me angry, too. I needed a partner with bedrock steadiness.

When I referred to him as Thomas's "uncle-daddy," he stiffened. "That's what you think I am?" He walked out of the room. He wouldn't talk to me for hours.

What was his relationship with this baby? We still hadn't discussed it. I had added to this confusion—acting like a hyper-vigilant mom, while inside, terror reigned. I had read books about parenting, that was all. I had grown up as the youngest child on an isolated dead-end lane; I had never cared for younger children, nor had an opportunity to babysit. Not once.

Still, I knew at a cellular level something was different, something was wrong with Thomas—perhaps it was the hospital experience; perhaps there was a more profound cause. I called and questioned the doctor more than once, but he said no, Thomas's reaction was to be expected. I didn't know babies, but I did know my own son. He did not act like the same infant.

## Settling In—December, 1974

The morning began like so many others—levitating out of bed as the piercing screams of my four-month-old infant rose in volume. Worn down from pacing the hallway with Thomas three times in the night, I rubbed the sleep from my eyes as I hurried barefoot down the hall to his little bedroom. I could never hold myself to a walk when I heard that potent cry.

Thomas quieted the moment he saw me, and I sang to him as I changed his diaper. The shaved patches on his head—where the nurses had repeatedly poked, and failed, to put in intravenous lines—had not filled in yet, so his receding hairline was juxtaposed with his innocent, interested gaze. He watched my every move with that serious expression of his—wide-open eyes, dark as polished walnuts, and rows of little wrinkles on his raised brow. For a moment he pursed his lips and splayed out his fingers as though holding a cigar. He looked just like a miniature Winston Churchill.

His body never stopped moving, but now I had experience, and successfully corralled his limbs into the crimson T-shirt and bright blue overalls. As I buttoned the straps, I played "borey-borey," a game of my father's when I was a child. Chanting the words, I spiraled my finger down to tickle Thomas's stomach. Just as I touched him, he chuckled out loud—his very first smile and giggle, all in one. Filled with relief, I laughed back, picked him up, and flew him in a circle high in the air. "You are so gorgeous when you smile," I told him. Then I bundled him up and took him for a ride in the neighborhood, trotting behind his umbrella stroller as fast as I could. Usually he widened his eyes at the speed but kept his sober expression—this day, he kicked his feet and screeched with joy, as though he had found new muscles that tickled with delight. All day, he broke into wide, gummy smiles, and each smile brought me fresh snatches of hope. If he could find joy like this, he just might have the strength of heart to stay here with me.

Life settled down, and comforting patterns emerged. We even got a dog from the pound to join our family. Thomas wailed every day when the sun set—right at the dinner hour—but if Ray or I flew him high in the air like a busy little airplane, he broke into riotous giggles and then at least one of us could sit down and eat. We took turns until our arms tired. I was happy to forsake a warm dinner to fly him again and again. I needed that joy.

## Chapter Two

### Check-up—June, 1975

We make a morning trek into San Francisco to see the cardiologist. Note to myself: the traffic is backed up past the rainbow tunnels above the Golden Gate Bridge in the morning; in the future, schedule for the early afternoon.

I sit for a long time in the waiting room. Ray paces. Gerri, the receptionist, says Dr. Lindstow is talking to a parent whose baby had complications during surgery. I say a silent prayer of thankfulness that I am not that parent, and then feel bad for my ungenerous thought. Finally, we are shuttled into the examining room.

Ray folds his arms and leans against the wall as the doctor listens to Thomas's heart in six different locations on his chest and back, a process that takes more than ten minutes. Lindstow feels for pulses in his feet and ankles to check circulation, then he turns to me, frowning. "He's ten months old. He still doesn't crawl?"

"No," I say, "but he rocks on his hands and knees. He creeps on his belly, uses his right arm to propel himself forward. Really fast." I demonstrate the move, but he has turned back to Thomas. I realize with shock that he stopped listening the moment I said "No." More bad news to come. I know that as well as I know the face of my own son.

He hands plastic keys to Thomas over and over again. Each time, my son leans forward and eagerly snags them with his right hand. The cardiologist's expression changes incrementally, each shift more dour than the last. My insides tremble.

"I want him to undergo neurological testing," he says finally. He focuses over my shoulder instead of meeting my gaze. He is not looking at Ray, either.

I feel my face go pale. My chest constricts so I can barely whisper, "Why?"

Now he stares at the floor, or maybe at his fingers, which are making a fist, easing, making a fist, over and over again. "Thomas is showing unusual handedness. He only uses his right, no matter how I offer him the keys." He demonstrates again, this time shaking the keys directly in front of Thomas's left hand. "At this age, children reach with the closest hand." Again Thomas snatches for the bright colors with his right. Ray steps forward, grabs the keys, and tries the experiment himself. Same result. Again. Again.

A hard chunk of resistance, grief, and unwillingness settles in my body. I pick up Thomas and plant him on my right hip. Ray walks over and puts his arms around both of us as though to shield us from Dr. Lindstow.

"No invasive procedures," I say. "I won't allow it, not this time." My words sound ragged, harsh.

The cardiologist finally meets my eyes and sighs with impatience. "I want you to go to the Agency for Infant Development. AID. It's near you, in Marin County. Just talk to the physician there. Dr. Liebermann can put you in touch with them."

We ride down the elevator in silence. I am screaming inside. I let Ray drive. I lock the door, and huddle in the car, holding Thomas instead of putting him in his car seat. "It's got to be okay," I whisper. "How much more can we take?"

Ray doesn't answer my question. A few minutes later he says, "That man is filled with gloom."

My bones knew, though. The same bell of doom tolled as on the second day of Thomas's life, when Dr. Lindstow avoided telling us his serious heart diagnosis and gave it to our pediatrician to deliver. This man pawns off bad news.

On two consecutive Wednesday mornings that bracket his first birthday, Thomas is evaluated by the physician and the occupational and physical therapists at AID. The process takes two hours each time, and involves mostly play—getting him to stretch, reach, and balance as best he can. Dr. Stowe finally calls me in for a conference. I sit Thomas on my lap facing outward, so we can both see her. She talks about "increased tone in his extremities and left-side stiffness" contributing to his not crawling.

"Okay," I say, "but what is this called?"

She strokes Thomas's dark hair, and rests a finger under his chin, staring at him. "The blanket term is cerebral palsy," she says softly, after a pause. "Brain damage that affects his motor skills. Some people may call him spastic, but that isn't correct." She pointed at Thomas. "Notice that his left arm wanders behind him? That's athetoid motion."

I shake my head, unable to absorb anything after her second sentence. "Brain damage? *Brain* damage?" I repeat. I feel my heartbeat flutter near my throat. Someday, someday in the near future, I will be forced to decode these words, and figure out what they mean for our lives. Not today. Today the words bounce back and forth inside me like an out-of-control racquet ball.

As I leave the office, I keep saying to myself *he is the same precious baby; I just know more now.* Instead of balancing him on my right hip, our usual mode of travel, I hug him so close to my chest he squirms. I cannot imagine how to break this news to Ray. He will cry; he will rail; he will not cope well. I only hope I get the chance to grieve.

## Intervention—August, 1975

I hung up the telephone in our communal living room, padded across the hardwood floor, and snapped off the radio, silencing John Denver mid-song. Dr. Liebermann's receptionist had telephoned me; our pediatrician wanted me to come in for a consultation *without* Thomas. I had never met with him alone. What was this about? Had there been another disastrous discovery about my son's health? Taking a deep breath, I made the appointment. My dog, Arthur, must have sensed my unease; he nudged his cold nose into my hand. I scratched his head mindlessly as I chewed over the phone call.

Thomas's just-diagnosed brain injury had presented a new snake nest of unknown challenges. My gaze lifted to take in our peaceful neighborhood, and I hugged myself like a vine clinging to a trellis in a stiff wind. One more piece of devastating news would tear me loose.

Three days later, I left Thomas with my housemate and pushed open the door into the impersonal scent of alcohol. I sat among sneezing and coughing children—a long fifteen minutes—until Dr. Liebermann ushered me through the doors to the familiar examining rooms. Instead of entering one, he led me into his private office. This didn't bode well. Hesitantly, and for the first time, I stepped over the threshold onto the thick avocado shag carpet. I faced a gleaming, mahogany desk and wall-to-wall bookcases filled with black, hardbound medical books. No plants softened the place or added a breath of air.

I jumped as Liebermann shut the door behind me. He sat down at his desk and gestured for me to sit across from him. I did so, then couldn't figure out what to do with my arms and legs. I crossed, uncrossed, re-crossed them. I blew a breath quietly through my mouth to still my skittish heart. The muted cry of a young child filtered in from the waiting room, but the force of Liebermann's gaze denied the sound. I did not know how I could hold my own under his persistence.

"Your son just turned a year old and seems to be thriving, despite the cerebral palsy and the seriousness of his heart defect," he said, tapping the pads of his thumbs together. "In fact, he's doing better than any of us expected."

My heart kathunked, waiting for the "but." What I got was a pause. He had said "better," I was sure he had. If this wasn't awful news about Thomas, why was I here?

"You, on the other hand, have aged ten years in the past twelve months." Liebermann measured every word. He continued to demand my gaze, but sat in silence while his pronouncement wedged through my resistance and rattled inside of me.

Ten years. *Ten* years? Tears sprang to my eyes and I willed them down. I would *not* cry. Not now; definitely not here. Why did I feel accused and found guilty, as though my weariness were somehow negotiable, a choice I had made, and my fault? I scooted up in the chair, tried to straighten my spine. I felt like a scolded child.

"You're exhausted," he continued, in a softer tone.

The sneak attack loosened the stiff matrix that held me together. I couldn't bear that; I'd always relied on my rock-hard core to press forward through each new wallop that life dished out. The sharp boulder in my throat broke loose and tears escaped down my cheeks. I dashed them away, but he noticed—of course—and handed me a box of tissues. I sat beleaguered in the face of his compassion. And I could feel he wanted something from me. He was requiring it, but I didn't know what "it" was.

"If your son died," he said, in an even tone, "would you feel relief? Wouldn't your life be easier?"

"No!" Indignation, rage, and shock bubbled at his question, and my feet uncrossed and rooted on the floor—like ivy, no longer some tenuous flowering vine. "*Not* relief. Of course my life would be a lot easier, sure," I snapped. "I apparently didn't get drafted for 'easy.'" I snatched another tissue from the box and blew my nose. How dare he? What was his point? Where had his usual kindness gone? I yearned to slam my way out the three doors—*whack, whack, wham*, into the hallway, the elevator—and escape.

"Thomas needs you," he continued. "and he needs a healthy mother, long term. Frankly, I'm worried about you. Changes are in order."

I glared at him, this adversary, this other. My feet remained solid on the floor, but my arms crossed in front of my chest, walling him out. "Easy for you to say," I said, surprised by the nip in my tone. "Exactly what changes did you have in mind?"

"You can't get up three times every night. It's debilitating. Thomas must start sleeping." He pursed his lips, folded his hands on the desk. "It'll be hard, but you have to let him scream it out. You can sit right outside his door. It will take no more than seven nights."

Not comfort Thomas? "No way!" I said. "He will scream for hours. He'll have a heart attack screaming that hard and long."

"He won't!" he said, smacking the desk with his palm.

I jerked back.

"He'll be just fine," he went on, rubbing his hand, looking sheepish. "He's strong. You may feel as though *you* are going to have the heart attack, listening to him." He smiled for the first time.

His attempt at humor, ignoring the severity of my son's health problems, galled me. Thomas, at one year old, weighed barely fifteen pounds. I could picture him screaming full tilt, grabbing the crib rail and hauling himself up to his tiptoes, since he had difficulty planting his feet flat. He would grip the top rail for stability—his baby knuckles white with abandonment and rage—his mouth a huge frenzied "O," screaming until the far ends of the universe rattled with the sound waves. He could rhythmically drag on that rail—the wood creaking and squealing—until the crib rocked like a boat. In the hospital he had screamed until snot poured from his nose, globbed on his face, and his breaths turned to raspy gulps.

How could this man expect a mother to eavesdrop on misery for hours without comforting her baby? "I can't do that," I said, broken. My arms, already crossed in front of my chest, now wrapped around my body. "You don't know what you're asking of me."

"Yes, I do. I raised five children," he said.

My chin dropped and I stared at him from under my brows. "*You* have?" I finally spit out. "Your *wife* has. *You're* in this office all day." He pursed his lips and considered me. A moment of silence hung in the room, but he ignored my hostility. "There's more. I want you to get out of the house. Leave Thomas with a sitter. Go back to college, at least part-time."

I shook my head, sorry I'd told him about leaving school. "I can't afford that—tuition, books, childcare, for heaven's sake. Who would care for him? He's cranky, difficult, and fights every nap."

"We've been going along on a no-charge basis." His measured words were smooth, like cream. "Let's continue that for now, and you can apply that money to your schooling." I sat for a long, uncomfortable moment. We had never spoken about his not charging me. The office had never sent a bill.

It seemed forever until he said, "You can find the right childcare person; you will. There are saints out there." He stood up. "Ray can help. I know he came into the picture late in your pregnancy, but he seems dedicated to both you and Thomas."

I swallowed, smoothed the hardwood armrests before I met his gaze. "We separated," I said.

His eyebrows twitched in surprise, and he sat back down into his chair. "I wasn't aware of that. I'm sorry. Oh my."

"Ray—" I stopped short, exhausted at the thought of trying to explain, then tried again. "He gave up everything for us, even quit school. I couldn't figure out why. Now he's miserable and angry."

"Of course the two of you will get counseling," he said.

"I'm willing; he's not." My words came out thick, like glue from a tube. I desperately wanted to change the subject. "I thought you were my *son's* doctor," I said.

"I attend to children *and* their families," he responded. "Your family needs guidance."

"Gee, thanks," I said, with sarcasm. "Someday, I might appreciate it."

"I know," he stood, and coming out from behind his desk, touched my shoulder. "Tough love. Perhaps I've been a bit hard on you. You're a good parent—very attentive—but when parenting debilitates you, Thomas suffers, too." He opened his office door.

I clamped my mouth shut, nodded, and marched out, trying to keep my shoulders back and my chin up. I felt chastised.

I hunched in my Datsun in the parking lot under the medical building, awash in a waterfall of tears and self-pity. Ray had stalked out a month and a half before. Thomas quit nursing the same week Ray left, snatching his head away from my breast and howling; apparently a mother's stress can degrade the taste of breast milk. Losing a partner is difficult enough; having my baby reject me felt very, very personal. I grieved for weeks. And now this. My baby's doctor giving me lectures. My baby's doctor, usually a support, making unrealistic demands.

I leaned into the firm, cool comfort of the steering wheel, and may have even dozed in that position. The shrill bleep of my own car horn shocked me back. My limbs weighed so much I could barely pick up my foot to work the clutch, or my hand to shift the gears.

My housemate took one look at me when I arrived back home and offered to watch Thomas a while longer. "Take a nap until dinner," she said. She had a son just two months younger, and the boys spent time together every day. I gratefully stumbled down the hall, flopped onto my waterbed, and slept soundly for two hours.

The fragrance of curried middle-eastern food drew me into the kitchen. The two little boys played happily in the midst of toys strewn on the living room floor. I leaned against the wall to watch them. Jesse, a plump, easy-going blond boy, patted a stuffed cat beside him. Thomas, all bones, sinew, and quick, anxious movement, poked at it. Liebermann was right; I did need activities independent of my son, and finishing college *was* my next step.

I quailed at the thought of asking my parents for financial help. Three times my pride prompted me to drop the phone back onto the cradle without completing the call. I couldn't imagine how to retain even a slip of dignity and still ask. After all, from my parents' point of view, I had decided to keep this baby without weighing the long term consequences. If I raised my child as a single mother, it would burden the rest of my family. I had assumed I'd have a healthy baby, and would scrape along as single mothers do. I didn't understand that casting into the gene pool is like gambling the tables in Las Vegas. There are no sure bets.

At last I telephoned my parents. Mom conferred with Dad, and then they called back with questions: who would care for Thomas? (I didn't know. Dr. Liebermann said "a saint.") What would my major be? (Child Development.) Would it lead to a job? (I hoped so.) They assured me they would provide the financial boost. Finally, a decision of mine they were happy to support.

I contacted the university about reinstatement. Then, to support my plan to attend school two or three days a week, I placed an ad in the local newspaper and interviewed babysitters. I found Janine, a cheerful woman about my age who cared for two other small children, and was willing to try Thomas. I did not mince words about his indomitable spirit—no point in that, she would find out soon enough.

She told me she had been a wild teenager—warning bell—but had found Jesus, and felt nurturing children was her calling. The warning bell shrilled. I asked for references, and called every parent on her list. They seemed genuinely pleased with her care.

Even so, that first day I dropped Thomas off with trepidation. I obsessed and worried during the drive into San Francisco. The busyness of classes, buying books, meeting new people distracted me for a while, but when I returned later that day to pick up Thomas, her face seemed worn and worried.

"My, that boy can holler," she said. "Don't get your hopes up; he didn't smile once. I'll give it a two-week try." I took him from her, and he snuggled close to my shoulder like a snail clinging to rock. I snuggled back, all the way to the car.

Thomas woke only once that night, then fell asleep in the middle of a bottle. He must have howled most of the day. So, no heart attack after extended screaming. Liebermann had won that round, too.

After ten days, just as I was imagining defeat, Janine was able to get him to chuckle. Thomas had come through on his own, found a way to be happy in childcare. With relief, I settled into school, a challenging routine of commuting and studying in addition to parenting. It was even more tiring than my previous life, but I found adult companionship in college. Although I had to study every day—often late into the evening—tendrils of hope grew that I might actually graduate.

I might have been willing to let Thomas cry at daycare if necessary, but I didn't leave him alone to scream out his separation blues at bedtime—neither he nor I were ready to face this step, and it seemed unfair in a communal household where the other four adults needed, and had every right to, a good night's rest.

At the next checkup, Dr. Liebermann seemed satisfied I had accepted part of his advice. This time we met in an examining room—more equal ground than his formal, claustrophobic office. This room had the friendly smell of baby powder. He crossed his arms and peered at me over his Ben Franklins. "You think your son is tough? You are every bit as tough—but not invincible," he said. "*Please* take naps. Nap when Thomas does."

I stared down at my active, alert baby who fought every nap. "When my homework is done. I have to keep up with school, too," I said.

## Chapter Three

### Uneasy Reunion—March, 1976

Ray and I got back together when Thomas was nineteen months old. I deeply wanted my son to have a father, and Thomas remained our glue-pot. I had trepidations—but flat out ignored them. The three of us moved into a second floor apartment in a brown-shingled house in San Rafael, seven miles north of Mill Valley. No more communal living, no more roommate buffer, no more live-in playmates for Thomas. We even had to find a home for Arthur. We were on our own.

Two months later, Ray asked me to marry him. The question had seemed inevitable; it hung in the atmosphere of that apartment. We stood in the kitchen, and the room constricted when he said, "So, do you want to marry me?"

"*Say no*," my intuition whispered. I responded to Ray's proposal in a low voice. "It's the next step, isn't it. Yes, let's get married." Where had those words come from? My body felt weighted down, squished flat under many feet of water.

### Stand-off—May, 1976

Three months later, Ray's mom came from Southern California for the wedding. Her gray hair was neatly permed, and she wore practical, thick-heeled black pumps. She shook my hand, but didn't meet my gaze. Her distaste was evident. She knew my child had been born out of wedlock, and she was angry and disappointed that Ray planned to marry me. When she met Thomas, surely her heart would soften. Who can resist a toddler? After all, she had raised twins.

My mother and father, who had arrived earlier, walked in from the living room and sat down with the three of us at our small wooden kitchen table, knee to knee over cups of coffee.

Dad seemed far too large for the room. Our second floor apartment had no air conditioning, and the last week of May had been unusually warm. He pulled out a pressed cotton handkerchief that matched his full head of wiry, neatly trimmed white hair, and mopped his brow. He wore a navy blazer with gold buttons, and a conservative red patterned tie—neat and snug at the neck.

"We just got back from Paris. Have you ever been to Europe?" my mother asked Mrs. Arnold. My upper back got very tight. I wondered where she was going with this. This didn't feel right.

"No," Mrs. Arnold said, "I haven't had the opportunity."

Mom patted Dad's hand. "We used to think that people who didn't travel were very parochial," she said. "But we've changed our attitude over the years."

Had Mom really said that?

Mrs. Arnold's gaze flashed toward Ray and then dropped to her coffee. Her mouth contracted, the little wrinkles above her lips pressing into sharp paper folds.

I flushed first cold, very cold in the pit of my stomach, then my head got hot. I stared at my mother and saw her in a way that I never had before. What arrogance. My whole childhood had been built on the framework of snobbery.

Mutters, moans, then a sharp cry came from Thomas as he awakened from his late nap. Relieved that I could leave that stuffy room, I rushed to get him and stumbled on my shoelace as I hurried down the hall. I thunked against the wall, but regained my balance, and grabbed a diaper on my way to the crib. My heart pumped fast as I changed him, whispering to him to be extra cute. I strained to hear what was going on in the kitchen. No warm conversation, only Ray's tight voice, talking too fast about the wedding. He tried to make our planned hippie ceremony and reception on Mt. Tamalpais sound appealing.

As I carried Thomas into the kitchen, he jabbered and pointed, his large, bright eyes taking in the new faces. Mrs. Arnold's mouth did not soften. Her hard gaze bounced off him, returning to Ray. That glance frightened me. I hugged Thomas close to ward off the effects, then passed him to my dad, who broke into a delighted grin. His large, square hands gently closed around Thomas's chest as he settled him on his lap facing outward and bounced him on his knee. Thomas struggled forward to touch the morning paper which displayed a tire advertisement. "W-w-wheel!" he said, stabbing his finger on the picture. "Wheel!" He looked up at Ray's mother, trying to get her attention, but she sat stiffly, ignoring him.

"Ray tells us you live in Southern California," my mother said, her tone both casual and proper.

Mrs. Arnold stretched her neck high. "In an apartment in Chula Vista." *I dare you*, her chin said.

Thomas made a buzzing sound and smacked the picture of the tire with his palm again and again.

"How nice," Mom replied. She paused, then tried again. "I understand that your husband died when Ray was a teenager."

"Yes," Mrs. Arnold said. Then she relented and added, "It was difficult. Ray has a twin sister, you know."

"Oh my, yes. Did you have help?"

Mom's words hung in the air. My stomach went cold again with disgust and shame. I prayed that Mrs. Arnold wouldn't take my mother's meaning. Thomas began babbling, softly, then louder and louder as though he needed to replace the rampant tension in the room. Ray would surely understand my mother's meaning; he would rant about her attitude; the only question was how soon. And for once, I wholeheartedly agreed with him. We could band together.

"Do you mean help, as in servants?" Mrs. Arnold's clawed hands rested on the table, frozen twigs that might snap in a breeze. "Oh no. No servants."

Ray's body went stiff. "Will you excuse me? I've got rings to finish," he said. He didn't look at any of us, just stomped into his small jewelry studio off the kitchen. I could hear him tap-tap-tapping with the small rounded hammer. My heart shrank; my hope shriveled. He was tapping all that rage straight into our wedding bands.

## Family Ties—May, 1976

On May twenty-eighth, a soft, warm day, Ray and I were married. Our parents sat on the margins, on folding chairs we had provided for them. Mom kept her legs neatly crossed at the ankles. My father stood out, the only man in a sport coat and tie. Ray's mother sat nearby, not close enough to make conversation. Her face was frozen into a small, forced smile. More than one hundred people sat on the hillside around the glen we had picked—friends, and friends of friends. I did not even know some of the people. My closest chums, Susan and Sondra, wove a halo of daisies for my hair.

Richard, a poet who became a minister by joining the Universal Life Church, officiated. John, Thomas's godfather, held my son through the formal vows. I heard one person whisper, "Too bad her son is crippled." Shock spiked through me. I swiveled around to see who had spoken, but that person already had melded into the crowd.

I do not recall the words or even the feeling of the ceremony. The light filtered through the trees, and I made a fragile wish that light could bring us luck. We needed all the luck we could get.

A week after the wedding, Ray and I rushed to another urgent appointment with the cardiologist. Thomas had been happily pulling books off the living room shelf. Then, a moment later, agitated and crying, he squatted on the floor. I was shocked to see his lips were tinged blue—this was his first "tet spell," something Dr. Lindstow had warned us about. Children might have one or two of these without harm, but they point to the need for immediate surgery to ensure a steady supply of oxygen to the body. Thomas had recently reached twenty pounds—the minimum weight for undergoing the open-heart procedure.

The date was set two days later, June eighth. Instead of our planned week-long honeymoon, the hospital—again. It was time to give more blood. Susan and Sondra stepped forward to donate, along with other friends whom I knew were squeamish about even the smallest cuts.

Thomas entered the Moffitt Hospital pediatric care unit as an alert, feisty child, jabbering in his own language with a few decipherable words mixed in: wheel, Mama, Daddo, and 'nana (banana).

Dr. Ebert, the lanky, stooped cardiac surgeon, came to speak to us. "I'll use a vertical incision here." He demonstrated on his own chest. He went on in his soft, measured voice. "Then I'll open his breastbone and stop his heart so we can put him on a heart-lung machine to keep oxygen and circulation going."

The cardiac team would patch the pea-sized hole between the ventricles and enlarge the outflow tract to the lungs, both with Teflon. They would sew him up. It sounded reasonable, sensible—and frightening.

Early on the day of the surgery, I went down to the cafeteria looking for my every-morning caffeine. Dr. Ebert sat at a small table, clearly savoring his black coffee and doughnut. I stopped in my tracks, horrified, wondering if his hands would shake as he operated on my son. Then it dawned on me that he, too, had his morning rituals.

The surgeon offered hopeful words as Thomas was wheeled down the corridor that led to the operating room. "I'll take real good care of him," he said. Smile lines framed his eyes. I trusted he would do his best.

Nonetheless, Ray and I spent three tortuous hours waiting in the hospital chapel, lost in our own thoughts and prayers. At one point, I glanced at him. Ray had aged as much as I. When I first met him, I had been impressed by his radiance—newly returned from six months of rural life in the Anderson Valley, he glowed tan and vigorous, his blond curls tipped white by the sun. Now the lines around his mouth were carved deeper, and I hadn't seen the smile that set off the spray of wrinkles by his eyes in a long time. All the light had left his hair. He didn't have the grit I possessed, and knowing that must have made him feel inadequate—which translated into anger. His fury grabbed him and wouldn't let go. But in this moment, he must have felt me looking at him. He reached over and covered my hand with his, gripping it gently in solidarity. "We'll get through this," he whispered.

The nurse finally signaled to us. We hurried down the hall in silence. I tiptoed into the pediatric intensive care unit, Ray a few steps behind. Thomas's color had degraded to gray. I felt my color drain away as well. The cardiologist had used smooth words and an even tone to describe what my child would undergo; he had not warned me that Thomas would look like he had been run over by a semi. A six-inch gash, roughly stapled, ran down the center of his tiny chest. His stitched-together heart pulsed rapidly just under the skin near the incision. He had four large drain tubes, a urinary catheter, a bag of AB negative blood, IV fluids, and heart monitor leads all attached to his twenty-pound body. A large smear of blood stained his stapled chest.

What had we done?

Ray stared at Thomas, then shook his head slowly and left the room, moving like a blind man. It was hours before he could drag himself back.

When Thomas awakened fully, he fussed and stared around the noisy room, eyes squinty with pain. Monitors beeped with mind-numbing repetition, alarms went off, and babies wailed. Thomas tried to jerk his right arm, but it was strapped to a board to prevent him from yanking out the intravenous line. There were too many wires to allow me to hold him, so I sank into the rocking chair next to his crib, stroked him, and talked in the calmest voice I could muster. "Big owie," I whispered. "You'll get better, I promise." Another lie. I had no right to promise anything. I was learning the hard way that life comes with no guarantees.

I asked the nurse for dampened gauze and oh-so-carefully swabbed away all the blood that I dared. Going near the staples was too daunting. I wound up his bedraggled music box teddy and snuggled it between his free arm and body to play its saucy tune. He hugged it tight. I barely stemmed my tears; they fell when I returned to the waiting room. It was hard for me to grasp that this amount of violence could fix anything.

Ray glanced over when I collapsed into the molded plastic chair next to him and pressed my palms to my temples. "How can you bear to go in there?" he asked, sighing deeply. He seemed folded in, distraught.

"How could I bear not to?" I responded. "He doesn't know the nurses. He needs us."

A week later, all cardiac signs looked good, but Thomas would only shake his head or scream. No words, no babbling. Dr. Lindstow hesitated to release him until he was sure Thomas's vocabulary was back, that he was neurologically normal. I knew he would not talk until the love and safety of familiar surroundings enveloped him—and me. My anxiety compounded the problem. Since he was physically healing so rapidly, I begged, finally convincing the doctors to let us take him home. When he saw Ray at the steering wheel, his little arms flew out for his daddo.

Sure enough, he began jabbering again, although those first few days, every other word was "No!" The traumatic scars of that experience were imprinted in more than the physical marks he bore. For years, he would not pull his T-shirt off in public—he even swam with it on.

Mom and Dad called regularly to check on their grandson and ask about his healing. Mrs. Arnold didn't call once.

Six months later, we drove to the hospital for a regular appointment. Trips to the cardiologist followed the same pattern: check in with Gerri, the receptionist at his office, then go to the third floor for an electrocardiogram and chest x-ray. To record his heart rhythms, they put gel—always cold—in a number of places on Thomas's tiny chest, and attached leads with brown suction cups about a half inch in diameter. They were stuck in sensitive spots under his arm, and tickled. Thomas giggled, squealed, and wriggled.

Then we traipsed back to the fifth floor to see Dr. Lindstow. When he came into the examining room, he wore his standard neatly pressed Oxford cloth shirt. His thinning gray hair always seemed to be the same length. He greeted us, of course, but I never felt as though he really saw me. I stripped Thomas down to his diaper, and the doctor listened to his heart and felt ankle pulses. This took about twenty minutes. Even though the results were positive—Thomas's heart was performing well and he was no longer on heart medications—the doctor maintained his usual austere attitude, talking to someone apparently over my shoulder. Once I even turned to see whom he might be speaking to.

"Come again in six months," he said. "If his condition remains stable, we'll start yearly visits thereafter."

In January, 1977, I finally graduated from San Francisco State University. I knew, the way my son's life was unfolding, there was no chance of my applying for traditional jobs. I simply needed more flexibility than a forty-hour work week could provide.

Thomas's next six month visit to the cardiologist was uneventful. Dr. Lindstow kept his word, and we were put on a yearly checkup schedule.

## Tie-breaker—July, 1977

Our marriage lasted just over one year; perhaps it was doomed as soon as Ray's mother called me a "chippie"—a whore—and Thomas a bastard. She never phoned to ask how he was doing, nor sent him a birthday present. Even when Ray decided to adopt him, she did not accept him as her grandson.

One day, as we stood in the kitchen together, Ray hollered, "You don't know what it's like, not having financial backup. You've always had it."

"And that's my fault? Please don't yell!" I retorted. "It doesn't solve anything." He wheeled around in rage and socked a hole through the lath and plaster wall.

The social worker's report in preparation for the adoption said we "presented as a mild-mannered family coping well with a disabled child." She had not seen me gradually freeze up and turn more inward with each of Ray's frustrated outbursts.

The adoption went through. Thomas Blaine became Thomas David Arnold.

I stood in our bedroom in the little bungalow near the corner of Fourth and F streets. The window, which faced the concrete back wall of the Dharma Trading Company, was stuck shut with thick globs of white paint. That was how our relationship seemed to me—clogged, hard, dry. Every morning for the last year I had stared out that window at the flat, gray wall not four feet away, grappling with what had gone sour. We were wrong from the get-go. We met too late in my pregnancy, had no time to get to know one another or broach the difficult question of parenting before Thomas was born. I never found the courage to address those questions. I walked over to the window and rubbed my finger over the lumps of paint that prevented any fresh air—any life, really—from entering the room.

While Thomas struggled with heart failure that first time in the hospital, Ray had given up his art classes because he felt Thomas and I needed more of him. I begged him not to leave college; I told him the classes brought him joy and advanced his skills—that there was no more he could do for us, but he seemed ferociously determined to make the sacrifice. He stopped making pottery, packed away his jewelry tools, deliberately closed his path to creativity, to joy. Another kind of heart failure.

This left him depressed and angry much of the time. It felt like martyrdom to me; his mother had taught him well. It drew attention to him, but didn't help in any practical way. His sacrifice was supposed to tie us together, but his rage at his lost future burned the very bonds he hoped to foster. He yelled a lot, slammed doors. Whenever I spoke up, it seemed to set him off. Soon, I didn't want to offer opinions at all. I never felt physically threatened by him, and did not believe he would intentionally hurt Thomas, but his rage penetrated us. His verbal and non-verbal attacks turned the atmosphere in the house murky, like thick Southern California smog.

I thought his adopting Thomas might make a difference—if he felt recognized as a parent and Thomas carried his name, his demeanor would change. It did not.

I couldn't face living with his intermittent, unexpected venom for years to come. I wouldn't be able to let down my guard, never knowing when he would let loose. I felt like I would die if I remained married to him—wither and dry, crack and disintegrate. Blow away.

I turned and stared at the room that only had space for Ray's wrought iron double bed. I had never liked that bed. Its thin black iron rails reminded me of prison bars, like our relationship. I glanced up at his hundred-year-old Navajo blanket hanging on the wall above the bed. Hand-woven of extra-fine wool, perhaps eighty threads per inch, it glowed with a rainbow of natural dyes. Now *that* I coveted. If only our marriage could be that closely woven, have that much rich vitality.

Ray walked into the room, the usual scowl on his face. I couldn't bottle up my disappointment any longer. "I dread coming home to you," I said, turning toward him. "I can't watch you destroy yourself any more. It destroys us too." I touched his arm and looked him directly in his eyes. "We tried; it's not working. It's time to split up." Ray's face contracted into the expected rage, the very rage that was driving me away.

Now, I understand that the deep crevices on either side of his mouth spoke of failure and sadness too, not just anger. But that day, only the fury seemed obvious to me.

His body went rigid, his hands trembled into fists. His jaw muscles bunched. "*I'm* not moving," he said.

I bit my lip, breathed out slowly, and tried to quiet the quivering inside my chest. "Thomas has finally settled in," I said. "He's only waking up once a night." I gripped the bars on the bed, and watched my knuckles turn white. "Surely you wouldn't force change on him now." I glanced back at him. "Besides, I work right next door. A working mother couldn't ask for more."

Ray shook his head, his mouth pressed into a thin, hard line. "If you want to leave, you'll have to find a new place," he said, his tone rising. "I found this house when it was empty; I negotiated the rent; *I* made it happen!"

My face flushed hot. I knew he loved this house, but I paid half the rent each month; *I* had paid the last month's rent and cleaning deposit in order to secure the house for our family. I had as much right to it as he did.

At that moment, Thomas wailed, waking from a late afternoon nap. All that compacted rage between Ray and me had yanked him from sweet sleep. I threw Ray a dirty, how-could-you look as I stalked past him to get my son. *My* son. We would have to move? What father, what biological father, would unmoor his child from a safe harbor? But adoption had not turned Ray into a real father. No blood tie existed; only a legal document sealed their relationship. I picked Thomas up and patted him on the back, murmuring. My body shook with damped-down frustration. Thomas squirmed in discomfort as I walked back toward Ray. I must have been squeezing him too tightly.

"He needs dinner," I said. "We'll have to continue this later."

As I carried Thomas toward his booster chair, I heard the front door slam; vibrations in the floor rolled like a tsunami all the way back to the kitchen, right into my bones. The house was as rattled as I was. I set Thomas at the kitchen table and gave him his octagon shape sorter as entertainment while I scraped together something to eat. I sure wasn't hungry and, at this moment, didn't care whether Ray came back to eat or not. I pressed my hands against the refrigerator to still their shaking. This argument wasn't about leaving the house, not really.

While I scrambled a couple of eggs, I shook frozen peas into a small plastic dish and set them in front of Thomas. He squealed with delight and shoved the brightly colored toy away. He focused on pinching one pea at a time, concentrating so hard a sliver of drool hung from his lower lip. One by one, the peas vanished into his mouth. A few he flattened on the table, mashing them down with rumbling grinder noises. I tested the temperature of the eggs and slid the plate in front of him.

As soon as he gobbled his eggs, he looked up with an eager, impish grin. "U-uppie?" he asked. His dark eyes gleamed. "W-wheel?"

"Okay," I said, chuckling at his boundless enthusiasm. The tension ebbed from my shoulders. "We can go out and play on the backhoe for a while."

I carried him out into the hot, late afternoon, and turned toward the dusty lot, home to the piece of heavy equipment Thomas insisted on visiting at least twice a day. What would we do when the city moved it to a different location? The backhoe, with its huge scraping bucket in front and a smaller digging one in back, had served as a regular playground. Then it struck me: we might leave first.

"W-wheel!" Thomas hollered as he pointed.

The industrial tires fascinated him most. A foot thick, they came up to my chest. He loved to pound on them with sticks, or ride them like a horse and hold on to the fender.

"D-Daddo!" he squealed, trying to wriggle free from me.

Startled, I glanced up. Ray sat hunched in the seat, his face in his hands. He looked beaten. I should have known he would come here, to be in the driver's seat. He avoided meeting my gaze—but reached out for Thomas, who had already thrust his arms in the air in anticipation. I raised my brows, silently asking if I could have a break. He nodded. I stood for a couple of moments watching them, assessing Ray's body language. Right now, he seemed more collapsed than enraged, and his eyes had brightened when Thomas raised his arms. In his own embattled way, he did love this little boy.

I turned to go back to the house. I heard Ray say stiffly, "We'll talk about this after he goes to sleep." I nodded my head, but kept walking. Yet another exhausting round to go.

A month later, I sliced open another packing box in my new garden apartment. It had a high wooden fence enclosing a grassy yard, safe for my crawling toddler. And I could afford the rent. Just. Ray made no financial contribution for Thomas at all.

I let Thomas watch TV and play with his box of birch blocks as I organized the new kitchen. From the sounds I could tell he had changed the channel from *Sesame Street*.

"M-Mama!" he called. Hearing the urgency in his voice, I rushed into the living room. His eyes were huge, and his wandering, affected arm jerked with excitement. He pointed to the TV. "T-th-there! Been there!"

On the program *Lifeline*, in an operating room at Moffitt Hospital, an interviewer spoke with Dr. Ebert, Thomas's lean, kindly cardiac surgeon. My heavens, Thomas remembered.

"Yes, that's right," I said, ruffling his dark hair. "He fixed your heart. There, in that very operating room." I snuggled down next to him on the floor, and spellbound, we listened as the surgeon described the challenges he faced operating on his tiny patients. When the program ended, I changed the channel back to *Sesame Street* and returned to unwrapping a few of the handmade ceramic pots Ray had given me. I smoothed my fingers over the surface of one that had survived the move. I set it on the shelf to begin a fresh and fragile peace. Thomas returned to his wooden blocks, building a large, unstable tower.

# Chapter Four

### Change of Heart—June, 1978

We drove to UCSF to see the cardiologist for our yearly appointment. It was a relief to not have to worry about Ray's moods. Again, a good report. Dr. Ebert had done a fine repair on my son's heart. Now I worried more about the effects of the cerebral palsy than his cardiac status.

Living a half-mile apart had not eased Ray's and my interactions as much as I had hoped. Thinking perhaps more physical distance from him would soften the tension that bound us, I rented a small house further north, in Petaluma. Ray's disappointment, fury, and sense of failure at my leaving bled into every interchange. I ended up thin-lipped, stubbornly attached to my positions.

"You're taking my son away from me," he said, his voice blade-sharp. "He's not even four. How can you do that?"

"Jeez, listen to your tone," I snapped. "It's exactly why I need distance."

Ray left "his" house to which he had been so bound, and moved to west Marin, thirty miles away, hoping, I think, that a return to the country might invite back the peace he'd found in the Anderson Valley. If only he had made that move when we split up, leaving Thomas and me in San Rafael. Instead, we had weathered two moves in less than a year.

Driving became a part of our weekend routine. On Saturday mornings Ray and I met midway, on a narrow road in the rolling hills of western Sonoma County, to exchange our bright-eyed son.

"D-Daddo!" Thomas squealed, stretching his arms high to be scooped up for a long hug. And again on Sunday evening, "M-Mama! M-missed you!" One day he tugged my hand, pulling me closer to Ray, and tried to press our hands together, looking back and forth. Ray's eyes filled with tears and he stared at me reproachfully, as though the separation, the distance, our son's hungering eyes—were my fault. Perhaps he was right. I had walked out; I had moved a county away. I was unwilling to try again. My body rigid, anxious, I picked up Thomas and turned away. I was not willing to renegotiate. Not ever.

## Grace—August, 1978

Telephone bill. Gasoline bill. Thank heavens, no toy store bill yet. I fingered the fattest envelope. The number ten business variety, it was addressed in my mother's hieroglyphics: each *w* an *m*, each *u* an *n*. Her handwriting was as hard to decipher as she was. I smacked the envelopes against my thigh as I plunked down on the front porch to sort through the other mail. I ripped hers open first. She had not included an article or newspaper clipping from the society page as I had suspected. Instead, I pulled out airline tickets. I gulped with surprise. At the bottom of her note, she had written the briefest line saying they were thrilled to get to see Thomas, signed "Love, Mom."

During our last phone conversation, we talked about the easiest time for me to leave work, but I had not expected them to fly us back. If it weren't for my son, I would never accept these tickets, yet I was so relieved not to add another chunk of debt to my credit card. I was thirty-three years old, and still not financially secure. I worked selling yarn, baskets, and dye at the Dharma Trading Company for little more than minimum wage. For Thomas's sake, I would have to swallow hard, then call and thank my parents. Most important, they would get to see their grandson at this energetic, curious stage. They had not visited us in California for more than a year, and he had changed so much. Though still not walking, he had developed a way of speeding across the floor—not a standard crawl because he couldn't put his left hand flat on the floor, but successful, nonetheless. And he was talking in full sentences.

Death stench from the nearby rendering plant pressed down. I plugged my nose. Thank God my parents couldn't smell this. I could imagine my mother's pity: not only the smell, but also because I didn't own my own home in a lovely neighborhood. Other than the foul odor a couple of times a week, we were comfortable enough living on Jessie Lane, surrounded by brilliant poppies and, in the evening, serenaded by crickets. It mirrored the country oasis where I grew up, but on my basic budget. I walked back into the house, musing about which of Thomas's new birthday presents to pack.

Two weeks later, I sat with Mom and Dad on their patio in Cincinnati. Thomas ranged on his hands and knees, pursuing a beetle near his grandfather's feet. I sat near the bronze sculpture of two sea horses, one large, one small, nestled together. It reminded me of sitting in bed with the covers pulled up to my neck, and Mom reading *The Little Engine That Could* from a nearby chair. I read to Thomas on the couch so he could snuggle and help turn the pages, soak up my motherly closeness like the warmth of a downy quilt. It filled me up as well, and I applauded myself for being a more affectionate parent than my mother.

I reached out to stroke the sea horses, to feel their cool, bronze patina. The sculpture stood for all I had grown up with and couldn't afford at this time in my life; every penny I earned selling yarn and weaving equipment to wealthy women went toward my most basics: food, rent, clothes, and toys for my son. Some months I did not earn enough to cover the bills. I had taken to prowling through used clothing stores to outfit myself—although for this trip, I had gone to the mall and splurged on a pristine pair of white gabardine slacks.

From where I sat between my parents, I saw two other sculptures. A rough-textured granite hippopotamus—so like my dad—stood stolid on a low stone wall; it bore the nasty weather Cincinnati dished out.

A stylized glass bird sculpture on a pedestal in the living room, cool and refined, resembled my mom. Dad had put Mom on a pedestal.

She repeatedly told us appreciation of art and music had been in our family for generations. I wanted to *make* art, not simply appreciate it. Dad and I held a common desire—to work with our hands. I had chosen weaving, and he had built hardwood furniture on weekends for our childhood home.

Mom brought out cocktails and hors d'oeuvres—fruit juice for Thomas, gin and tonic for the two of them, and a rum and water for me—adult fare finally, I thought, as I swirled my glass. Nice. She had made my favorite party snack—large pimento-stuffed olives wrapped in bacon, broiled until crisp—their scent preceded them. This would test my commitment to being a vegetarian, I thought.

"Here's some cheese and crackers for Thomas," she said. "He probably won't like the fancier fare." But Thomas had developed a yen for arcane foods like barbecued oysters and, figuring he would love the giant bacon olives as much as I had as a child, I handed him one. Mom looked startled, but he avidly sucked it down, tugged on my pants, and asked for another. I let him have three more while I nibbled on the cheese and crackers.

For a few minutes we were silent, soaking up the warmth of the sun and family connection, staring out toward the bend of the brown Ohio River in the distance. A tug pushing a heavy load began a wide turn upriver. I could relate to that tug, churning along, making only slow headway.

More than two years had passed since I had last come to Cincinnati, and even though this was not the house where I grew up, the moist scent of the surrounding trees filled me with memories of building forts in the woods, prowling after my older brother and his friends, and swinging on grapevines over deep ravines, delighted and terrified. I set my hand on Mom's arm. She patted my hand in return, and gave me a gentle smile.

"No more, you'll spoil your dinner," I said, when Thomas begged for yet another olive. A tiny smile tickled Mom's face. He peered hopefully at his grandmother. She pursed her lips and shook her head no. His face buckled. Dad crooked his finger at him and I plunked Thomas onto his lap for a grandfatherly bounce. Temper tantrum avoided.

I didn't get many respites like this at home. The single parent life meant I worked full-time, made the half-hour drive in the late afternoon clogged traffic to Petaluma to pick up Thomas from the babysitter, then began dinner preparations while distracting my cranky child. After dinner, I read to him, got him ready for bed, and fell into bed myself, exhausted. With Thomas, in Petaluma, I had created our own sense of home—a very casual lifestyle, unlike the formality I had grown up with.

Right now, I felt pulled this way by childhood recollection, tugged that way by my full, adult life, replete with friends and holiday traditions invented on the spot. Yet the Cincinnati white-glove culture, with its careful, conventional ways, would always have a grip on me. As a child, the formality created a safe web; I knew how to behave in any given situation. As an adult, I'd left that stifling atmosphere behind, but the patterns and rituals were like marrow in my bones.

Dad raised Thomas high into the air and, gazing up at him, addressed me. "He's going to be just fine, you know. Nothing will hold this boy back." Thomas grinned down at him, a thread of drool hanging from his lip. "He's got a will of steel," he said, his tone more serious. I couldn't disagree; I confronted that unbendable rebar each day. Dad settled him on his lap for a minute and ran his fingers through Thomas's full head of walnut-colored hair. Then he set him down on the floor, his large, fleshy hand holding on to Thomas's little stubby one until he was sure his grandson had a grip on his pants leg with his good right hand.

"See how he stands on his toes? He can't flatten his left foot," I said. "The orthopods think if there's any hope of his walking, he'll need heel cord surgery."

Dad leaned over and squinted at Thomas's feet, then nodded. "Mark my words," Dad said. "He *will* walk." I smiled at him and hung on to those words, so grateful he had spoken them out loud. They floated in front of me. I needed to believe them.

On Friday, I went to my sister's across town for the weekend. Saturday evening, Maggie babysat Thomas so I could join my parents at one of their friends' homes for dinner. The table was covered with a fine linen cloth, and candlelight flickered in the graceful sterling silver settings. The evening went well until our hostess passed the roast beef, and I murmured "No, thank you"—no reason, in this company, to mention I was a vegetarian.

Dad turned and squinted at me. "No roast beef?" he asked in a sarcastic tone. Then he turned my choice into a heated monologue about religious beliefs, of all things. This was so unlike my restrained, usually gracious father. I shrank from the tight faces of the other guests.

When Dad denigrated my Sufi path—he sneered and referred to them as "the Stufis"—I did not have the wherewithal to let his comment slide past me. Instead, I took the direct hit, raised my voice, and snapped back. "You should be glad for my spiritual beliefs," I snapped. "We focus on love and harmony in a world that needs more of it. You have no right to make judgments!" It was the first time I had ever stood up to him.

All through dinner, I had listened to stories of the other families' successes—brilliant and athletic grandchildren, friends and classmates with prestigious corporate positions. I noticed the silences that followed my answers when they asked tentative questions about my life. It was hard enough, with my minimum-wage job and disabled child—and now divorced—to keep my sense of self-possession in this crowd. I wasn't about to stand for having my spiritual practice, one of the few sources of comfort in my life, trashed.

Dad tucked in his double chin and pursed his lips, the deep line between his eyes now a chasm of disappointment. Mom shook her head at me and whispered, "Mind your manners. Not here!"

I flushed. "What about Dad's manners?" I muttered.

Mrs. Maguire slid her well-manicured hand over her mouth. Mr. Brennan peered down and fiddled with his napkin. His wife looked down her nose at me. Mr. Maguire stared at my father, probably waiting for his retort.

It was humbling to be a grownup, facing serious parenting challenges, and to be treated like a child by my parents, in this company in particular.

Today, I understand that I humiliated my father in front of his oldest friends. I broke their rules, in their home, at their dinner table. Now, I can see my parents' point of view—I had dropped out of Vassar College to marry, then divorced, gotten pregnant out of wedlock, had an affair while pregnant, married and divorced again. I appeared to have rejected all their social conventions—niceties that were important to them—and showed no sign of finding stability and happiness in the same way they had. Although I hadn't rejected their deep, basic values of kindness and honesty, they couldn't see that. I wanted happiness, yes, but not happiness bound up with the wooden rituals of their society.

The morning after the dinner party, I slipped Thomas into the high chair at my sister's house, snapped the tray in place, and cut up a pancake for him. Secure in her warm support, I shared the evening's events. "It was hard enough at dinner," I said. "Their friends asked careful questions about Thomas and me after bragging about their own children. They clearly didn't want to hear my answers."

Maggie nodded. I got up and paced.

"Most people are afraid, you know? It's like Thomas and I are a plague to be shunned; if they even *ask* about our lives, they might catch the unlucky disease."

Thomas swallowed his last piece of pancake, and I got him another one from the warm plate in the oven. Then I pressed my hands down on the table. "I was already on edge," I said. "Then Dad started in. I couldn't figure out how not eating meat rolled over into religion, but he made some convoluted link. I've never seen him attack anyone like that." I plunked down again. "You know how purple flushes up his neck? He got that pissed-off last night. I should have given in, confronted him later, in private."

"That wouldn't have rocked the boat so badly," Maggie said. Seven years my senior and a family therapist, she offered perspectives that were often illuminating.

"I blew it," I muttered. "But I'm sick of being humiliated. Damn, it's about time I stood up for myself."

"He had *no* right," she said.

The strength of her assertion so startled me that I fumbled my mug and sloshed coffee on my expensive white slacks. Thomas burst into giggles. Maggie grabbed a dish towel and sopped up the puddle. I stripped off the pants and frantically scrubbed them in the sink. Finally, I gave up. Not even bleach would get that stain out. My new pants were ruined. Tracing around the edge of the huge blotch, I hoped the fight with my dad would not have similar, indelible consequences.

My sister drove me back to Mom and Dad's so I could pick up clothes from my larger suitcase. I was to come back and spend the second night with her. Thomas dozed in the car seat. While we were driving, Maggie said, "Families have fights, even though we were raised not to believe that. It's normal. Healthy, even."

"But the way I broke the rules…."

"Irish tempers flash hot. He'll get over it. Probably already has."

"Maybe," I answered, unconvinced.

We pulled into the circle driveway. I turned around to peer at my son. Thomas was still sound asleep, head pressed into the padding on the side of the car seat. I caught Maggie's eye, and she nodded. I walked up the path, paused, then knocked and opened the door. Dad came into the hall—he must have seen me hesitating—because he strode forward. With outstretched arms, I ran straight into his embrace.

"I'm so sorry, Dad." I wrapped my arms around him.

"I wasn't playing fair," he said.

"I do love you," I said, holding more tightly.

We stood hugging—and I will always remember his tall, thick body, his wide, warm hands pressing against my back, the scent of his Old Spice aftershave. Always.

This was not a meeting of the minds; Dad would never change his opinions about my spirituality, or vegetarianism, for that matter. But he had apologized for the first time in my memory; our relationship had shifted. Standing up for myself made an impression on him after all.

"I love you too, sweetheart," he said, kissing my cheek.

The next morning, Thomas and I returned to my parents' house. Dad had flown to Florida on business. Mom said he hadn't wanted to go—not while we were in town—but felt he had to attend a meeting with an important customer. It was only for the day. He would be home, "quick as a wink," he said, "in time for dinner."

Mom and I packed a lunch and she drove us to the zoo. I worried whether there would be residual discomfort, but she kept to the old family rules, never mentioning the argument, so I focused on making it a special day for my son. It was his first zoo trip.

When we arrived, I buckled Thomas into the stroller, but he didn't stay settled.

"M-Momma!" He rattled the stroller and pointed. "L-lookie! Big cat. With spots!"

I leaned close to him and turned to see where he was pointing. "Sure is. Can you say jaguar?" I asked.

"J-jakuar," Thomas repeated, stumbling over the unfamiliar word. "Jaguar."

"Good job!" I said.

Mom smiled at me. "So motherly."

The day seemed to brighten around me—a halo of sunlight. I felt secure, her equal. I straightened my shoulders and smiled back. I didn't carry that sense of myself as an equal adult within me. I still needed to see it in her eyes, have it reflected back. It was often hard not to feel like a soccer ball, kicked from one side of the field to the other. Child, adult. Child, adult. For now, I could set that aside and simply enjoy her perception.

About an hour into our visit, the loudspeaker blared, "Mrs. Blaine, please come to the white kiosk. Mrs. William Blaine, to the phone at the kiosk."

Mom fixed her gaze on me, her eyes as huge as Thomas's. Puzzlement gave way to crinkles of concern. "Who could possibly know that we're here?" she asked.

"This is Alma's cleaning day, isn't it?" I said.

"That's right; I left her a note."

Our glances locked for one long, silent moment, and then, steering carefully, we hurried past the concessions with their heavy scent of fried food.

The kiosk attendant surrendered her chair to my mother. Mom's hand trembled as she took the receiver. "Yes? This is Mrs. Blaine." She squinted and covered her other ear, trying to hear amid the office buzz. Thomas, kicking the metal desk which he could just reach, added to the din.

She looked at me, eyes glazed, and mouthed, "Dad's had a heart attack." I tried to distract Thomas by fiddling with the toys on the bar of his stroller—he was still fussing, not understanding why he had been ripped away from the animals—but I didn't take my eyes off my mother. Her color faded to gray as she set the phone down carefully in its cradle, and stared through me.

"Bill's dead," she said in a soft, flat tone. "Your father's dead. He died on the airplane. The pilot diverted the plane to Atlanta." She rested her forehead in her hands. "The Delta Airlines person just kept repeating, 'He expired.' I couldn't figure out what she meant." She dragged her gaze back to mine. "Will you drive me home? I'm so sorry to ruin our day."

Thomas pounded on the front bar of the stroller as we left the kiosk. "C-cats," he hollered. "W-wanna see the jaguars again."

"Mom...." I began, but my voice trailed off. My father, gone? No more hugs from that big, comforting body?

I had no idea of what to say; I could not imagine a union of forty-two years ended by an abrupt phone call in a public place. Now I know there is nothing to be said. Words would have been only platitudes; my actions sufficed. I went over and steadied her, my arm around her waist. Thomas was standing up and rocking back and forth—I had neglected to fasten the seat belt. I rolled the bucking stroller and kept my other arm snug around Mom as we pushed through the crowd entering the zoo gates. I managed to locate the large beige Lincoln in the parking lot. Thomas screamed and arched when I snapped him into the car seat, distraught that his special day had come to a rude end.

I climbed into the driver's seat and closed the door. Thomas's screeches grew hideously loud. I noticed our packed lunch on the floor near Mom's feet.

"Thomas, hey, please," I said. Desperate to distract him, I chucked the brown bag into his lap. "You can eat that, sweetie," I said, watching him in the rear view mirror as I turned the key to start the engine. Primitive as tossing food seemed, it was all I could do: the next, tiny thing. Try to quiet my son. Surprised, he stopped bellowing and fiddled with the bag.

I was not sure how to get back to my parents' new home and felt intimidated by this huge car with power steering and power brakes. I took a deep breath to steady myself, put it in gear, and eased out of the parking spot.

The last time I had driven Dad's car—when he was teaching me to drive seventeen years before—I stomped on the brakes and launched him into the windshield. For weeks he had teased me about his bloody forehead, but he never offered to let me drive his car again. Now, for his sake, whether I felt inadequate or not, I had to master this beast—so similar in size and style to the car back then—and deliver my mother safely home. At the parking lot gate, much to my relief, delicate footwork brought the car to a gentle stop. An unfamiliar intersection lay before me. Now I had to navigate a confusing landscape that had burgeoned in the decade and a half I had lived out of town.

I glanced at Mom slumped in the seat next to me, her fingers rubbing her forehead, repeating, "This can't be happening. We have so many plans."

My relationship to my mother instantly shifted. This woman, who never got lost, who handled maps all over Europe on vacations—and prided herself on her independence—now she needed the baby of her family to take over. I was certainly willing and, if you had asked me the day before, would have jumped at the chance to get behind the wheel, to wield a piece of large equipment. But under these circumstances, I wasn't so sure. Puzzling my way through the city, at different intersections I had to ask which way to turn. She glanced up each time, pointed, and said "That way." Her voice was steady, but flat and hollow.

I heard the paper bag tearing in the back seat. If lunch was going as usual, Thomas was smearing peanut butter and raspberry jelly sandwiches on Dad's leather upholstery. I'd better clean it up before … oh my God. I was thinking "before Dad sees the mess." I shook my head. Dad, gone. My mom's mother had died the year before at ninety-eight; she'd had a full, long life, and her death seemed natural to all of us. Dad was only sixty-four. I didn't know how to respond, or what to expect, and had no idea how to feel, either. Looking back, my feelings seemed suspended in static, like a video put on pause. Shock had blunted any initial response.

From behind me, all I heard was munching. Truce-by-food still held. For once, my child had stopped screaming when I needed him to. He emanated an easygoing calm, just as he had when he clutched my dad's pant leg on the patio. Maybe Thomas felt Dad's presence here in his car. I did. Dad lived in that rich scent of leather; I could still see him stroking the soft tan upholstery with the tips of his fingers. He lived in the large, secure presence of that Lincoln.

As I drove, one hand on my mother's arm, moments with my father from the last few days popped into my mind. I blinked back sudden tears: he would never see his grandson toddle across the floor.

I realize now he had not only been speaking about Thomas. He must have seen the determined support I gave my son, and maybe, just maybe, had been quietly acknowledging my parenting.

My dad and I did not understand how to be with each other as adults, so I had no sense of immediate, crushing loss. He had only tolerated who I became as I came of age; my clear sense of faith and active spiritual path grated painfully against his chosen atheist stance. But Dad had buffered me from the world with his large presence—both his physical size and take-charge attitude—and I had hidden behind him, in the family safe zone. Now that zone was shattered, and I stood raw and unprepared.

I parked the Lincoln in front of the kitchen window. I wasn't about to try pulling it into the garage. Alma must have been waiting anxiously; I saw her fling her apron on the counter, press her hands to her gray permed hair, and rush in the direction of the front door. As I helped Mom out of the car, Alma burst outside, trotted down the walkway, and offered a hand. "Oh, Mrs. Blaine," she said. "Come inside and sit down." Then she paused, and taking in our expressions, cupped her hands over her own heart. "No! At the zoo? On the telephone?"

I nodded.

"I told the airlines not to phone the zoo," she whispered. "I'm so sorry." Relieved that Alma could help Mom, I reached into the car to extract Thomas from his food orgy. Alma crooked her elbow and, patting Mom on the forearm, walked slowly into the house. I followed, mentally ticking off phone calls I must make. Perhaps Alma could watch Thomas for half an hour. I needed to get Mom settled; I had no intention of leaving her alone. I asked Alma to fix her a glass of iced tea. Mom passed by her own reading chair in the living room and sank into Dad's.

Abigail, Mom's golden retriever, bounded into the house. As she made her way across the living room, her tail dropped with each step until it was pinned under her legs. She scootched next to the chair and rested her nose on Mom's knee.

I grabbed a tissue, wiped Thomas's sticky hands, and set him on the floor with some blocks. Then I sat down in Mom's chair and reached my hand out to her.

"Please phone your brother," she said. "I can't face calling him, and I need him now."

I nodded. "Of course." I drew away.

Mom stroked Abigail's nose. At this moment, her dog could give her more comfort than I. Ice cubes clinked in the kitchen. Sitting in that oversized chair, Mom seemed shrunken. She covered her downturned mouth with her fingers, but I never saw her cry. Unspoken family rule: crying is a private matter.

Alma took charge of Thomas, and I went into the study and sat at Mom's desk. I moved the slider from M to H on her metal telephone address book. Each click echoed in the room. I found Harry's number at his new business, Software Solutions. I reached for the receiver, then pulled my hand back as I considered how to break the news. How would I have preferred to hear about Dad's death? Would I want the warning, "please sit down"? Probably. It seemed corny, but at least it would prepare the body for bad news.

I rested my forehead in my palm, thinking over the past two days. A permanent coffee spill on my new white slacks was all that prevented an unmended rift. If I hadn't returned for clothes, I wouldn't have gotten that conciliatory hug. My last memory of my father could have been his deep frown as I argued with him in front of his friends. I can only imagine the sleepless nights I would have berated myself; meals picked at and shoved away, appetite gone; the hollowed-out sense of life-gone-wrong; tears, but no resolution.

Grace shows up in such simple, everyday ways.

I picked up the telephone and called my brother.

## Complication—September, 1978

I bundled Thomas into his car seat, whistled for Nisa, our new pup, to get in the back, and rushed to the weaving studio I shared with Kathryn at her house, about a twenty-mile drive south. We had our first client, and a large order to fill. It had been three weeks since my father's funeral—but life zipped on as though nothing had happened. Somehow it should hold still for a bit—give me a chance to breathe.

Kathryn and I became partners in a weaving business six months after we met at the Dharma Trading Company. She sparked my creativity, and when I found out she was a skilled weaver, I hooted with joy. My grandmother had been a weaver; I had recently inherited her loom and had been teaching myself.

I wanted us to plow ahead into a weaving business. She felt the creative connection too, but was far more cautious about diving into a new venture because her husband, Andrew, earned his living as a self-employed musician—some months they were flush, more months were very lean.

"But I think we can manage it," I said. "Think of all the fun we could have, forging our own way in the world. Hand-weaving is popular now."

"I have to have a full-time job," she said. If we want to do this, we need to start with evenings and weekends."

She owned a large floor loom. Although I shuddered at the expense, I purchased a similar one. Kathryn had named my first smaller loom "The Blazer," because it wove so easily and fast. We shoehorned all three looms into their master bedroom—the only space big enough: Andrew's grand piano, cello, amps, and other equipment overfilled the living room. They moved into the guest room, and the main bedroom officially became our weaving studio. We worked together, sampling dye and weaving fabric samples, three evenings a week, plus weekends.

This particular evening, Thomas seemed cheerful, making up stories in the car. He finally drifted off to sleep, head lolling to one side. When I pulled into Kathryn's driveway, I reached over and brushed his bangs out of his eyes. I wiped the ever-present drool from his lip. Disheartening. That drool just wasn't going away.

When he fell asleep in the car it made our arrival and digging into work easier. I lugged him into the house, got him nestled down in the spare bedroom. I turned Nisa into the back yard with Kathryn's dog.

A woman in southern California had discovered our weavings in a show. She wanted us to weave unique fabric for her elegant clothing designs. I had opened her first order a week before—for large quantities of hand-dyed, hand-woven cloth for the high-fashion market—in quite a different style than either of us was used to. Kathryn had a lot of experience with dyeing, but never in this kind of lot size. Until now, we hadn't considered tackling quantities this big. But since a real honest-to-gosh order had fallen into our laps, we feverishly taught ourselves how to warp sixty yards of length-wise threads on the looms. Then we could weave long rivers of cotton fabric before having to stop and re-dress the loom again, saving more than a full production day. My fingers fumbled at these new tasks. I doubted whether I could learn fast enough to fulfill this order, but kept this worry to myself. Kathryn split her time among dye tests, stirring skeins of cotton in dye buckets in the garage, and weaving with me.

I lost myself in the rhythmic interplay of beats between Kathryn's loom and mine—the swish of the shuttle in the shed as it sped from one hand to the other, a soft whack as the beater met the fell line of the cloth to press the thread into place, the wooden clack as my feet raised different harnesses to create the textural pattern. We were weaving a sweet friendship as well, and I soaked up the companionable silence as readily as the yarn in the garage soaked up dye. The women friends in my life had been trustworthy, kind, and wise beyond their years. Why had I picked men who were such a bad match?

Around 11 p.m., I thought I heard Thomas cough. My breath caught for a moment; over the years, he had been prone to croup. I got up from the loom and checked on him, patted his back, felt his forehead, snuggled the covers closer. No fever. Probably just my imagination. Thank heavens—this would be a terrible time for him to get sick. Not now, not while we struggled to produce our first order.

I returned to weaving. An hour later, Thomas bolted awake, his screams interspersed with seal-like barks. Jumping up from the loom, I called over my shoulder to Kathryn. "That's croup. Damn!"

Croupy coughs have such a deep tone, it's hard to imagine such a guttural sound can emerge from a little chest. I picked Thomas up and crooned to calm him so I could assess how bad the croup was this time. His crying stopped, and only the growling, thick coughs remained. My heart beat rapidly. The illness, usually viral, can progress quickly, and there was always the threat of his throat swelling shut. Children have died of croup. The best palliatives are moist heat or cold air.

"Kathryn, please turn the shower on hot," I hollered. I stripped off my clothing, then Thomas's, and stepped under the water as soon as it warmed up. In moments like those, my anxiety fell into the background, and I simply took the next obvious step. When the spray hit Thomas, his snuffling turned into howls, but it could not be helped. I cupped my hand and pounded rhythmically on his back as respiratory therapists do to loosen the phlegm in his lungs, but the deep yelps persisted. Fear twisted inside me.

Kathryn brought bath towels.

I called out, "Open the window, would you? The cool breeze hitting air this hot should make more steam." Eventually the room filled with the needed hot moisture, but if anything, his cough worsened. I stepped out of the shower, bundled him in a towel, and handed him to Kathryn. I yanked on my jeans and T-shirt, then dressed Thomas in his footed pajamas. "I have to take him to the emergency room. He's scaring me."

"I'll go too," Kathryn said.

"No, stay here. It's late, and you have to work in the morning."

"Are you sure?" she asked.

"Yes, but can you help us into the car?"

"Sure—leave Nisa here with Padnah," she said. "The dogs will be fine. Call me."

"I'll call first thing in the morning. I don't want to wake you up; we'll be fine once we get to the hospital."

"Andrew won't be back from his gig for hours," she said. "I won't be asleep—I'll be working anyway."

I hesitated. Here we were, at a crossroads in our business, and I couldn't hold up my end. I met her gaze, and my pain and confusion must have showed on my face.

"Don't go there," she said, softly.

How can I not, I thought.

Kathryn held Thomas while I moved his car seat into the front. It wasn't as safe, but I wanted to keep my eye on him while I drove. I buckled him in, and she tucked his hand-woven blanket around him. She stood in the driveway waving, concern creasing her fair, Nordic face as I backed out. On a rational level I knew she was worried about Thomas, but I also realized she would stay up late and do my share. And I'd left her master bathroom a mess—soaked towels everywhere. More work for her.

Coughs racked Thomas, yanking my attention back to him. I reached out a hand and patted his small, knobby knee. "We're almost there," I said.

I pulled into the Marin General parking lot and rushed Thomas inside. It was near midnight and the emergency room was busy, but his nasty cough attracted attention.

A nurse quickly moved us from the waiting room into a curtained cubicle with a narrow bed. "The doctor will be in soon," she said.

"Thank you," I whispered, relieved we hadn't had to wait.

Once they rigged up a medicated moist-air tent over his head, Thom stopped struggling so hard to breathe and gradually the ragged gulping movement of his chest eased.

I took my first deep breath too. Crisis averted. I sat with my head in my hands, wondering how my life had gotten this complicated. Nothing seemed organized any more. Everything revolved around my son, as, of course, it needed to. But I felt so out of control—afraid to plan because plans fell to shambles—and unable to get ahead. Ray offered no financial help; he could barely support himself.

Although I had a full-fledged, adult job in parenting, I couldn't take charge of my life like a thirty-four-year-old should. I was beholden to Dr. Liebermann for providing free service, but certainly *that* would not go on forever. I felt caught in the downward spiral of my own making—after all, I had gotten pregnant out of wedlock; I had decided to keep this child and raise him.

Thomas dozed, his face like a mirage behind the plastic tent. His thick bangs stuck to his forehead, and dark smudges stained the hollows under his eyes. He's more exhausted than I am, I thought. My head was too heavy to hold up any more; I bent over and rested it on the bed.

When I was growing up, I wanted to be special, to make a difference. Apparently I got what I asked for. Lots of people recognized the bedraggled mom in their community struggling along with her little disabled boy. Certainly I made a huge difference in his life. I wanted him, but it was not the kind of special I'd envisioned. I could see no way to improve our situation in the future. Even though I had graduated from college, I couldn't hold down a high-paying job and get the benefits accorded such positions because my unscheduled absences—like the one tonight—would not be tolerated.

I wanted a partner, but couldn't blame men if they weren't interested in my package. I brought a heavy load. It seemed as though Thomas's and my life would continue this maze of intermittent chaos until he became an adult, if he survived childhood. He certainly didn't seem to come with the same fine warranty details as other children.

I pressed my eyelids tight, trying to rid myself of hopelessness. I needed to trust more, that was all, to dig down and find my faith again.

Finally the pediatrician on call swept back the curtain of the cubicle. "Take him home," he said, handing me some antibiotic samples. "But watch him carefully."

The doctors gave Thomas antibiotics for everything. I suspected they were afraid if they didn't, he could get endocarditis—an infection of the heart lining—and they'd be sued.

I glanced at my watch—4:10 a.m. I prayed that Kathryn had gone to bed. I pulled myself up, heaved an exhausted Thomas onto my hip, and wearily headed out the emergency room door. Maybe I could find that faith tomorrow.

## Chapter Five

### Directional Shift—July, 1979

On a blazing hot day in July, I picked up the telephone to hear an unfamiliar male voice.

"Skye? I'm Nate—from the Ranch," the man said. "Lauren's friend? I know this is a weird request, but I play in a baseball league in Petaluma, and Lauren told me I might be able to shower at your house." He hesitated, then went on. "I have a meeting, and I don't want to drive all the way home to Novato."

Lauren had told me this guy was really nice. Single, too. Five years ago, she had moved into the commune where he lived, ten miles south of my house. If anyone but Lauren had endorsed him, I would have turned him down flat, but I'd known and trusted her for years. His voice sounded friendly, too.

"You're nicknamed 'Hawk,' right?" I asked. I wanted to be sure this was the person Lauren had raved about.

"News gets around."

I could sense his smile over the telephone. "Okay," I said, "Sure. Come on over."

I opened the door to meet a lanky man with a crooked, sheepish smile, and curly dark hair smashed under a baseball cap. As Lauren had said, he did have a thin, beaky nose. We talked before and after his shower. He was casual with a bright, intelligent gaze. I could tell by the smears on his uniform he'd slid into base a couple of times.

Hawk sat on the couch scratching Nisa's chest. Thomas scrambled into the room on all fours, then hung onto the coffee table and pulled himself up.

"Hey, big guy," Hawk said. "What's happenin'?"

"B-building a space ship with blocks. W-wanna see?" Thomas asked shyly.

Hawk followed him into his room, and I heard him exclaim, "Wow, look at that. Hit the moon yet? You're awfully short to be an astronaut."

Thomas giggled. "I-I'm five!" he said.

Hawk won points with me for that interaction—he seemed relaxed and natural with my son. After that day, he just kept stopping by. Each time I felt surprise, then delight. I loved watching him play with Thomas. They developed a favorite game, nicknamed "the claw"—roughhousing on the couch. Thomas's squeals of joy tickled me.

Hawk invited me to the Ranch for a Saturday evening dinner one weekend when Thomas was with Ray. I drove down the long dusty gravel drive and parked in front of the house. Since he lived in a hidden-away outbuilding, he was waiting for me on the tree swing out front.

"Welcome to the Ranch! Want to take a tour?"

"Sure do. Lauren told me about your organic garden."

He gave me one of his engaging crooked smiles, and we followed a dirt track around the house, past two cabins, then left on a path to the garden. The dirt road continued up a rise, ending at a rickety barn that overlooked the property. The vegetable garden was huge—more than a quarter acre, I guessed—fenced high with wire to prevent the deer from raiding. Zucchini and crookneck squash, tomatoes, chard, kale, strawberries, corn, melons, pumpkins, salad greens, many kinds of peppers—seemingly endless beds, neatly weeded and beautifully tended, lay before me.

"Wow." I stared. "Do you handle this all yourself?"

"Folks help weed and water, but the prep and planting mainly fall on me," he said. "I love it."

"Clearly!" I said, wandering down one row and admiring an unfamiliar flowering bush with vivid blue flowers. "What's this?"

"Borage. The flowers are great in salads, and it's a good companion plant." He saw my questioning gaze, and went on, "It helps with pest control, attracts beneficial insects. Want to help me pick for dinner?" We gathered a bounty of tomatoes, squash, and lettuces. Hawk was not a wordy man—thank heavens, after Ray's diatribes—but he was happy to share his garden knowledge. I loved seeing him in his element.

That evening, we settled on an old couch in his large chicken coop room. He'd hung Indian bedspreads to create a closet and provide some privacy for his queen-sized bed from the entrance. With the unspoken open door policy on the property, I bet he'd been walked in on more than once.

"Wanna get high? I've got some organic Northern California pot."

I smiled and nodded, still taking in the orderly surroundings.

"Hold this." He handed me a small, hand-blown glass pipe with psychedelic swirls of color. It nestled in the palm of my hand. He leaned over me, pulled out a baggie from a drawer in the side table. "Smell?"

The buds were enormous, larger than I'd ever seen. I opened the bag, and the rich aroma cascaded over me. The buds, sticky and green, looked very alive.

"Gorgeous."

"Pinch off a tiny bud. We don't need much." He stuffed half of what I gave him—about a quarter teaspoon—in the pipe and slipped the rest back into the stash. "Here." He handed the pipe to me, struck a match, and lit it. "It's strong. Careful."

I inhaled lightly. The sweet smoke penetrated. A few seconds later all the day's cares vanished, and I floated on the sensation. "Wow."

He slipped his arm around me, and snuggling me closer to his slender body. "Nice, huh?"

"Better than nice."

He put one finger under my chin and brushed my lips with his—just the lightest touch, a question. A rush of pleasure flushed through me. Just as softly, I kissed him back.

A few weeks later, Hawk told me that he, Lauren and the others wanted to purchase the Ranch, and were looking for money for the down payment. The property included the rambling one-story farmhouse, where one family lived. One of the three refurbished chicken coops—not the one Hawk lived in—had two tiny bedrooms and its own bath. I had recently inherited some money from my grandmother, and was interested. Our current rental was surrounded by gravel and concrete. Thomas was hanging on to anything in reach, and he fell down a lot; he needed large expanses of grass as a landing pad. Nisa would love more room to run. I offered to contribute half the down payment for a share of ownership if Thomas and I could live in the cabin with the bathroom. A deal was struck, and the Ranch became our home.

Right after the move, Thomas and I drove into San Francisco for his yearly cardiology appointment. Once again, he received a stable report. Spotting the rainbows painted on the Highway 101 tunnels on the way home—always a beacon—I celebrated the good news.

Over time, we settled in comfortably at the Ranch. The three other children accommodated Thomas easily because of their age spread—from two to nine. As a band of kids, they had widely differing abilities. Thomas didn't stand out as much as he did in a group his own age.

Three months after I moved in, Hawk eased his clothes from his room into our little cabin. I wasn't going to make the same mistake of avoiding difficult issues like I had with Ray, so one evening, after Thomas went to sleep, we sat down for a serious talk.

"You've seen my belly scars; I can't have more children." I said. "If you want your own bio kids, we'd better stop this relationship now. It would be easier now than later."

He thought for a minute. "Having my own kids isn't important." He reached over and picked up his pipe, packed it full.

"You're sure? Thomas and I are getting attached to you. I'd rather know the hard truth now, particularly for his sake."

He lit a match, and offered me the first toke on the pipe. "That's the truth," he said. "Really."

I stayed quiet. Sometimes silence makes the other person uncomfortable, and they'll fill the space. What comes out can be revealing. But Hawk didn't seem to need to say anything else. I decided to trust what he'd said.

Although Thomas was half Italian and Hawk came from a Jewish family, in body type and coloring, they could have been father and son. It delighted me to walk down the street in town together, knowing we looked like a family. I yearned for Thomas to have that long-term family experience, as I had growing up. Then I could feel like a better parent.

Fourteen months later—September 7, 1980—a day as hot as the first day we met, Hawk and I were married on a shady, grassy area near the main house. I had woven our wedding shirts for the occasion. The garden provided large bunches of flowers and beautiful food for the potluck. Hawk's parents seemed to get along easily with my mother, and were gracious with me. His mom brought Thomas a little gift, and made a real effort to get to know him. My hope burgeoned that this marriage might have enough ground to last.

## Caught in the Maelstrom—November, 1980

Dr. Beech, the head orthopedist at Stanford Children's Hospital, and a specialist in cerebral palsy, spoke; the time had come for heel-cord surgery on Thomas's left ankle. Beech said, "Don't count your chickens." From his lips, the colloquial statement sounded like a formal pronouncement. Thomas, now six, still wasn't walking independently. Children who do not walk by four often end up wheelchair-bound. He said this surgery might make the difference between walking free—unlikely—or ending up in a chair. It was worth the risk and pain, he thought. Now there lay a double message.

I dreaded putting Thomas through another operation. Open-heart surgery seemed more than enough for one body, yet how could we not try? His positive cardiac evaluation in October, an additional appointment required prior to surgery, had cleared the way. California

Children's Services had signed the pre-authorization; they would pick up the whole bill.

I called Ray. "Dr. Beech says now's the best time."

"It's good you're living communally. The women at the Ranch can help you out."

*Yeah, so you don't have to.* Then I felt bad for my mental unkindness.

Hawk and I sat down that evening. "It's your decision," he said. "I'll do whatever I can to support you."

Clearly, parents must make a decision of this weight for a young child, yet I still needed to present the plan to Thomas. I wondered how much he recalled of his open heart surgery. I knew he must have cellular memory, but didn't know how conscious those memories were, or if they would make him fearful now. He was a strong-willed child, and I had to choose my words carefully. Trying to gather my nerve, I put off talking to him for a couple of days. Finally, we sat down on the small, dusty deck between the two chicken-coop cabins and I tried to explain what was going to happen. He sat like a frog—feet poking out sideways behind him—as he always did. It provided a solid sitting base.

When I described in simple terms what would happen, he frowned and shook his head hard. "N-no!" he said. "N-no more owies."

One look at his hunched shoulders, his little pinched, worried face, broke me. "Don't you want to walk?" I asked. I had no intention of mentioning walking! I didn't want to get his hopes up and yet, in an effort to make the surgery appealing, to convince him to face more suffering than any kid should have to endure, I held out the top prize without a moment's hesitation. If only I could have taken the words back. I was so busy thrashing myself I almost missed his answer.

He peered at me earnestly. "Y-y-you can't promise that," he said.

I jerked so hard I almost catapulted off the edge of the deck. How could a six-year-old know that much? The answer came right on top of the question, flooding me with knowledge I could not deny: he held wisdom beyond his years because he had already faced immense disappointments. He knew there were no guarantees. Every day he experienced firsthand how different he was from other children his age: he couldn't walk; he couldn't talk as clearly; his left hand didn't work.

Oh my. This conversation might be harder than I had imagined. If he refused, how would I convince him? If I couldn't persuade him, would I simply drag him toward the operating room? I dropped my face into my open palms and took a deep breath. "You're right," I said softly. "I can't promise. But we can hope and pray. If you were able to put your foot flat on the floor, it would make a big difference."

He nodded slowly. "W-w-will it hurt bad?"

"Yes," I said. "But the doctors will give you medicine to make the pain less. Good medicine."

He dipped his head and thought for a long time, dragging his finger on the dusty, splintery wood. The deck must have once been new, sturdy, filled with promise. Along the line, people stopped caring for it, and it fell into a decrepit state. I wouldn't let that happen to my son.

Shouts from the other children cavorting in the front field floated over us. They had no obvious worries. Life wasn't fair.

"Y-you'll stay with me?" he asked. "In the hospital?"

"While you're awake. If they'll let me, I'll stay part of the night, too. Otherwise I'll sleep at the Ronald McDonald House. We visited there once, remember? The place with the clown paintings on the wall?"

He ignored my question. "W-w-will Daddo come?"

"Yes, he will." I did not add that his presence might make the atmosphere more difficult. When Thomas was in pain, Ray got angry—not at Thomas, at the situation—but still, his anger was one more challenge for me to deal with. Unnecessary difficulty, I thought. I would have to mediate between Ray and the nurses, Ray and the doctors, Ray and Thomas. I quailed at the thought.

"Okay," Thomas said. His shoulders were still hunched, his face pinched. His mouth pressed into a flat line. He looked older, filled with grit I had never seen before.

I put my arm around him, drew him to me, put my head next to his, so we looked out at the same view. "We'll get through this," I said.

Three weeks later, we dropped luggage off in the Ronald McDonald room first so Thomas would know exactly where I was when away from him. I was relieved to see single beds on opposite sides of the room. Ray might want to catch a nap when he came to Palo Alto, and neither of us could afford a second room. Even though we were ex-spouses, we'd have to deal with sharing. I sighed. Well, we weren't the first un-couple to face this.

I wheeled Thomas in the stroller over to registration. I liked this low-slung, unobtrusive building amid madrone trees. It only had two floors—ground level, and one below. Wings divided orthopedic patients, usually there for a week or so, from the more chronically ill.

Both beds in his assigned room were empty, so Thomas chose the one by the window. It looked out on a small deck and into sun-speckled woods. Leaves hung limp on the trees. We needed the relief rain brings, and I wondered when it would come. The woods needed it; Thomas and I did, too. We all needed to be washed clean.

I put him back in the stroller and we wheeled to his four o'clock appointment. I glanced up at the fluorescents and knew they contributed to his color shift—but fear did too. I wondered if my face reflected the same pallor.

As we wandered down the halls, wheelchairs flew past us and around the corridors as children visited and explored the hospital floors. They seemed to be on a mission to have a good time, and long hallways did not stop them. I could see bald heads didn't scare the other patients, neither did body casts nor the rhythmic pounding I heard as we passed by respiratory therapy. The children seemed curious. They were embattled; all faced the terrors of needles and general powerlessness, and each child seemed to recognize the others as belonging to the same club. But amid the toys and bright colors, it smelled like any hospital—a mixture of alcohol, industrial cleaning supplies, and anxiety.

Once in Dr. Beech's office, I helped Thomas strip down to his underwear. He looked so skinny and insubstantial without his clothes, the sinews and tendons of his legs rigid with the tension of the upcoming appointment. His knees were knobby chunks larger than his calves, and his left arm jerked repeatedly in the air, punctuating his staccato stuttering. He was pale and withdrawn. Dr. Beech asked to see Thomas "walk" one more time, so I outfitted him in short-shorts, but left his shirt off because the doctor wanted to see his whole body move.

Dr. Beech's office was situated in the hospital, but the maestro took Thomas into the long hallway instead of an examining room. With a team of residents observing, Thomas teetered down the corridor holding my hand, then we turned back toward the doctors. He tried to maneuver a wheeled walker they provided. Walkers had never worked for him because he had so little control of his left arm, so I stayed close in case he toppled the whole apparatus. Thomas's large brown eyes seemed more astonished than usual, but he said nothing, struggling along, mouth pressed shut.

Although I respected the famous doctor for his abilities, he also irked me. Today was no different from previous appointments. He lectured his entourage in a pedantic tone, displaying my son as an object of curiosity. Starched white interns hovered, pointing, poking, prodding. I knew it was a teaching hospital—one of the finest in the country for orthopedics, but how did this make a small boy feel? I knew how it made me feel: he was treated like a lab animal. On stage. Embarrassed, and uncomfortable. Couldn't Beech take the time to address him directly?

"Notice the chicken-claw position of his left hand," he said, "how the tone in the boy's fist changes when he's under stress." Hearing the word "chicken-claw," Thomas jerked his head to peer up at me, stumbled, and ended up in an awkward pile on the floor. I caught the walker in mid-air so it did not land on him. Beech looked on in clinical fashion, waiting patiently for me to get Thomas up so the observation could continue. The hallway seemed very cold, and Thomas, with no fat on his bones, shivered so hard he shook. I pulled a sweatshirt out of my backpack and helped him into it, talking to him to relax his left arm so I could pull the sleeve down. Beech even used that as a teaching device. "Mrs. Arnold is an engaged parent," he said. I bristled. I had never used "Mrs." on medical forms, and I wasn't an Arnold any more. And what parent who came to the hospital with their child didn't appear engaged?

Finally, he released us. I could feel my back muscles ease. "I feel sorry for that man's children," I whispered to Thomas as I pushed the stroller back to his room.

"M-m-me too," he whispered back. We grinned at each other.

Surgery was scheduled for the next morning. I stayed with Thomas during the evening until the sedative took effect, and then meandered back to Ronald McDonald to get some much-needed sleep. The next day would be tough. I wrapped my arms around myself in the chilly air and stood peering up at the night sky, wondering what the worst outcome could be. I had to prepare myself. Maybe the surgery would fail. Maybe my son would never walk. And the hardest thought of all: he would undergo general anesthesia; he could die.

The stars were just popping into view. I desperately needed a lodestar that night. With relief, I found Venus, bold, bright, and hopeful—then watched fog sweep in from the west and cover the light.

Ray arrived early the next morning. "Hey, kiddo," he said, hugging him close. Thomas snuffled the moment he saw his dad, then tuned up to wail, but the squall started and ended quickly. The staff let him keep his music-box teddy bear. Ray and I walked on either side as the intern pushed him down one hallway, then another, toward the first set of double doors leading to surgery. We knew what the double doors meant: separation. I kissed Thomas and ruffled his hair. When the end of the narrow bed pushed opened those doors, I could swear the scent of ether wafted out, a memory from my childhood tonsillectomy. We stood back and watched the gurney recede into the distance, my son a small lump under white sheets, clutching his bear.

In heel-cord surgery, the surgeon nicks the Achilles tendon so it will "unwind," or lengthen a bit; hopefully neither too much—causing "foot drop," a permanent problem that seriously impedes walking—nor too little, requiring repeat surgery.

"He may have some cramping," Dr. Beech had said.

"He may have some cramping," the resident said.

"Thomas, you may have some cramping," I told my son.

The Achilles, I have learned since, is the most powerful tendon in the body, and one does not mess with it without major repercussions—powerful spasms that even large doses of Valium may not touch.

Thomas caterwauled as they pushed him from the operating room to the recovery room, full lung power, no holding back, howls of agony. Ray and I heard it through three sets of double doors and catapulted from our chairs. This was not "cramping." We had been misled, and worse, I had passed on that lie—in good faith—to my son.

Ray went rigid with rage that someone had hurt his boy that much. I put my hand out to touch him, then drew it back. He seemed capable of throwing a punch at the first available person; I did not want it to be me. I left him and ran down the hall searching for a doctor, a nurse, someone, anyone in a uniform. I arrived at the recovery room door just as the gurney did. The resident was giving tight, rapid-fire commands to the nurses.

One of them paused to speak to me. "He's not really awake," she said, trying to pitch her voice over his screams. I stared at Thomas's cavernous mouth, his wide-open eyes. I did not believe her.

I marched into the recovery room, ready to throw my own punches if they tried to keep me out. I spoke through jaws gritted so tightly my muscles ached. In despair, I sat on a stool next to Thomas. He was not fully awake yet, only enough to bellow like an animal being butchered. I had homeopathic medicines with me; when the nurse wasn't looking, I slipped some arnica pellets under his tongue. The nurse administered IV Valium. It mildly reduced the spasms, but not the screaming. When he finally came to, he was as livid as a six-year-old who has experienced betrayal can be.

"Oh my God, I am so sorry," I said, smoothing his forehead, touching his shoulder, my hands trying to be everywhere at once. He stared through me, and did not say a word. His eyes were glazed with pain, yet I could see he no longer looked to me for unfailing protection, or all the answers, for that matter. That day, in his eyes, the idea of "the mother who knows everything" shattered. Comforting him could not take away that intensity of pain, and I had no idea how long the agony would last.

Ray could not face that much wretchedness; he paced close by in the waiting room. When I walked out for a short break I could tell that being alone had not reduced his distress. When I looked at him I saw my own face: carved out, drawn, blanched. Aged.

## The Ceremony—December, 1980

I plodded down the hallway toward Thomas's hospital room, dreading going back to face his piteous crying, and my inability to ease his spasming Achilles tendon. Then I spotted a halo of blond curls coming toward me, and recognized my closest friend, Susan. We wrapped our arms around each other. I clung for a moment, soaking up her courage, wisdom, and understanding. She could make me laugh, take me away.

Although I sighed when I stood at the hospital door and watched Ray head for home, deeper feelings collided—resentment he could leave, yet vast relief he had. I had spent the past nine hours vigilant to every nuance of his mood. When he had bellowed at Thomas's main nurse, "Fuck! Can't you stop this misery?" I placated everyone so Thomas had the best chance for a positive outcome. But the nurses scurried down the hall and out of sight to complain about us behind our backs. Thomas and I took the rap; except for the jobs licensed staff must do—medications and changing intravenous fluids—they left Thomas's care to me. I mopped his face, held the urinal and the small harvest gold vomit pan. I crooned songs to him. My knees shook with exhaustion and fear—and undirected, unexpressed, unmollifiable rage. Knowing Susan had answered my S.O.S.—as friend, confidante, support—felt like balm spread on festering sores.

She pulled away to get a good look at me. "How is he? You seem wiped."

"It's bad." I took her hand and walked toward his room. My feet slogged along the floor. "He tolerated the anesthetic, but he's been in agony since before he even fully woke up." I stopped and sighed, wondered where I would find the strength to take in more air. I tried to straighten my shoulders. "I'm not blowing this out of proportion, either. Listen—you can hear him from here."

She paused, cocked her head. "Oh my," she said, "poor kid. Poor you." She dropped my hand and looped her arm through mine, drawing me closer. "I'm here for you, remember?"

I leaned into her.

We sat with Thomas until nightfall. Finally, between morphine and exhaustion, he dozed. After leaving my room number at the nursing desk, Susan and I trudged toward the Ronald McDonald House. We didn't talk. My child's shrieks rang in my head. I knew he would wake in the night, and guilt plagued me he would have to endure wracking pain with only brief interventions from impersonal nurses. I would be talking with my good friend, snuggling in a warm bed, maybe sleeping the whole night through. Nonetheless, I *had* to have this break.

I opened the door to the room and staggered inside, grateful for the inexpensive, clean accommodations. That didn't change how I felt about the framed clown who sneered above the bed. His picture hung in every room, and he gave me the creeps.

To save money, we'd packed sandwiches for dinner. When I snapped open Thomas's Star Wars lunch pail, the musty smell squelched any appetite I might have had. The limp tuna sandwich stuck to my fingers, but I forced myself to chew and swallow. I was grateful to be away from the bustle of the hospital, the stink of Pine-Sol, the regular alarms and beeps from the medical equipment. We ate without talking, somber and shell-shocked.

I'd brought precious objects from home to try and change the atmosphere and steady me: a polished worry stone, prayer beads, and a sage and lemon balm stick, so I could waft cleansing smoke through my room. At the last minute, I added a tiny carved box to my suitcase. The contents of this box plagued me. I turned my bedside table into a makeshift altar, placing these items on it for safekeeping. Reaching over to touch my prayer beads, and running my fingers over their buttery, olive wood surface, I picked up the box instead.

"What's in there?"

I closed my eyes for a moment. This was embarrassing. "My wedding ring from my marriage with Ray."

"Really!" She leaned over and smoothed her finger on the box's carved surface. "Why are you holding on to it?" she asked. "And why did you bring it here?"

I opened the box. "I can't just throw it away—doesn't feel right, or honoring. My son may be about to walk on his own for the first time in his life. Five years late." I rubbed at the nagging, chronic pain in my low back, the result of carrying him. "It's past time I'm my own person, too." I unfolded the forest green velvet, and touched the ring. "I loved this man; this ring symbolized our caring and commitment, even if it didn't last."

She tilted her head and frowned at me, mystified. "I've seen Ray act downright mean to you. Hanging on to his ring is beyond strange."

"Yeah, you're right." I had been clinging to misery.

"It seems really important you finish with this."

"But how?"

Susan pondered my question, and we were silent for a while. She had gained strength and faith in herself the hard way, through the loss of her children and the courage she'd mustered to get through it. She always had valuable insight to share.

"A water ceremony?" she suggested. Curious, I stared at her. Her gaze held a wicked quality I'd come to recognize and love.

"Come on," she said. "We'll tidy the bathroom first, and burn the sage to purify the space. Then we'll sit on the floor and create your ceremony."

I nodded, slowly. I glanced up and grimaced at the clown, then stood on the bed and turned the painting to the wall. That clown would not be privy to my ceremony.

The bathroom already looked clean, but it needed to be *my* clean. I found Comet, a rough scrubby, and even rubber gloves under the sink. Susan and I worked on every surface, inside and out. I vented my frustration at Ray on that toilet bowl, scrubbed until I had emptied the day's rage out of me. Then I lit the stick; the sage and lemon aroma dissipated the acrid stench of both the cleanser and my bitterness. We settled ourselves on the tile, on either side of the sparkling toilet.

I opened the little box and fingered the pounded silver band. My chest went tight. I remembered the tap-tap-tap of his jeweler's ball-peen hammer. My sense of dread still felt fresh in the marks of the hammer. "It feels awful to flush something he made."

"Could you give it away, or sell it?" she asked.

"Not in good conscience; passing along unhappiness feels like really bad juju." I turned the ring and peered at it closely in the light. I could see a shadow of myself in its surface. He was still hammering on me today.

"What have you learned from Ray?" she asked.

"I saw his potential. I learned a hard lesson—you'd better love your mate exactly the way he is, with no expectation of change."

She pursed her lips. "What did he take from you?"

I turned the ring slowly. "The confidence that I know how to pick a loving partner."

We sat for a while. It was so quiet, I could hear the loud tick of my Little Ben alarm clock.

"What did he give you?"

"He gave too much," I said. "He gave himself away, and then hated himself—and me—because nothing was left." I held the ring and offered prayers for Ray, that he would find his own way, and peace would enter his spirit.

"You ready?" she asked.

I nodded, dropped the ring into the bowl, and watched it settle to the bottom. Then I pulled down the handle. The water swirled and flushed. Susan and I both rocked forward and stared into the bowl. The ring had not budged. I flushed again. The ring sat stubbornly on the bottom, its hammered surface reflecting the round ceiling light above.

I pressed my fist against my mouth to stifle a nervous giggle. I whispered, "Now what?"

Susan met my gaze, her eyes wide. Then a titter burbled out of her. Soon we were both laughing uncontrollably. Tears poured down our faces. I gasped for air. I wasn't laughing at the ceremony. The anxiety of the day had simply erupted; that kind of pressure requires venting.

It took ten minutes for us to regain control. My sides ached, and my cheek muscles were rigid from laughing. I unrolled some toilet paper and mopped my eyes.

She peered through the water at the ring again. "I hope it's not an omen."

"Omen?"

"An omen of how present he will be in your life. Like he won't go away."

"He isn't supposed to go away; he's Thomas's dad." I said. "But I'm afraid of his temper."

"What's underneath?" she asked. "Even deeper down?"

I closed my eyes. Resistance still clogged my heart. "I have a responsibility to set boundaries, for both Thomas and me."

"Yes, you do."

I pushed up my sleeve, plunged my hand into the bowl, and grabbed the ring. It felt different now, not so sacred after its sojourn in the toilet. Admitting my weakness, hearing it spoken out loud, had girded me. "This sucker has to go," I said. "Now." I wrapped it neatly in toilet paper, set it lightly on the water's surface, and flushed again. I held my breath. The water swirled, whirled, and down it went—ring, paper, and all.

Gone.

## Endurance—December, 1980

To be fair, even the doctors were dumbfounded by the power of Thomas's spasms. I could tell by the way they talked among themselves. Dr. Beech was so concerned that the contractions might rip the tendons away from the bone that he cast Thomas in a straight leg, non-weight-bearing cast contraption. "Only for a few days," he said.

The rest of the time is a blur. I remember repeatedly nodding off to sleep with my head on Thomas's hospital bed; I remember Ray coming and going, one day ferrying old pants that I could slice up and pull over the cast, another day bringing Thomas's favorite brand of yogurt that we had not found nearby. Hawk made the two-hour drive to visit.

I remember Thom's plaintive, endless weeping, a side effect of the Valium. Day rolled into night into day again. I lost count. A couple of times when his crying punctured holes in my reserves, or he shoved away food and would not eat, I snuck into an outdoor alcove and furtively smoked a joint. The change, any change, made it possible to re-enter that room and face my son again.

Some days I stumbled back to my room to shower; other days I could not bear to leave him except to go to the bathroom. And then, miraculously, the spasms abated enough to back off the high doses of Valium.

"You may go home," Dr. Beech said, in his imperious tone. "I'll sign his release papers."

As our last stop in Palo Alto, we pulled into the parking lot of the California Café. Ray joined us there. Taking great care not to bump the cast, we eased Thomas into the stroller. Without a word between us, Ray and I stared at him, then back at each other. Even with the cast, we could tell he had shed weight he could ill afford to lose. He seemed just plain bony. Rain sprinkled as we wheeled toward the restaurant, then thickened as we hurried forward. I gave Ray the handles of the stroller so that he could get him under the eaves to keep his cast from getting soaked; and for a moment, I turned my face upward and allowed the fat drops to cleanse me.

After we sat down, Thomas said, "M-Mom, r-read me everything on the menu!"

I couldn't deny that hopeful face. When I finished the long list of entrees, he ordered the fresh prawn plate, which included a huge mound of pasta and fresh sautéed vegetables. It looked gigantic compared to his slight, six-year-old body—and he ate every bite. I ordered the same plate and could only take a few swallows.

Thomas piped up, "E-eat your lunch, Mom; you need your strength."

I laughed; I cried; I tried to force down a few more bites.

Seven weeks later, a technician sawed off Thomas's cast. We both stared at his leg, much skinnier than before, with its red, angry, zipper scar running up his Achilles tendon.

## Jubilation—February, 1981

All the adults from our communal family—all my loving eyes and ears—crowded around the chipped table in the main kitchen. We bantered with each other, some of us drinking fresh drip coffee, some herb tea. The room had a homey, lived-in smell, sweetened now, because as usual, we were passing around a hand-rolled joint. As usual, I felt myself relax and wondered at the back of my mind, where's Thomas? But I didn't have to worry, I told myself—ten acres to play on, and he's as happy at the Ranch as I am. Although the cast had come off, he still was not walking free yet. He managed on two feet when he looped his arm through someone's elbow. The kids could leave him behind in a flash.

Hawk and I had been married for five months. He had finished his commodities trading for the day, and lazed with his bare feet up on the table, the old-fashioned kitchen chair tilted back. This particular day, he was decked out in a tie-dyed shirt and pants. The shirt exploded with cobalt and orange. The drawstring pants flared red and purple. His dense, almost black curls, overdue for a haircut, frizzed out. He fingered the joint, inspected it before he took a drag, and then passed it on to me. I took a toke, sniffed the sweet, skunky aroma, and stared out the window at the crisp winter day. Children shouted and squealed nearby on the property. But I couldn't discern Thomas's voice. I strained to hear farther into the distance. Where was he playing? Were the other kids including him? The Ranch's three other children were happy kids—but any group of kids can turn on one of their own from time to time.

I waved through the smoke that hung above our heads to disperse it. "We need a treat," I said, "to celebrate the end of that dreary patch of rain."

"We have pumpkins left," Lauren said. She knotted her hair up off of her neck—the hairdo a casual, reckless affair.

John, undergoing radiation for lymphoma, was preparing to leave for a trombone gig and had donned his wig for the occasion. "Pumpkin pie?" he asked. He raised his eyebrows and peered pointedly at Lauren. He adored Lauren's pie—warm and comforting, in a circle of close friends—nothing better than that.

Lauren picked up John's wig and planted it back down on his head sideways. "You're a sucker for pie," she said.

He chuckled, leaving the wig askew.

More hollers from the children, farther away now. It sounded as though they were chasing each other up near the barn, or maybe in the vegetable garden. I still could not distinguish my son's voice in the mix. Familiar unease tickled through my chest. If only I could feel completely free to let him roam with no concern; the other mothers were able to do that.

"Yeah, Lauren—pie," Hawk said. "Yours are the juiciest."

Out of the corner of my eye, I caught a flicker of movement.

"Did you see *that*?" Lauren pressed her hands on the table and half rose, craning her neck to peer out the kitchen window. "Good Lord, Skye," she whispered.

For the briefest moment, fear spiked through me. Then Thomas's head bobbled by the window, a shock of thick, dark hair rising into view, sinking out of sight, rising into view again.

My six-year-old son.

Walking. For the first time.

My breath caught in my chest, stopped. My heart pounded in my ears.

No one shouted, no one spilled out the kitchen door. The banter hushed into awe as I pressed against the window. People packed in behind me. Thomas turned at the end of the long porch and headed back toward us. He pushed up on his strong right leg, paused as he swung his weaker left one forward, his shoulder sinking as he planted his left foot on the concrete. His left arm and hand floated behind him like ballast. He glanced up and saw us. A grin danced across his face, exposing his incoming, oversized front teeth. He straightened his shoulders and raised his chin. His smile stretched broader. As he reached the near end of the porch, he dropped his gaze to concentrate as he negotiated the turn. Walking, back and forth. Back and forth. Six years old, two years past the doctors' last expectation.

So much for grass to fall down on. He had needed a concrete surface after all.

Hawk slung his arm over my shoulder, pulled me in close. "Look at that," he said, his voice low, cracking a little. "Look. At. That."

My throat thickened. All I could think of was what my father had said just a few days before he died—"Mark my words; he will walk."

# Chapter Six

### Blood Bath—September, 1981

The telephone rang in the living room as I was stuffing laundry into the washer—including many T-shirts from Thom's latest spate of nosebleeds.

"This is Janet French, the school nurse. I have Thomas here—he has a bloody nose and I can't seem to stop it. He said to phone you." I heard my son's muffled voice call out, "T-Thom, not Thomas!" He had shifted to the nickname on his seventh birthday.

I began the litany. "Is he lying down?"

"Yes."

"Tip his head back, and put firm pressure above his upper lip against his nose. It seems like forever, but if you hold it for five minutes by the clock, it'll stop."

"You know, if you got his nose cauterized, this wouldn't happen," she snapped.

I could hear Thom's loud "N-n-no! No more surgery!" His volume crept up, the fear audible through the telephone line. I gave a long sigh. Minor elective surgery was not an option.

As mandated by law, Thom had been mainstreamed into first grade in regular public school. Although the staff did its best, they were not trained to respond to the needs—physical or emotional—of handicapped children. It seemed simple enough: kids are kids. Above all, support his normalcy. Treat him like other children whenever possible.

Allow him to discover his boundaries. Don't speak in an artificially loud tone; he has a heavy limp, he's not deaf. I spent a lot of time patiently, or not so patiently, educating the educators.

"Someday, perhaps," I said. "But not now. Call me back if the bleeding doesn't stop." The vessels lay very close to the surface—not a disease or condition—simply more bad luck.

Thom didn't want me to rush to school for little incidents; he wanted to be like any other seven-year-old. He especially did not want me to tell the story of his walking independently for the first time only eight months before, once he could put his foot flat on the ground.

"Th-the kids will make fun of me, Mom," he said. "B-bloody noses are bad enough."

But he wasn't like so many other seven-year-old boys. They had carefree mothers who took their children's stable health and mobility for granted. I again weighed the balance—step in on his behalf and, by doing so, make his differences more obvious, or back off and perhaps miss an opportunity to support him.

The minutes ticked by; the nurse did not phone back. I rested my forehead in my hands. I didn't know any young adults who left home still dealing with nosebleeds. At some point, he'd probably outgrow them.

## The Business of Shunning—October, 1981

All week, Thom and I anticipated Olive Elementary School's back-to-school night to meet his teacher, his first in a mainstreamed setting. Since he was a year older than the others, I was glad he was small for his age. He wanted to show me his desk, his colorful painting the teacher had pinned on the wall, and his latest workbook exercises. I secretly hoped he could also show me he fit in, was accepted, and had made new friends.

I parked our aged but tenderly maintained Datsun amid the Volvo wagons and Jeep Cherokees. Late September sun slanted across the parking lot. As I helped Thom out of the car, I anticipated he would grab my arm to steady himself—and as he did, I braced to keep us from falling. Then we took off down the walkway toward the front door. I glanced at his elbow scabs from a previous spill on concrete, and shuddered at how thick and inflamed they still were. Though he rarely complained, he usually carried wounds on top of wounds.

As we entered the busy classroom, I paused to get my bearings. The classic scent of chalk mixed with the pungency of whiteboard markers didn't quite smell like the school room of my childhood. Dozens of able-bodied kids milled, some in clutches of friends, some chattering with their parents. Thom dropped to the carpeted floor, threaded his way on his hands and knees through the crowd to his desk. At his previous school, all the kids had physical disabilities and got around with power chairs or crutches, rolling walkers, braces, and canes. In that universe, when Thom leapfrogged across the floor under his own steam, he shone like a galaxy.

When he noticed I wasn't behind him, he reared up on his knees and waved me over. I saw a couple of mothers stare at him, then peer to see what kind of creature I might be. Their expressions told me they did not see the same shining galaxy. When it dawned on the women I was watching them watch us, they turned away and busied themselves in conversation. I tried to shrug off the tension knotting between my shoulder blades.

Thom was waving even more energetically, so I walked over and sat on his chair. Now closer to his height, I snuggled my arm around his shoulder. I admired his lined practice sheets, wrinkled—true—but smoothed out. The pencil had torn through the paper in more than one place, and his letters jagged painfully across the page—T-h-o-m A-r-n-o-l-d. His sheets looked much like his kindergarten papers. I visualized him leaning tight-shouldered over his desk, holding his mouth just so—holding his breath as well—taking painstaking time on each letter, determined to finish his name.

"Hey, great concentration," I said. "I know it's hard work." But my gaze slid to the papers on the desk next to Thom's—smooth practice sheets, clean, identifiable loops spelling the name Kirk. I took a slow breath and wrapped my arms around my chest. It's fine, I reassured myself. Do not compare. But I always compared. Even in his kindergarten class I noted with pride the easily distinguished letters Thom had formed, while his neighbor's sheet had been scribbled with a fisted pencil—no identifiable letters at all. That's what parents do. Compare, and notice where their child shines.

These parents were no different. From my perspective, thirty-plus years later, I can understand my shock. These parents were also measuring where my child fell short. I was used to Thom being in the "better than" position at school. Now that he was mainstreamed, I sensed this evening was the prelude to the full underdog experience.

Thom busily sorted through his drawings. "I-I gotta find the one about the story I told you in the car this morning." He enjoyed hatching great yarns when we rode together.

As I waited for him to locate the picture, I stood up and pressed my back against the wall, drawing strength from the concrete blocks. My body shook in this new environment. I took a moment to absorb the vast difference in this classroom—no walkers, wheelchairs or crutches. Thirty students instead of ten. On the other side of the room, a cluster of parents surrounded his new teacher. They seemed happy and relaxed, and she chatted with them easily. I wanted to be a part of her circle.

"I'll be right back," I said, and smoothed my fingers across his shoulder before I picked my way through the traffic jam. She saw me coming. The smile on her face contracted. I could tell she was sorting through her mind for some breezy, brush-off welcome. Neither of us had a handle on this mainstreaming business, and now was not the time or place for meaningful dialogue. I yearned to stand among those parents and greet her as easily as they had, but she stepped away from the group and met me one-on-one.

"There are so many parents here," she said uncertainly. "I know you must have questions about Thom, but tonight we have to be brief."

*As if I didn't know.* "Yes, of course. What a roomful."

She seemed to soften.

I wondered how he was being treated by the others. How did she encourage him? "I have lots of questions. I'd like to set up a meeting."

As my words sank in, the flesh around her mouth tightened again, and she drew herself taller. "I'm doing the best I can." She enunciated each word with care.

"Of course you are," I said. "I'm sure it's challenging."

Her gaze queried whether I really understood the depth of the challenge. I didn't feel ready to answer. I couldn't imagine facilitating a roomful of thirty normal children, much less including disabled kids. "I'll call to schedule," I said, and made my escape.

Re-crossing the busy room, desks filled with lined-up pencils and tidy work, I entered the warm chaos of my son's territory again—jacket, pencils, and backpack, strewn on the floor. Even though his son's desk touched Thom's, Kirk's dad carefully avoided looking at us. Thom had located his drawing, and he excitedly told me his story, complete with sound effects. He had covered his paper with shaky stick figures and many explosions.

"Wow," I said, "your drawing radiates energy." He looked up at me and nodded, grinning.

Kirk's dad tripped on Thom's backpack and bumped into his own son's desk. A pencil rolled off onto the floor. I picked it up and held it out to him. "I'm Skye," I said. "Thom's mom. Kirk writes beautifully."

"Yeah," his dad muttered. He took the pencil, slid his gaze over Thom, and turned away from me.

Trembling, I mimicked "yeah" to his back as he moved off to join the pack of fathers across the room. I wanted to yell "How dare you ignore us!" but couldn't face causing a scene. If the incident happened today, before he strode away, I would have tapped him on the shoulder and said in a firm tone, "Please. Tell me about your son. Is Kirk adjusting well to first grade?"

Dead space opened up around Thom and me—in this cheerful, conversation-filled, crowded room—four feet of space in all directions. We were the lone galaxy spinning toward a black hole. From where I stood, light years of distance separated the other parents from me. Over the next few minutes, several mothers managed weak smiles in my direction, but none came over to introduce herself. I glanced down at my beaming son, eyes filled with pride in his work. He didn't seem to notice how alone we were. For his sake, I pushed my shoulders back and lifted my chin, but my courage had crumpled.

The divide was too great. They weren't reaching out to me, and sadly, I didn't know how to reach out to them. Thom seemed comfortable enough; in his own resilient style, he had adjusted well. I was the one struggling to fit in, to be accepted. I had not made new friends here. The only "friend" who would matter, really, would be Thom's teacher. I would call tomorrow to make that appointment.

## Scant Rest for the Weary—July, 1982

Ray had picked up Thom for an overnight. Now I could relax, get high without a second thought, and enjoy my thirty-hour respite from parenting—no responsibilities, no obsessing about Thom walking in and catching me with a pipe in my hand. When he was younger I wasn't concerned—but lately, when he caught me, he turned away with a disgusted expression, so I stopped smoking around him.

While Hawk set up his straight-backed chair and music stand in our living room, I threw my legs over the padded arm of the sturdy 1940s couch, flopped back, and rested my head on a seat pillow. It took me a moment to let my head relax, let all the tension loose. I knew Hawk would load up the pipe for me before he played. We'd share, and feel deliciously close.

He lifted the classical guitar from its case, stroking away a speck of dust from its glossy surface. Then he set the instrument in the guitar stand and folded his slender frame on the couch near me. He rested his hand on my shoulder for a moment. It felt soft, familiar, touch that required no words. Hawk knew how badly I needed this break; he knew I wanted time alone with him—he, too, had been living through the Thom experience. His touch said it all. When he lifted his hand to reach in his pocket for a baggie of pot, his glass pipe, and some matches, that spot on my shoulder felt bare.

"This will ease the hyper-vigilant mom," he said, stuffing the pipe full. He lit it, took a deep toke, and handed it to me. "Besides, music's always better with a little buzz."

I scooched into a sitting position, smiling at him as I fingered the cool glass. I inhaled as he relit the pipe for me, grateful for the sensual fingers of the drug. My constant concerns softened and faded into the backdrop; only a trace of worry about Ray's mood remained. He'd been uptight when he picked up Thom. I shoved that to the back as well. Thom could handle it. If his dad got too out of line, he'd throw a fit. Time for me to relax—lie back without minute-by-minute interruptions, breathe with no parenting worries, allow my mind to wander.

"You were practicing something different this morning," I said. "Aren't you still learning the fugue?"

"I set it aside to work on the Seixas Sonata in A minor. My teacher thought it would improve finger dexterity. Hand me that pipe, would you?" With a matchstick, he emptied it into the ashtray and refilled it. "I'll play it for you. The beginning reminds me of Bach, but then shifts. It's tricky."

He stared at the pipe he had refilled, then set it down without relighting. "If I smoke any more, I won't be able to play at all." He smiled that crooked grin that made me laugh, and leaned over me. "I can still kiss you though," he said.

Our lips felt good together—a feathery, tentative touch at first, then a more robust meeting.

"Hmm." His voice grew more modulated, rounder. "We'll have to pursue this later. Music first." He rolled off the couch and ambled over to the chair. His joints seemed looser, as if his leg bones were barely attached to his ankles.

His first few notes were hesitant, but then he found his rhythm, and rich tones poured from his fingers. I closed my eyes and soared on the music until he came to an abrupt stop. "Sorry, that's all I know so far. Nice, though, huh?"

"Mmm-hmm. Play it again, would you? I love it when you serenade me. You know the way to my heart." I'd learned Hawk couldn't express his feelings with words, but sure could with the guitar. I yearned to hear his music.

"Once more." He ran through it again, this time a subtler rendition, then put the guitar back on its stand. "Now I have the munchies," he said. "Cook for me? It's the way to a guy's heart."

We shared many household tasks, and most evenings, we cooked together. So this afternoon, a momentary prick of disappointment caught me. I didn't want to look after anyone right now; I wanted to be pampered. But I heard the voice of my mother in my head: just as our men take care of us by providing, we need to take care of them by nurturing.

"What did you have in mind?"

"Chili rellenos."

Thinking about all the work—pre-roasting the peppers, grating the cheese, assembling, baking—I said, "Jeez, you don't want much." My hopes of dinner out were dashed.

"Our Anaheim peppers are so heavy they're about to break the plants. They're begging to be eaten," he said. "After all, I grew them for rellenos."

I sighed. "Before you go pick, might as well ask around and see if the others want to eat. They'll get wind of rellenos and show up anyway." I lit the pipe one more time, to delay pushing myself into motion. "Guess I'll have to cook at the main house; the oven's bigger," I said, finally. "I'd better check the supply of cheese and eggs."

Hawk set his guitar back in the lined case, smoothed the velvet cloth over the top, and snapped the lid shut. He walked over to the couch and reached out his hands to mine. Feeling heavy and lazy, I let him bear some of my weight as I stood up. He dipped me back and kissed me. "Thanks for saying yes," he said.

"Okay," I said, but my heart wasn't really in it. "You grew 'em. You pick 'em; I'll cook 'em."

After checking supplies in the refrigerator in the coop, I started over toward the main kitchen. Hawk hollered from the garden, "Everybody said yes, plus Robert and Camille. Can you handle eleven? I've got plenty of peppers."

Eleven? I rubbed my temple. Oh sure, why not? One pan or two, didn't make much difference, and we'd have a great party on a kid-free Saturday night. Change of plans. My plans. I gave him the high sign and turned back to the coop to fetch the eggs and cheese from our refrigerator. Lauren and Camille would help with cooking. Jan might too, if she got back from her nursing shift. The women always pitched in.

I hoped Hawk and I could relax alone in the morning. If I had to, I would insist on it.

## A Walk in his Shoes—September, 1982

I tried to slow myself to Thom's pace as we crossed the Novato shopping mall parking lot—we had only a fifteen minute window before an appointment at home on this blazing afternoon. Longs Drugs was having a sale on toys, and we needed to pick up an eighth birthday gift for a friend of Thom's. They were both the same age. As usual, Thom dragged along a few steps behind me.

"Hi Thom!" An older kid shouted across the parking lot. Thom gave him a brief glance, but did not respond.

I stopped short, prodding him with my elbow. "It's unfriendly not to say 'hi' back. How would you feel if you were that boy?" I asked, trying to coax him into action.

"H-he's no friend of mine," Thom said, indignant. "I-I've never even met that kid."

His comment silenced me. I chewed on my lip, feeling sad and unsure how to respond. Everyone in town recognized Thom—they had seen the deep limp, toed-in foot, sagging shoulder, wandering arm. But they did not know him personally; Thom was right about that. They had never held a conversation with him, or chuckled with him behind a teacher's back. He was recognized for his difference, his variance from the norm. Welcome to my son's world.

"It's still rude," I finally said. "Can it hurt to just say 'Hi'?"

"Y-you don't know what it's like," he said, shaking his head. "Y-you have no idea."

That pinched my heart. He was right. I had no idea. As much as I wanted to, I could not walk in his shoes. I had tried to imagine a thousand times what he must feel like; I had ached for him those same thousand times, but imagining and experiencing are nothing alike.

Dejected, Thom turned and limped slowly toward the car. I followed him. Neither of us had the heart to pick out a gift that day.

The next morning, I dropped him off at school. He tripped on the gravel that edged the parking lot and went down hard. His face squinched, and his hands cupped his knee. I ran to him. Knelt beside him.

"I-I landed real hard on that," he said, rubbing his knee and pointing to the offending stone. I discreetly planted a kiss on my hand and covered his knee. He wanted me to do this, but to not be obvious about it in public any more. He whispered, "Th-thanks, Mom." As he rose and limped toward school, I fingered, then secretly pocketed the stone.

None of the children ran up to Thom. The boy who had spoken to him yesterday turned, noticed him, then swung back to his own little clique. Thom glanced at the boys, then straightened his shoulders and walked into the building alone.

When I got home, I stuffed the stone into my shoe. For the rest of my busy day, I kept it there. It hurt my foot, and as the day wore on, the discomfort traveled up my leg until, like my son, I limped on the left side of my body. How differently people behaved toward me. As they did with Thom, people swiveled their heads to stare, curious—and then, uncomfortable, looked away. Embarrassed. No one lacked a reaction of some kind. No one. I was not part of their human race. They turned from me, and loneliness flooded my body. Based on past experience, being shut out was a reality Thom and I could both predict.

That loneliness stayed with me as we once again headed to UCSF to see Dr. Lindstow. None of my friends faced yearly medical reminders of their kids' serious challenges. Their children were able-bodied, playing soccer, and hanging on the jungle gym. But at least Thom received another stable report.

## From Cub Scouts to Karate—September, 1983

At the beginning of the fall term, Thom mentioned the boys in his third-grade class were sporting Cub Scout uniforms, and I had to agree they did look snappy. With multiple patches sewn on their sleeves, shiny pins on their hats, and smug smiles, the Scouts clumped together in self-important groups. It didn't dawn on me that he might want to join a pack until he hung on my arm and begged. Foreboding crept up through my gut and inched all the way to my mother-heart. Not this. Could this possibly end in any way but humiliation of one form or another?

I suspected that the Cub Scouts were not educated in working with children who had physical disabilities. The den mothers were moms just like me; undoubtedly they had their own child's best interest at the forefront of their concern. I peered at Thom's bright, curious expression, the curve of the smile that had spread across his face and exposed his two adult front teeth, still out of proportion with his other features. I wanted to whisper, "Oh, Thom, don't ask this." Instead, I said in a matter-of-fact tone, "Well, all right, if you want to try it. I suspect that a lot of the tasks are two-handed."

"M-my dad will help," he chirped.

"That would be nice," I said. I kept my tone upbeat, but I had no real hope that Ray would engage in the process. He loved his son, but the challenges in his own life usually took precedence over attention to an ongoing project on Thom's behalf.

Anticipating the problem of the uniform necktie, I jumped in and taught Thom the rabbit-hole chant for knotting it. He paced our converted chicken coop muttering, "Th-the rabbit runs all around the tree, u-up through the hole, then d-down through the knot and you're done!" I could hear my father's voice as he and my brother stood in front of the mirror, Dad behind, with his freckly adult male arms substituting for Harry's, demonstrating a Four-in-Hand knot. They had repeated the process again and again. Harry's young voice piped in with Dad's; they discussed how much longer to leave the fat tail at the start—and always on the right—plus how to wrestle the knot properly snug at the neck. I had stood on the sidelines feeling left out. Mom grabbed the Brownie camera and took a picture of my brother's elfin grin when he mastered the skill. Now also the mother of a son, I understood how precious that moment was for her.

Ray loved to tie knots, and had developed advanced skill; one of the first gifts I gave him was a hardcover edition of the *Ashley Book of*

*Knots*. He made beautiful monkey fists that looked like woven cabinet pulls. At first, he was excited at Thom's interest; then he got frustrated by the process of helping him figure out the one-handed approach to a Four-in-Hand. He had adopted Thom; he wanted to call himself Thom's father, but he couldn't maintain a grasp of the specific difficulties Thom had. One day he would underestimate what Thom could do on a given project, and the next day his expectations skated far too high. I wasn't surprised at Thom's difficulty; he had not yet mastered tying his shoes, another two-handed knotting task. Clearly, he understood the principle, but hadn't found a way to adapt the turns and twists for one hand with modest coordination, and the other that could barely pin down a shoelace.

And then, irritatingly late, I made a huge discovery—the uniform's tie did not require a Four-in-Hand at all—it came with a slide to push up the tie to secure it at the neck. What a break, I thought. I bet Thom can do this; he could pin down the tie with his left hand, and run the slide up with his right. That would help him fit in. Maybe, oh maybe, this Cub Scout business would turn out all right.

Thom joined the pack and became a Bear Cub. How he loved that uniform! I pressed his shirt repeatedly, even added spray starch to get it to behave in an orderly manner like the other kids'. The problem was not the shirt; it was Thom's gimpy body. No matter how he tried to straighten himself in front of the mirror, his sagging shoulder and the compensating tilt of his neck pulled the shirt lopsided.

At the first meeting, I learned the Cub Scout Promise is to "help other people," and the Law of the Pack is "The Cub Scout gives good will." But the leader of the troop barely disguised her resentment at having to include Thom; in fact, with a self-righteous attitude, she ignored him much of the time. I saw neither the Promise nor the Law being upheld in our pack: no helping, no good will. She required my presence at every meeting—as though he were a Tiger Cub, a first-grader—instead of nine years old. The den mother said she could not sit next to Thom and help him keep up. She was not willing to ask other boys to assist either. I held my tongue. I wanted Thom to have the experience he craved, and I was afraid if I spoke up, even privately, the situation would become intolerable for him or, even more humiliating, they would kick him out.

My memory of the meetings is of tables filled with craft projects. I held the paper while Thom labored to cut out the pieces, then I finished the cutting so he wouldn't fall behind the others. Thom desperately needed an activity to do on his own, one where he felt included and successful. At Cub Scout meetings, a zone opened up around him—the boys were good-natured enough, but they were eager to earn their own badges and pins, not assist Thom with his. I couldn't blame them, they were just children trying to meet their parents' expectations. But the pack leader offered no guidance, provided no role-modeling. Today I still get hopping mad when I think about that woman—mad at her, and mad at myself for not educating the Cub Scouts.

Ray looked forward to the Cub Scout Pinewood Derby competition—he had participated when he was a boy. The cars are made of wood and about eight inches long. Gravity-powered, they shoot down a wooden track. Rather than use the standard Pinewood Derby kit the other children chose, he built Thom a car for the competition styled after an antique model, one of Ray's passions. As they sanded, polished, and practiced, I prayed Ray would follow through on this project. It was so important to Thom. And I have to hand it to Ray; this time he came through. Both of them were keyed up when Pinewood Derby day arrived.

I stood at the bottom of the hill to watch the cars cross the finish line; perhaps the weight of my intuition told me to do so. I wanted to see the outcome with my own eyes; but mostly I wanted to cheer Thom at the end no matter how his car scored, champion him, and surround him with all the love I could. Ray often got overwrought by excitement so I encouraged him to stay with Thom at the top as he launched his car.

The cars sped down the hill. Parental cheers of encouragement rang through the crowd. My eyes widened as Thom's antique model clearly came in first by an inch. Then the leaders, with a large fanfare, announced another pack member as the winner, and Thom got second place. In the chaos and crowd at the bottom, our den mother turned toward me. Our gazes locked like the horns of fighting rams.

She saw that I knew. We all knew. No one spoke up for Thom. I'm appalled that I wilted as she stared me down, but I am not ashamed that I never disclosed the unfairness to Thom. One look at his beaming face, and I knew what I must do. I swallowed the bile creeping up my throat, gulped back curses, clenched my wagging finger into a fist, and celebrated his thrill with his second-place win. I could see no possible good coming from disrupting the proceedings and making a fuss. Perhaps if there had been a videotape—some impartial proof we could all review—but thirty-plus years ago there was no instant replay. The dispute would further alienate the group from Thom, and spoil his day.

When Ray threaded his way through the crowd and got to the bottom, he said, "Didn't Thom's car come in first? I could have sworn it did."

I looked him straight in the eye and lied. "It was very close," I said, "but apparently not."

Now, in 2015, I read the Cub Scouts have a detailed plan for including disabled children. Kids with disabilities can earn Eagle Scout certifications; all kinds of accommodations are made. Helping and good will are present today—but not because of my efforts.

A few weeks later, the Scout pack visited a karate dojo in our town. The atmosphere held an air of respect. Students bowed as they moved on or off the mat. There was little extraneous talk. Thom's eyes widened as we entered the space and saw the sensei in his black outfit, black belt knotted at the waist. Although Mr. Ito was a small, wiry man, his calm presence gave him a larger stature. Thom and the other boys settled into quiet awe around him. They didn't rustle or poke one another. Surrounded by centered people focused on a centering practice, my body relaxed. I felt safer and more comfortable than I had in years.

After a brief tour of the dojo, Mr. Ito encouraged the boys to take their shoes off and sit near the mats in the front room. The advanced karate students—wearing brown and black belts—swept onto the gray vinyl pads and demonstrated their moves, wonderful high kicks and punches accompanied by loud cries called "kee-eyes." Their reflections danced in the huge bank of mirrors behind the mats. I could see Thom's face. He watched every move, eyes wide in admiration.

Mr. Ito gave a talk to our group, and I appreciated his serious approach. "Karate is for self-defense only," he said. "My hope is you are never put in the position to have to use the skills we practice day after day. In fact, our practice is not about fighting at all."

At that comment, some of the boys looked at each other, surprised.

"The goal is peace, not conflict," Mr. Ito said.

I thought back to the Pinewood Derby and felt a hard knot ease behind my heart. I had affirmed peace.

Thom's hand shot up into the air. His stammer increased when he felt under stress, and I prayed this question would go easily for him.

"H-h-h…." He stopped. A couple of the boys tittered as he struggled to get his words out. Thom tried again. "H-h-how l-long d-d-does it take to get to black belt?"

Mr. Ito raised his eyebrows and fixed his gaze on the boys until they quieted. He waited patiently through Thom's stammering—did not try to put words in his mouth—and carefully answered his query. "It's very individual," he said. "But the easy answer is years and years. Only a few students make it to black belt."

Thom could barely contain himself as we made our way back to the car. "M-Mom!" he said. "C-can I take karate?"

I saw an opening, a possible way out of an increasingly unpleasant situation with the Scouts. "Maybe," I said. "I need to speak with Mr. Ito. But *if* he says you may, I cannot afford both Cub Scouts and karate lessons. You'll have to choose." It was hard to hide my secret delight at his interest. Having to choose *was* the truth; I wasn't sure how I would manage to pay for even the ongoing karate classes.

"K-karate," he said, with no hesitation. "I want to learn how to protect myself. C-call him today, okay?"

"I'll call," I said, "but I want to go in and talk with him in person."

"Mommmm!" Thom frowned and set his right hand on his hip. "L-l-leave it alone. D-don't make me different from the other kids." He fisted his left hand and stuffed it in his pants' pocket.

"Hey!" I said, "Give me a break! I'm not simply going to hand you over for instruction without asking some tough questions. Any mother would."

"Okay," he muttered. He was silent, pondering what I had said, but he snuck hopeful glances in my direction as I drove. I mulled the whole way home. I *did* draw additional attention to him that probably made his life harder; it was difficult to parse the fine line between skillful and overbearing intervention. My view, my experience, was certainly different from Thom's.

On the telephone, Mr. Ito remembered my son, and unlike the den mother who could barely look at him—he was welcoming—so welcoming I could not stop smiling. He suggested I bring Thom to the dojo the following day after school. When he heard the news, Thom threw his arms around me and squeezed very tight.

That night, I lay in bed and described the day to Hawk.

"You're really jazzed about this, aren't you?" he said.

"This seems like the most positive turn in a long while," I replied.

The next day, Mr. Ito greeted Thom first, then me. I liked that. Thom squared his shoulders and shook his hand. Mr. Ito met my gaze and gave me a firm handshake. He suggested Thom take off his shoes and get on the mat. "I want to see your moves," he said with a smile. He leaned against the wall near the mirrors, his casual body language belying his intense interest as he watched Thom pick his shoelaces open and wrestle his high-tops off one-handed. His left hand waved high in the air behind him for balance. The sensei's level of attention pleased me.

Thom limped onto the mat, up on the ball of his left foot, which toed-in badly. Mr. Ito took note, but made no comment to Thom, and no aside to me, much to my relief. Then the sensei moved onto the mat as well, and demonstrated how to fist one hand into the other and bow, the proper greeting when the teacher calls the class to order. When Thom had difficulty getting his hands in the correct position, Mr. Ito asked him to show what he could do. Thom thought about it, then tried again, and the sensei said his solution was just fine. No talking down—nothing but basic problem-solving, respect, and interest—so different from Cub Scouts.

"I want you to meet Cindy," Mr. Ito said. "I couldn't run this place without her." He invited a middle-aged woman over and introduced her. She seemed close to my age, maybe a few years older. Motherly. Cindy wore a white karate uniform and a blue belt. I had glanced at the belts hanging behind the desk—I assumed in rank order—white to the left, and black to the right. A blue belt signified her rank as an advanced student. Not a black belt yet, but far along. You could feel the deference—and love—she beamed toward her sensei.

"Cindy teaches the white belts; she would be the one to work with Thom directly," Mr. Ito said. "She gives them a solid start, and I teach the advanced students. The dedicated ones. Lots of kids drop out, unwilling to apply themselves." I felt a rush of disappointment. Mr. Ito would not be teaching my son. Thom's face clouded for a moment, and he looked back and forth between them.

Cindy gave us a smile. "I'm partially deaf," she said, "so please look directly at me when you speak, so I can catch your words." I could hear the tiniest sibilance as she spoke. That got my attention—an adult with an obvious disability, and so direct about it. Great role-modeling.

"I-I-I stutter," Thom said. "I-I get stuck at the beginning of sentences."

"Then we're quite the pair, aren't we? That makes it more important you look right at me," she said with a grin. "Can you do this?" She gave a low kick in the air, then noticed Thom's posture, and switched to kick with her right leg instead of her left. I held my breath. Thom gave it a try, although his foot barely cleared the ground before he lost his balance. "Now this," she said, standing directly in front of him and holding out her palm as though directing him to stop. "Punch my hand as hard as you can."

Thom peered up at her, eyebrows raised. "Are you sure? I'm strong."

"Yep, I'm sure."

He let loose with a punch, and the smack rang out in the room. Cindy's hand shot backward. I pressed my lips together to keep from grinning with delight at his success. Laughing, she rubbed it as she spoke. "What about the left?"

"I-I-I can't," said Thom, a frown spreading across his face. His stammering, which had subsided, returned.

Come on, Thom, give it a try, I thought. Demonstrate your courage.

"Show me," Cindy said. Thom gritted his teeth and pressed his arm forward, but he couldn't get it stretched out in front.

"Okay," Cindy said. "You've got one solid punching arm. The important thing is you tried. Now, can you bend your knees like this?" She squatted down, her knees wide, fisted her hands, and turned her wrists toward the ceiling.

Thom did pretty well imitating her, although he lifted out of the stance after a few seconds. "Th-th-that's real tiring," he said.

"You bet it is. But you'll get stronger with practice." She turned to her teacher. "We've got plenty to work with here," she said. "We'll do just fine."

Thom grinned at her, then flashed his eyes toward me. They were bright, alive, excited.

"How do you discipline the kids?" I asked the sensei. The children had seemed so well-behaved, so respectful. I wondered how he cultivated that.

"We teach the children to develop patience, to be willing to repeat a move again and again." He looked at Thom. "Students pass into higher levels at very different rates. Our motto is 'discipline the mind, body, and spirit.' Students are never allowed to hurt one another. Too much force and we send them off the mats."

He leaned against the front desk. "And we encourage more advanced students to assist with beginners. It's good for both of them."

"Th-this is what I want, Mom, can I?" Thom asked. "F-forget Cub Scouts."

I would be delighted to never think of Scouts again.

"I'll run it by your dad, but I bet it'll be okay," I said. "Maybe your grandmother will give you your karate outfit for Christmas."

"It's called a 'ghi,'" Cindy said. "He'll need it to start, though. In class, no one comes on the mats unless they are properly dressed. The black T-shirt, too. Some of the kids do chores to pay for theirs." She gave Thom a gentle poke with her elbow.

"Fine idea," I said, nodding at my son. Taking on chores at home would be valuable experience for him—but it wouldn't make any difference in my money outlay.

"M-m-may I see a ghi?" he asked.

"It looks exactly like mine," Cindy said, "except with a white belt. But check this out." Cindy held up a black T-shirt with a lunging white tiger imprinted in a circle on the front, the same logo as on the sign outside.

Thom gasped. "W-we all get to wear those?"

She assured him everyone wore this same shirt under their ghi. "In the beginning, all students wear a white belt," she said. "Then you work toward your orange one."

Thom tugged on my sleeve. "M-m-maybe I can earn enough for the tee shirt," he said. "Th-those ghis look awfully expensive."

I nodded. "Sounds fair to me." I took a deep breath. I had to make this happen.

I turned to Mr. Ito and told him I would like to observe a class. He said both beginning and advanced classes were scheduled that evening, and we were welcome to return to watch.

Thom and I did go back, and Ray drove up to join us. Ray seemed calm and interested this time. We sat on the sidelines through the classes, the first taught by Cindy, the second by Mr. Ito. Their style was supportive, but firm. One child fooled around on the mats. He was asked to go sit on the sidelines, where we were. No shaming, though. Just a simple, "Sit out, please. Calm yourself down."

Terrific, I thought.

Mr. Ito's movements on and off of the mats were so fluid and graceful, the simplest action made elegant, I hoped he would do a demonstration.

Ray agreed the classes seemed like a good idea, although he made it clear he could not contribute money. I was relieved he could see the value of the practice; I had no expectation he might help pay for lessons. I would find a way to cover the expense for as long as Thom wanted to attend.

Thom could not settle down to sleep. Ecstasy rolled out of him in giggling waves.

The next day, I talked to Kathryn at our weaving studio and got an advance so my check would not bounce. After school, Thom and I went to the dojo to purchase his official karate uniform. Cindy insisted he try on the pants, and admired how terrific he looked in the tiger T-shirt. Then she helped him on with his new jacket.

Mr. Ito stood behind him—as my father had with my brother—and showed him how to tie a square knot in the belt. Thom faced the mirror, practicing again and again, squinching his mouth as he struggled. Although a couple of students watched, no child in the dojo smirked at him. By the time we left, he had figured out a way to complete a respectable knot, and the huge grin that swept across his face made Mr. Ito smile.

That evening, I called the Cub Scout den mother and announced Thom was dropping out of the pack. I don't know who was most relieved—the den mother, Thom, or me.

# Chapter Seven

## Straighten Up—March, 1984

The raw cough descended deep into my chest; I felt it drop overnight. Bronchitis, again—the fourth time in the past twelve months, and four times the year before. My daily marijuana habit had caught up with me. Most of my friends smoked pot, but as I sat on the side of the bed, hunched and hacking, I had to admit I smoked more regularly than they did. With the enormity of each new discovery of Thom's deficits as additional work was demanded of him in school, I yearned to smoke often. Getting stoned eased my worry and disappointment. It dampened my flaring rage at the tactlessness of the medical community, the failure of his teachers, and the heartlessness of the strangers who shunned him in public. My beautiful son. I could feel our unique connection each time some thoughtless act occurred. It hurt physically, as though I had been struck.

Pot also blunted awareness of my own failings. The more I smoked, the less I chose to be directly involved with Thom, whether it was homework or an art project, reading out loud or gardening. I wanted to sit on the couch and float.

The hard, deep cough wracked me again. My lungs ached. They felt heavy and full of gunk. I could get lung cancer if I continued abusing my body. Lung cancer! I rubbed my palms on my jeans. I had not allowed myself to consciously think those words before. If I became ill, I would be unable to protect Thom, stand between him and the uncomprehending world. Was I so tired and frustrated that I unconsciously wanted to die and escape? I tasted the thought of being a quitter, of letting my son down, the ugliness sitting like sour orange juice at the back of my throat. No, I didn't want withdrawal through illness. That wasn't the kind of solution I sought.

I called Susan, who had kicked the habit the year before. "How'd you quit pot?"

She hesitated, silent for a long moment. "I went to meetings," she finally said.

Shock reeled through my body, prickling my skin. "You never told me! Regular meetings, the whole deal?"

"Uh huh," she replied. "The whole deal. Alcohol, too."

I didn't want to go that route yet. But clearly my poor lungs needed a break. Now. The temptation to smoke stalked me fifty times a day. In my relationship with Hawk and the community we lived in, marijuana was plentiful. Alluring.

I hungered for grass's soothing effect, but it was clear I needed to quit for good. Purge every last molecule of it. Not just try, but succeed. I owed it to Thom.

For one week, I didn't smoke. Then I wavered. I wandered into the living room and plunked down in my worn platform rocker. An overflowing ashtray sat on the apple crate table. I leaned over, told myself I was just looking. The sour smell, reminiscent of sewage mixed with roofing tar, accosted my nose. Repulsive. I kept staring. The receptacle itself was smeared with oily black residue. No wonder my lungs hurt. Little stained roaches—stub ends of joints—filled it, along with blackened wooden matches, a rubbish pile of sticks and seeds, and crumpled gum wrappers. A long, long week ago I had fished around in there for a smoke. Imagine.

I tapped my thumbs together. My cough *has* improved, I thought. I reached for Hawk's glass pipe, lying on its side by the ashtray. Its iridescent rainbow colors were no longer recognizable under a tacky layer of tar, but I didn't care. I filled it with two pinches of marijuana from a baggie nearby, and tamped it down. I hesitated, set the pipe on the ashtray, and picked up the open baggie, lowered my nose and breathed in the sticky, sweet, earthy smell. The scent had a subtle underbelly similar to descriptions of wine. I sniffed again. One toke wouldn't hurt.

Wait a minute! If I picked up smoking again, Thom might want to get high as well. What would stop him from choosing the habit, maybe not this year, at nine, but at thirteen? I dropped the bag on the table. I could not do this to my son. He knew the distinct odor; he had figured out what I was doing. I had seen his downcast glance when I sneaked outside for a toke, and then zoned out on the couch. He didn't approve now, but he'd been around pot for so long, his attitude could change any day. He would be tempted to experiment.

I pushed the pipe away, and got up from the rocker, sick with shame. Yet I could hardly imagine a future that did not include the softening effect of pot on my ragged emotions. Days imagined without it, or dinner without wine, felt so empty, even lonely, unfeeling events, without the companionable, tingly warmth. Before I could change my mind, I called Susan again and asked to go to a sobriety meeting with her.

I drove the ten long, rainy miles to San Rafael, and met Susan outside the door of the meeting room at the Fifth Presbyterian Church. I hesitated, staring at the door. She waited patiently by my side. At least this was an all-women's meeting; a bunch of male heroin addicts would have scared the shit out of me. Their macho posturing, shut-down emotions, tracks on their arms—I had seen guys like that loitering around the door of a recovery house I walked past in this town. I'd hurried to get away from them. I told myself I was not anything like them.

"Do I really belong here?" I asked her. "With *addicts*?"

She raised an eyebrow. "Truthfully. Does pot get in the way of your everyday activities? This is your best friend asking, remember."

Of anyone in the world, I trusted her. I leaned against the wall. Just getting in my car this morning, I could smell the stuff. Ten days before, I had taken a couple of tokes from a joint in my car before walking into a parent-teacher conference. I wondered at the time why Thom's teacher had frowned and backed away a step. She must have smelled it on me. She knew. The whole staff must have known. The hierarchy of people who planned for and assisted my son—I imagined them talking behind my back. *Poor Thom, with that addicted, pothead of a mother.*

Every time I saw a police car, my steering wheel got slippery with sweat as I imagined them pulling me over, finding the baggie under the seat. Last week—seven soul-pinching days, 168 dragged-out hours—I had ached to smoke. This morning I had finished the antibiotics for the current round of bronchitis, and finally my lungs no longer hurt. Yet I hungered to light up right now, feel the hot curls of comforting, numbing smoke penetrate my being before going into this meeting. I didn't care if it started the cycle all over again. I craved pot. I wondered if I would always want it.

I raised my gaze to Susan, sighed, and nodded slowly. We walked inside. Eighteen women sat around a long line of tables shoved together. Most seemed to be between twenty and forty; I was thirty-seven. They greeted me with smiles, more welcoming than the PTA or Cub Scouts. When my turn came to introduce myself, the words stuck. I had to clear my throat and force my voice past a stammer like Thom's. A hand on my shoulder. Nods around the table.

"Keep coming back," one woman said, after the meeting. "It gets easier, I promise." Her encouragement felt like a mainline transfusion of hope. I hadn't experienced this much open-hearted warmth in a long time. With support like this, maybe I could break this habit. No. Be real, I said to myself. Addiction. Break this addiction.

I waited until I had attended five sobriety meetings to assure myself I had the strength for my next step. After dinner, I broke the news to Hawk I would no longer smoke pot—or drink wine—with him. His expression went from astonishment to frustration.

"Why are you doing this?" he asked. "Don't expect me to stop smoking around you. It's always been okay, and suddenly it's not? You're on your own." He turned and left the room. I shook my head in amazement and disappointment. So different from the acceptance I received at meetings.

Home didn't feel safe anymore. Certainly not comforting. One after another, friends discounted my decision and downplayed my health concerns. Only one couple in the crowd of Hawk's friends did not use pot. I prayed they'd be at the party we would attend in a few days.

When we showed up at the party and our sober friends were not there, I felt abandoned. Vulnerable. For more than a decade, pot had damped down my introverted shyness, made hanging out in large groups easier.

At dinner, some of the guys made teasing comments, most ignored me. While they smoked, I sat on the sidelines, arms wrapped around myself. Where were my kind? The more pot was smoked—followed by alcohol—the louder and more incoherent the scene became. I fingered the talisman in my pocket, the "chip." In my meeting I had received a silver-dollar-sized plastic disk with ONE WEEK emblazoned in gold print. Chocolate chip cookies might just stave off my loneliness. I headed for a table loaded with comfort food.

It wasn't any better in my daily life. The most difficult times revolved around my son—after I picked him up at daycare, or shopped with him at the mall—enduring the questions and sidelong stares. Thom ignored those conversations, but I patiently answered and educated wherever we went. The strong desire to smoke still tugged. I wanted to retreat to the familiarity and privacy of our property. There I could dream of packing a pipe full of sticky marijuana buds, lighting up, and waiting for the gentle fingers of the drug to smooth away my nagging worries. How would Thom ever get a decent education? It hurt to watch people either ignore him or jump in to finish his sentences, not giving him the space to express himself.

But I managed not to smoke, only to dream about it. I made sure no residue of other people's smoke hung on my clothes before I met with doctors or teachers. As the weeks passed, I took satisfaction in small milestones. My first school meeting with no toke beforehand—my new confidence with his teacher—I could meet her eyes again. I could meet everyone's eyes, especially my son's.

A friend commented that I seemed livelier and had more color in my cheeks. I smiled as I thought about the one month chip I received the day before. I slipped it into my change purse where I would see it often. That chip gave me the strength to be around Hawk when he smoked.

One night in mid-April, two months after I quit, I woke in a sweat, jerked to a sitting position, my heart knocking my chest wall. I had felt the tissue-thin paper in my hand, the sensation of rolling the buds into a lumpy joint, the paper sticking to my tongue. I was sure I had experienced the heat of the smoke in my lungs, the delicious skunky sweet smell in the air, the first rush of high as the pot surged through my body until it tingled in my fingertips, the feel of passing the joint to the person next to me. All so real.

Then, as the outline of bedroom furniture and my dog asleep on the rug clarified in the moonlight, I sank back, quivering with relief. Hawk snored softly beside me. Marijuana might still be exiting my cells, but it certainly had not been freshly inhaled this night. Relieved, I hugged the pillow to my chest. I felt like a salmon forcing its way upstream, arcing with all its energy to make the next level of the waterfall, falling back, trying again.

My "rewards" seemed so slim—an upset husband, an awakening knowledge of how seriously I had abused my body, and the daily grief that I could not turn to any of my habitual salves for stress.

As I look back, I was embittered and closed down as well. Neither Hawk nor I found a pathway we could walk together that felt safe enough to explore these painful divisions.

Yes, there were long-term benefits to sobriety, far down the road. Perhaps my son, when he became a teenager, would turn away from drugs because I had; maybe I would live a longer, healthier life. Certainly I was breathing better. In the meantime, I clung to every small reward and slogged through each day with a dogged determination to remain sober.

I had avoided picking a sobriety sponsor, but after this dream I knew I needed one. My sober compatriots, fearful on my behalf, were critical of my willingness to put myself in situations where people smoked. I chose Judy, a former marijuana user like me. She seemed different from most of the other women—vulnerable, soft-spoken, focused on the positive, present when she looked into my eyes.

She challenged me to develop new friends.

"That doesn't happen overnight," I said. "Friendships take years, decades, to deepen."

"Eventually, you'll have to," she said. "Don't expect this huge change in your life to rub off on anyone else."

"It's not that easy. I'm married to a pot smoker with pot-smoking friends."

She regarded me steadily. "Long term, that may or may not work for you. Only time will tell whether the bond you have with your husband is strong enough to survive this upheaval."

My body lurched with the fear of recognition. She saw this, too.

She pursed her lips and went on. "You are making your sobriety so much more difficult. You're in a very tough situation."

My mantra became "Life *will* get better. Everyone will get used to this change in me." Friends stopped going in the other room to smoke, or hiding joints behind their backs when I walked into the kitchen.

One evening a month later, a guy lit up in front of me again, handing me the joint to pass along to the next person. I fingered it for a moment. I felt both resentful and relieved. He and the other smokers obviously didn't understand the struggle I faced every day, but at least they weren't actively excluding me. As I passed the joint along to the person to my right, it struck me that he would climb behind the wheel that night, stoned, when he and his wife drove home. I couldn't judge him; I had driven loaded so many times. Now I understood the risk for him and other drivers on the road. My need to be included overpowered my willingness to confront my smoking friends. I stayed quiet, trying to rationalize that I was taking the karate way, peace instead of conflict.

Thom never broke the unspoken taboo at the Ranch about children mentioning pot—either my previous use of it, or my new sober outlook. But I knew he noticed, and I got what I needed from him—respect.

Hawk did not adjust. We had fewer reasons to share activities. He chose to visit friends without me, began to move in circles where I was not included. We used to hang out on the couch while he watched baseball, chatting during the commercials. Without sipping wine or smoking a "J," our companionable times dwindled. I held judgments about pot smoking now, and although I knew better than to voice them, those judgments were fully alive in the unspoken realm. The grubby paraphernalia, the litter that accumulated, the sloppiness I perceived when a group of people got stoned—now it repelled me.

He applied to computer programming school, completed the intensive program, and took a job in San Francisco. This was a huge change for Hawk that I was not able to properly knowledge at the time. He chose this path so he could support our family, and perhaps biggest of all, get health insurance. My failing weaving business certainly wasn't providing for us.

More and more, we led unconnected lives. The life force was bleeding out of our marriage, and I was the one who had opened the vein. Hawk was not willing to help me close it. He still roughhoused with Thom, but even that felt more like a way to avoid interacting with me. The shift had been gradual, but Thom was aware of the tension between us.

One rainy Sunday in May, I heard the Honda door slam. Hawk left the property without saying goodbye. Normally he would find me, ask if I needed anything from town. We had not been quarreling; nonetheless, the gap had widened. I huddled on the couch and felt sorry for myself. I had become the first of my kind—this new sober self—and by changing, I had separated from the rest of my tribe. My community.

I suspected where Hawk had stashed his baggie of pot. Even now, I struggled against the urge to hunt for it, to light up. Instead, I focused on the improvements in my life. Wanting to survive to see my son grow up, wanting to be a good role model for him, had kept me strong so far. I was resolved in a new way not to medicate my painful feelings.

While I was still curled on the couch, Hawk's college friend, Roger, called. He and his wife had moved to the Sierra foothills, and we had been out of touch since January.

"You don't sound so good," Roger said. He proceeded to draw the events of the last few months out of me and seemed surprised I had remained pot-free.

"On one level, I'm good. But plain-Jane-sober can be raw," I said. "I've got nowhere to hide—particularly from myself. It's nasty looking at my history with pot and how it's affected my parenting. Sometimes I choose smoking over Thom."

"I feel cornered," I went on, swiping away tears. "Cornered in a community that isn't a good fit any more; in the wreckage of my marriage." I was glad Roger could not see my tears. "Not much space in this corner," I whispered.

"Turn around," he said, softly. "Your corner is much bigger than you think."

We hung up, and I remained huddled on the couch with my arms wrapped around my knees for a long time. His comment struck me as true, though at the same time I couldn't completely grasp what he meant. But his words wouldn't leave me.

Mid-afternoon, Roger strode into the chicken coop. Seeing him disoriented me—how could he be here when he was just there, on the other end of the long distance phone? I greeted him, dazed, shaking my head. But it was Roger, all right. He had pulled his long, blond hair back into a ponytail that accentuated his high forehead, and all over his head, tiny droplets of rain sparkled like a halo.

"Where did you come from?" I asked. "What are you doing here?"

He touched my cheek. "Worried about you," he said.

He'd come to transfuse me with courage, jumping into his truck and driving four hours to talk further with me. I felt this man's compassion in the tone of his voice. Here stood someone from my tribe, who lived on a continent I must rediscover for myself.

We went for a long walk in the mist. His compassion warmed me, and lifted me out of depression. And his words, "Your corner is much bigger than you think," became my new mantra. By dinnertime, when he got in his truck and headed home, my sober fortitude had returned.

## Courage—April, 1984

Thom looks tall for his nine years, but he's not—he's bone and sinew with a thatch of straight almost-black hair, and brown eyes so large I fall into them each time they turn my way. He stands by the side of the indoor pool, left leg slightly bent and toed-in, heel just touching the ground. His left arm wanders stiff and jerky behind his body. Knobby legs stick out of his trunks, and the heart surgery scar still reads purple in the fluorescent light. I watch the skin of his chest pulse fast just above his heart.

Mike, his Easter Seals' coach, stands in five-foot-deep water. In his twenties, well-muscled and athletic, he heads up the handicapped swim program. Thick blond hair on his outstretched arms catches the light, contrasting with his sun-browned skin.

"Jump, Thom, I'll catch you."

The boy, all trust and heart, flings himself outward and down, and true to his word, Mike catches him, holds him firm until my son has a solid grip with his right hand on the drain ledge at the edge of the pool.

Mike steps back in the water. Drops glisten on his face where Thom splashed him. I am not in their universe, but stand outside, an observer with goosebumps.

"Remember last week, how I held your arms and you kicked across the pool? Such a strong kick," Mike says.

Thom nods, teeth chattering. The pool is heated. The chattering is excitement, or fear.

"So here I am, only four feet away. I want you to shove off the edge and kick like mad. I'm right here to catch you."

Thom's oversized front teeth rattle together now. His breath comes fast as he gears up his body and his brute nine-year-old courage.

"You can do this," Mike says.

Rickity-tick go Thom's teeth as he nods again.

Push off—flailing limbs, head arched out of the water, sputtering.

"Keep coming! You're doing it!" Mike steps backward through the water.

My body, there in that separate universe by the side of the pool, wants to swim for my son. I hold very still as though, if I move, I'll break the spell. They make their way across the pool.

Thom sucks in air. Sprays of water dance from his errant arm. He smacks the other side of the pool with his hand, grabs on, and rears up, like a tsunami reaching shore. He shakes his ears clear. "D-did it!" he hollers. "I did it!" The sound swirls around the enclosure, joined by Mike's loud cheer.

I tremble and cannot stop. Now he is safer on the planet. He can swim.

## Behind My Back—June, 1984

Hawk and I loaded potluck dishes into his green Honda Civic. We were headed to a friend's home twenty miles away. As we drove down Atherton Avenue, Hawk seemed quieter than usual, and it made me uneasy. That much silence was never a good sign; perhaps he was going to hassle me again for giving up marijuana. We needed to get past this.

Finally, he cleared his throat and said, "Francie called me a few days ago. She knows a lesbian couple, and they want to get pregnant." His tone was low—without much intonation—but I felt a layer of energy, even excitement, underneath. He glanced over as though gauging my state of mind, then returned his gaze to the road. "She asked if I would donate sperm."

My chest felt cavernous, and I broke out in a clammy sweat. Of all the challenges I might have expected, I could not have imagined this; it struck deeper than Hawk could have possibly known. I had an immediate, strong urge to smoke a joint. Not even six long months of clean time could erase the memory of soothing smoke deliciously easing what was now rising panic.

But I took no relief. I had to endure the grief that bubbled under the surface. The image of a child, his child—a child my body could never give him, with his dark curly hair and beautiful beaky nose—made my heart ache with both yearning and sorrow. Even as I quaked inside, I chewed on my lip and tried to formulate a sensible response. I tried to keep my voice calm. "Why would you want to do that?"

He shrugged. "To help them out."

I suspected that wasn't the real reason. Was this to get back at me? No—Hawk was not unkind. Perhaps my huge shift toward a clean lifestyle had catalyzed unforeseen changes in him. More likely, his desire to father a child, dammed up and unable to flourish in our relationship, was forcing new pathways. I needed as much information as I could get. "Do they live in Marin?" I asked.

" I think so."

"So we could be walking around one day, and run into them on the street," I said. "A child who looks like you." My voice quavered. "Raised by people who are not you and me." I shook my head and blew out a breath. "I couldn't handle it."

"It would not be my child. I'm not talking about having sex, if that's what's worrying you. I would just donate."

How little he knows, I thought. He hangs it all on "just."

We drove past a farm, and the acrid scent of manure flooded the car.

"They'd be the parents. What's the big deal?" he said.

I stared at him, but he kept his eyes firmly on the road. I tried to picture knowing—for the rest of my life—that someone else was mothering my husband's child. That's how little he knows about the magnetism of pregnancy, birth, and parenting. "I'm barren, Hawk. I feel the hollow, scarred places where my ovaries used to be." I rubbed one fist into the other. My hands were sweaty. "You told me when we got together having your own kids wasn't important to you. I asked you specifically, remember? We were sitting in the living room."

He shook his head. "It's not important."

"You're sure acting like it is." The manure scent faded, but not the mess between us. "They can damn well use a sperm bank," I said.

He turned his head sharply toward me. "They want to know the donor, know the health history. I'd like to do this. At least let me do *this*."

"Why is their wish more important than mine? Why is your friend Francie's more important?"

He looked away; either he wasn't clear about why, or wasn't about to tell me.

"God! The very thought makes me crazy," I said. "Please don't rush to donate—we have to resolve this. Please, give us time to talk. Maybe I'll be able to work this out."

For months with my counselor I had delved into my grief and rage about being barren, what it meant to me as a woman. I didn't need the additional threat of turning a corner one day and running into Hawk's child.

A long hesitation. "Okay," he said.

We arrived at our friend's house, and I had the whole sober evening to ponder which direction I should choose. I couldn't focus on the conversations, and spent a long time alone in the garden.

For the next ten days, all I could think about was Hawk's child—the child we could never have—being cuddled and loved by someone else. The image puckered like a nasty, itchy scab that's not ready to let go. I picked at every side of it. Was it fair to deny Hawk this taste of passing on his genes? But I could not see what possible good his donating sperm would serve us as a couple. Our marriage should be more important than helping out people we didn't know. Supposedly, he didn't plan to be involved with this child. From my point of view, it was a mean whim. But my envy felt truly savage. And if he had intentions that he wasn't voicing about being involved with this child, we were tiptoeing on quicksand.

Friday evening at dinner, I played with my mashed potatoes but couldn't bring myself to eat them. I glanced at Hawk. He sipped his wine and stared out the window toward his vegetable garden. My appetite had fled days before. When I was this profoundly anxious, the mere smell of food made me as queasy as when I had been pregnant with Thom. Only now, I was pregnant with grief, rage, anxiety, and a very old humiliation. I felt sure anything I said would sound whiny, or worse, self-involved. My mother's voice—patiently explaining how self-centered I was because all the sentences in my letters from summer camp started with "I"—still rang in my head. From then on, I had been unwilling to stand up for myself for fear of being labeled self-centered. I could rise up on behalf of Thom, but repeatedly failed in executing self-love and respect.

I set down my fork and excused Thom from the table to go play with the other kids. He hadn't eaten with his usual gusto either; the tension must have gotten to him as well.

As though catching my train of thought, Hawk glanced over at me. I hesitated until Thom went out the door. "Can we please talk about your wanting to donate?" I asked. "The very thought of it makes me miserable; I can't even eat."

He looked down at the table. The muscles in his jaw humped up. I waited.

I tried again. "I'd like to have a conversation about it. A back and forth dialogue. I need to understand."

He chewed on his lip for a moment. "I wish you felt differently," he said, finally. He did not look at me; the conversation was complete.

"I wish I did too. This isn't just tearing us apart, it's shattering what's left." I got up and stalked out of the coop.

The following Sunday morning I startled awake with tendrils of a longstanding, repeating nightmare—being chased through dark streets, stumbling and struggling to keep my feet under me. Hawk's side of the bed was rumpled and empty. I reached over and touched the sheets. Cold. He must be in his office in the main house. Good. I threw my arms wide, breathed deeply, but my unease would not go away. I glanced at the clock. 9:15. Wow, late. Thom had gotten up and not awakened me—a first in nine, long years. A sign of his growing up.

Although I didn't know why, my agitation about Hawk increased and drove me over to the main house. I went to find my son, to see if he needed breakfast. He was sitting with Lauren at the kitchen table, which was littered with glasses, bottles of juice, syrup, and a plate stacked with pancakes. The cloying sweet odor made me gag, but I swallowed hard, and gave Thom a hug. As I glanced at Lauren, I had to clear my throat to speak. "Seen Hawk?"

Lauren nodded good morning. "Check his office. He fixed a cup of coffee and took it in there a while ago." A pause. "Are you all right?"

"I'm not sure." I went to find Hawk.

He wasn't there. I stood in the doorway and peered at his desk. Empty coffee cup, ashtray with a roach. Commodity charts, a couple of financial reports. It looked like business as usual, but my gut still cramped. Something wasn't right. As I headed back to our coop, a faded red Datsun pickup raised dust along the long drive. It parked next to Hawk's Honda.

I didn't see Hawk in our coop, but the atmosphere felt measurably different. As I leaned down to look out the narrow window toward the garden, expecting to see his bare back hunkered down, weeding, I noticed my nipples were hard. Aroused, but not in a good way. What was going on? I scanned the garden. No Hawk. The faucet turned on in the bathroom, and at the same time, I heard footsteps on the deck. As I swung around, the bathroom door opened. Hawk emerged with a small paper bag and handed it to the person outside. Over his shoulder, my eyes met Francie's.

"Oh, hi, Skye," she said, her voice high, forced, false. She waved at me. "Bye." Then she wheeled and fled.

Adrenalin gushed through my body followed by hot, red rage. I pushed past Hawk and strode to the main house to find John. I'd known him the longest.

"I need to talk to you," I said. "Right now." I couldn't still my body or my hands, shaking with violent tremors.

"Good God, what's wrong?" he said.

I tried pressing my hands on the wall, but they drummed a rhythm, so I wrapped them tightly around my body.

"Sit," he said. "Tell me."

"Hawk just beat off and donated," I said, through gritted teeth. "Before we came to an understanding about this! Handed his sperm off to Francie for some friend of hers. Jesus. I could kill him!" I paced back and forth, breathing fast, blowing out air, trying to get some kind of control. I couldn't see properly; everything seemed seared with red, and tears streaked my face.

"He what?" John reached out to touch me, to soothe me, but the sensation burned and I jerked my arm away.

"I've never seen you like this," he said.

"He went behind my back," I retorted. "I asked him to wait until we sorted this out. That never happened."

John looked startled. "Tell me everything," he said.

I spent an hour with John, pacing, raging, crying. He listened, only occasionally offering a comment or asking a question. After I'd quieted, we talked.

"What's with me?" I said. "Why do I feel so horrible?"

He set his hand lightly on my shoulder. "You feel like you were betrayed," he said.

The word sank into my body. I had been circling it, aware of it, denying it. I felt betrayed all right. And not just by Hawk. By Francie too.

Hawk avoided me all day. Lauren didn't ask any questions; she just scooped up Thom for a sleepover with her kids. That night I crept into our bed, alone, exhausted, but agitated. I had no idea where Hawk was. I lay awake for a long time, replaying the last two weeks; I couldn't shut it off; I kept trying to make sense of the facts, find a way to explain his actions, make them all right. If I hadn't caught him, would he ever had told me?

Finally he tiptoed into the bedroom. I heard his jeans drop on the floor. His presence reignited my righteous indignation. I certainly was not going to sleep next to this man. As he pulled back the covers and slipped into bed, I shoved him hard.

"We never even reached an understanding. What a shitty thing to do." I shoved him again. "Get out of my damn bed!" I was screaming now.

"It's my bed too," he said.

"Not tonight it isn't." This time I shoved him so violently he landed hard on the floor. I don't know where he slept, but all night I lay diagonally across the bed with my arms flung out, claiming my space.

## Setting Rage Free—October, 1984

Hawk's sperm donation left me at odds with the world, feeling unpredictable and ungrounded. I needed an outlet for my anger. From watching Thom's classes, I knew karate would be a safe place to vent—I could channel the rage into powerful kicks and punches without harming anyone.

The recipient had not gotten pregnant; I felt huge relief that our volatile energy would not have to impact the woman during a pregnancy so unwanted by me. Oddly, I had no rage toward her—I understood that hunger to bear a child—I focused my fury on Francie and Hawk. The incident tore a profound hole in the trust Hawk and I had built; I didn't know if it could ever be mended. If I could ground myself with karate, nurture my courage and self-esteem, perhaps I could open to trust again.

My respect for Mr. Ito and Cindy at the dojo grew over the months they worked with Thom. Cindy had recently told me "Thom has a *mean* elbow. It could get him out of a tight corner." That soothed a hard knot inside me. I wanted him to be able to defend himself. Now that he was ten, "d-double-digits," he said, I saw new self-confidence budding in him, new levels of courage. He showed me I could trust karate for my growth, and I certainly needed to get out of my own tight corner.

I asked Thom if he minded that I study at the dojo as well—it was important to me that he didn't feel as though I was intruding in his activity.

"Sure, Mom. I'll teach *you*! Show you the ropes."

I put my ghi purchase on a new credit card, and signed up for three months of classes.

The first time I slipped into the uniform and tied the knot in my white belt, I felt a flush of power. Agitation dropped from my overactive brain, and concentration that had scattered over the past few months felt closer, as though I might, just might, be able to reach out and grab it. I knew one day I would surpass Thom in karate skill, but my mother's heart thrilled that, at this point, he could demonstrate various stances and punches for me. I listened carefully when he critiqued my form.

Cindy worked us hard, and while my legs burned as I struggled to hold the unfamiliar positions, my rage flickered and flared inside. I drove that rage into a stronger stance, into more focused punches, into higher, more powerful kicks. My three-month contract called for two classes a week; soon I gobbled up three, arriving early to work out on the practice mat and staying an extra half hour to check out the form of more advanced students. Luckily, Thom enjoyed watching the older students spar as well, and we talked about what we learned. The first day Thom and I sparred together, I couldn't help comparing our laughter, my delight in learning alongside him, to my cool, stiff life with Hawk. I was not having fun at home. Our marriage was no longer a collaboration.

The dojo offered a new kickboxing class, so I saved up and purchased the necessary gloves, shoes, and shin guards. It provided my first experience with a contact sport, and another delicious opportunity not to be at home. We were taught to control contact with great care so we didn't hurt one another.

Karate practice allowed my rage to surface. It finally dawned on me that I was, at the core, a very, very, angry woman. It burbled thick in my chest, growled in my throat. I had long bottled up how incensed and frustrated I was with Ray; irate with the Cub Scouts; livid with Hawk; enraged at every doctor we'd ever come in contact with; and most of all, horn-mad at God. Controlled, yes; dangerous, no—unless cornered. I took delight when I learned how to stomp the arch of an attacker's foot, an immobilizing move. I reveled in my hot anger, and my kicks grew more solid as I practiced on the large gray punching bag that hung in the workout room. I mastered kicking head-high. I had taken charge of, and enlarged the corner Roger had spoken about—finding a powerful avenue for my growth, and pursuing it intensely.

One physical fact held me back: in 1980 I had cut the knuckle of the ring finger on my left hand, and an ensuing six-month infection ruined the joint and froze my finger in a half-bent position. Even surgery failed to repair it. The stronger I became in the techniques of karate, the more an interference this finger became. No bag punching for me. After nine months of consideration, I solved the problem: I had the finger amputated. The ring finger on my left hand. And to this day, I have no regrets.

When the photographer came to the dojo to take yearly photos, Thom begged to have a picture taken in a powerful stance with flames superimposed. "Of course," I said, and promptly signed up for those flames as well. My friends hooted. I didn't give a shit. My son still limped, but he limped with his shoulders back. And me? Let's just say—world, don't you *dare* mess with me.

## Parental See-Saw—December, 1984

Three days before, we'd trekked into San Francisco—this time in pouring rain—to the cardiologist. Gratefulness for Thom's stable report still clung to me.

I snuggled on the couch with my son, his fourth-grade reader open on his knees. Rain drummed on the roof. I sighed. "Hold the cardboard under each line like your teacher showed you," I said. "It really helps."

"B-but all the words above the line confuse me," he said. "It-it's a big jumble." He snapped the book closed, set it on his knees, and stared at the cover.

"Would it help if I cut a thin rectangle out in the cardboard, so just one line of text shows?"

Thom shrugged. "I-I-I don't know. D-don't think so."

"Well, try again."

"L-lost my place."

"How about starting at the beginning of the chapter?"

He blew out a breath and opened the book. Shuffled pages. Finally he rested his finger under the first line.

"Th-the dinosaur said," he began again in a halting tone.

"Had," I said, my volume rising. This was the third time I had made a similar correction in as many minutes. "The dinosaur *had* eaten one hundred pounds of vegetables." I ran my finger under those specific words. I frowned at him. "Are you really trying?"

"M-Mommm!" He didn't look up. He slammed the book shut and gripped the cover so hard his knuckles turned white. I could only see the edge of his long lashes, but he was blinking very fast. He finally peered at me. His face had turned a flat gray, and his mouth sliced a hard line across his face, failure written all over it. The muscles in his jaw clenched. "I-I can't read," he muttered. He slid off the couch and marched to his room, slamming the door. I sat alone on the couch. My heart squeezed tight in my chest. Why couldn't I have been more patient, kept my mouth shut?

The springs complained as Thom threw himself down. I pictured him huddled on his bed, confused and sad. I had made him feel like a failure, tearing away his confidence like a book from its binding. Patchable, maybe. Truly mended? Made right? Probably not. This time I had done real harm. Mothers know these things. I went into his bedroom, sat by his side and rubbed his back. "I'm so sorry," I said, feeling broken myself. "I do know you were trying."

We come from a family that holds reading both as a prime activity and a delicacy that makes life worth living. I cherish the memory of the library with built-in floor-to-ceiling bookcases in the house where I grew up. A casual "I'm reading" warded off all kinds of unwanted parental intervention. I thought this ease of reading transmitted from one generation to another. "We're a reading family," my mom said. "It's in the genes." Oh, what we take for granted.

Two weeks later, before Christmas vacation, the principal of Olive School called me in for a conference. "Fourth grade is a threshing ground for kids," Mr. Adams said. "A whole lot more is expected of them than in third." He paused and worked his plump interlaced fingers back and forth, back and forth across his overfed belly. "Dyslexia prevents Thom from keeping up. We need to transfer him to a special ed class at the end of this semester."

"Special ed," I whispered. If Thom felt like a failure before, this could devastate him. And me.

"It means switching schools," he added, not meeting my gaze.

I don't remember the drive home, but I recall stumbling up the steep hill at the Ranch to sit in silence at the top. I needed an expansive vista. I stared across Atherton Avenue at cows lying in the pasture in the chilly late autumn air; their universe remained undisturbed. I longed for their unwitting peace. I had to—somehow—get a fresh grip, yet again, on my faith. It had been swept away with the principal's words. There must be some good in this new crisis; I just couldn't see it yet.

The next week, at the end of the school day, Thom and I slipped into the special education class at San Ramon Elementary to meet Thom's new teacher, Miss Brown. I had to get a sense of her before this tectonic plate-shift rattled our lives. She glanced up from her desk with a warm smile, caught my eye, but spoke to my son. "Hello, I bet you're Thom! I've been looking forward to meeting you." Her warmth poured out.

"H-h-hi," he said in a low voice, hesitantly glancing around the room.

Her eyes followed his gaze, as though searching for clues to his interests. "Do you enjoy drawing?"

He nodded.

"Check out these supplies," she said, rising to open a cabinet at the side of the room.

"D-do I have to read out loud here, to the whole class?" He had a stricken expression.

Miss Brown turned to meet his question directly. "No. Most of the children have difficulty with reading, Thom. Would you be comfortable reading out loud to me?"

His body language softened. Mine did too. He nodded to her. This room and Miss Brown felt comfortable, direct, safe. This might turn out all right.

## Blood Brothers—January, 1985

Finally released from a freeway traffic jam, and running late, I squealed into the parking lot at Thom's daycare and walked through the winter drizzle toward the low-slung portable buildings California built when classroom space ran out. Thom crouched on the ground next to the outside wall. Something didn't seem right. Anxious, I jogged over to him.

"S-Sandy pushed me down and called me a cripple. Y-you should have heard him—like it was a dirty word," he said, pointing to his torn name brand pants and badly scraped knee. He fingered the long rent in the material. "L-l-look at my new pants." He glanced up, his brows pinched together, worried I might be angry. Relieved that he wasn't seriously hurt, I ruffled his hair and gingerly pulled the fabric back to get a better look at the wound. Taking a tissue from my pocket, I wet it on my tongue and dabbed at the grit. He grimaced, but under the coagulating blood the damage didn't look too bad.

Sandy was his new best friend. His mom and I called them "salt and pepper"—both ten, both skinny and the same height, but Sandy was a towhead, and Thom's hair glowed black walnut.

I tried not to take sides in kid disputes. It always takes two; for sure, my son was complicit as well. "What happened?" I asked with a mom's voice that required a truthful answer.

He met my gaze, his eyes wide and filled with wonder. "I-I didn't do *anything*, Mom." Thom shook his head, his expression bewildered. "N-not this time. His father left them a couple of weeks ago. S-Sandy's real mad at his dad and I think he took it out on me."

I looked into his innocent eyes and sat on my heels, startled that he knew so much, so young.

He understood firsthand what a split family felt like. He already had uptight, unhappy parents at home, where the energy was so potent and entangled it leaked all over him. Yet Thom retained this gentle curiosity in the face of adversity.

He stared at me with a perplexed frown. "Th-think Sandy will still want to be friends?" he asked, softly.

"I'd think so," I said. "But do you? After all, he called you names and hurt you, not the other way around." I realized I was talking about myself, as well. Why did I still want to be intimate with Hawk after he had betrayed my trust? I had passed along a generational disease—Thom had learned this misplaced loyalty from me.

"Y-yeah, I do; he's cool. K-kids bang each other up. C-comes with the territory."

I shook my head. Now where did he learn that? I must have been thirty before I had that kind of understanding.

He sucked his forefinger, then scrubbed cautiously around the edge of the wound. He peered with interest at the deep red on his fingertip, and wiped a streak on his pants. "G-guess we're blood brothers now," he said.

Instead of lashing out at his hurting friend, Thom had responded peaceably, and worked to understand his behavior. Karate had made a huge difference for him; I still had a long way to go.

# Chapter Eight

## The Question—January, 1985

My therapist requested I bring Hawk in for an appointment. "Each of you pick an issue," she said. As soon as Hawk arrived home from work and changed out of his dress slacks and jacket, I approached him. "Janine wants you to come in for a session with me, and discuss something that's bothering you. Would you be willing?"

He rubbed his chin. "Okay, I guess that's a good idea. When?"

"I made the appointment late next Tuesday because of work. Is 5 p.m. okay?"

"I'll go in to work at the crack of dawn and come back on one of the first commute buses. I can make it."

I arrived first. Would he really show up? Ray had never been willing to pursue therapy. Then I heard gravel crunching in the parking lot. Hawk opened the door of the waiting room, acknowledged me with his eyes, but didn't speak. My stomach churned as we sat in the cramped space.

Hawk hunched over, his hands clasped, thumbs tapping together in a steady rhythm. I hadn't noticed his curly hair now had a few gray threads.

Finally Janine called us in. "I asked each of you to prepare a question," she said. "Who wants to begin?"

I stared at Hawk, worried. Since Janine was my therapist, if I went first, he'd be sure we were ganging up on him.

He jumped right in. "I'll be the guinea pig," he said.

Surprise again.

"What's your issue?" Janine asked.

"If Skye won't adopt a child with me, I'll have to leave her," he said. His tone was even, as though he were saying, "We're having eggs for breakfast."

My body didn't know how to react, so it froze. I felt as though I couldn't move any part of it.

Janine sat up straighter, and looked from Hawk to me. She said, "Skye, you look really surprised. Haven't you two talked about this?"

"We talked about children from the start—that I couldn't have any more. Hawk said he didn't need his own kids. He has never even asked me to consider adoption," I said. "This is fresh news to me." I stared at him, stunned, then glanced at Janine. She looked nervous, clearly too inexperienced for the likes of us. I felt hysterical laughter boil up. Surely Hawk was teasing me. But another glance at my husband quashed that possibility. He meant it.

He raised his eyebrows. "I'll give you six months to make up your mind."

We spent fifty minutes talking, but all I heard was six months. Only six months.

Afterward, as I sat in my car, I realized his donating sperm should have been a bold warning. No matter what Hawk said earlier, fathering children was now important to him. If that were true, then adoption would be no more than a second best solution, a ghost of what he yearned for. He wanted his own children, and I could not give them to him. How I yearned to be able to! I leaned my head on the steering wheel as I blubbered and howled.

A man knocked on the window of my car, and I waved him away.

He hovered. "Are you all right?"

I cracked the window. "Fine," I whispered. "This cry has been ten years coming. I just want to be alone."

He shook his head and walked away.

I had chosen sobriety and been the first to change the rules of our marriage. Now Hawk had upped the ante big time. Putting a six-month deadline on this decision felt like a game, one I didn't care to play, considering the stakes. I had watched other couples and their ante-up games destroy their marriages and worse, their children's respect. I lowered my head and settled back into my long-needed cry. How would I ever find the strength to deal with this, and what would the new rules be? We didn't even have an experienced therapist to guide us.

## True Friendship—April, 1985

The clatter of treadling and rock music greeted me as I walked into HarmanBlaine studios. We had plenty of weaving orders, and could hardly keep up with the demand. All five looms held sixty yard warps, and weavers steadily knocked out yardage on each. Yet because of distribution problems—too many middle people—we couldn't make money; the business fell further into debt each month. The studio hummed with activity, but I was slogging through my work. Kathryn stirred our huge cauldron of a dye pot at the back of the studio.

I finished warping the dobby, the largest production loom in the studio, and the only one with a fly shuttle. Warping is a tedious process that can only be successful with careful attention and patience—one end of yarn threaded incorrectly, and the fabric is spoiled. Some errors can be fixed by cutting off the weaving and rethreading, others can be corrected in the finished fabric. Some cannot be fixed at all.

It was time to tie on the warp. I began at the center of the warp threads, tying a clump to the metal bar. The center completed, I knotted the next group to the left, then one to the right, until the whole warp, fifteen bundles in all, was tied on. Now for the exciting part: I laid in torn strips of sheeting, beat them into place to space the threads evenly, and was ready to begin weaving. I found my rhythm and wove two inches. I stopped to squint at the fabric growing in front of me. A distinct error in threading, as visible as the nap of carpet brushed the wrong direction, lay blatant in the fabric.

"Shit," I muttered. As I examined the warp more closely, I realized this was not a simple error of two twisted threads. A wave of anxiety roared up my body. The designer who had ordered this fabric had called up screaming for it—literally—the day before. "Kathryn?" I called back to the dye shop. "I need your help over here. I've got a crisis."

Kathryn gave one last stir, extracted herself from her rubber gloves, and made her way to me. She studied the threading problem, then she faced me, hands on hips. "A crisis is when someone gets run over by a car," she said. "This is a problem, a challenge. This is not a crisis."

There was something about the tone of her voice—no accusation, and I could feel her love—but the underlying grit surprised me.

"If you didn't refer to everything as a crisis," she went on, "perhaps you would have fewer of them in your life."

Quickly, before my knees could give way, I sat down on the loom bench. She was correct, I knew it—knew it in the inner recesses of my body, in the muscles along my spine—and could sense the profound difference this change in perception would make. A bad weaving error, not a crisis. Bills to pay at the business and not enough money, not a crisis. Thomas getting croup, like the time I had to take him to the emergency room, perhaps an impending crisis.

I looked up at Kathryn and without speaking, nodded. I valued her opinion. She was as close to me as a sister. I finally managed to say, "I get it." I felt hollow inside, bereft. I wondered when I had chosen to define my life by the markers of crises, and if I would feel alive without them.

Kathryn reassured me with a touch on the shoulder, then slipped in to sit on the loom bench with me. "Okay," she said, "let's look at this threading problem." She studied what I had woven, then squinted at the pattern in the heddles. "This is a tough one."

"Yeah. See there?" I pointed. "I think a whole section of the pattern is reversed."

"Yep," she said. "Time to hack off the weaving and rethread."

We batted ideas back and forth. In the end, it took eight hours crouched inside the loom's framework to rethread and straighten it out. A day in production, lost. A painful telephone call to the designer.

Moments of humiliation. But in the big scheme of things, not a crisis, only the kind of problems and events that arise in every life.

Kathryn's intuition was correct—when I stopped using the word, life smoothed and eased. Weaving was my avocation, and when it turned into a stressful job with too many deadlines and problems, it depleted my joy. But we had formed a partnership, suffered and struggled shoulder to shoulder, so I would learn this lesson.

The bereft feeling never came back, and I have not used the word "crisis"—in speaking about my own life—since that day.

## The Language of Love—June, 1985

Five months had passed since our joint therapy appointment with Janine, and three months since I'd begun individual sessions with Deborah, a more experienced therapist. Hawk and I didn't talk about adoption; we had no idea how to bridge a discussion, and hadn't succeeded in couples therapy. Sadly, we didn't talk about much. Neither of us had experience parsing feelings, particularly in marriage. Displays of difficult emotions, or back-and-forth serious disagreements had been squashed in my family of origin—I'd had no role models and hadn't learned the skill. I can't think of one intimate conversation with either of my parents, and it was much the same in Hawk's family. His dad joked constantly; I never saw him dip beneath the surface in the six and a half years I had known him. I suspected his mom had the capacity, but she didn't marry a man who brought that out.

So our lives went on, side by side—skimming the surface. We slept in the same bed—without cuddling or sex—ate meals as a family, pretended life was normal. Each morning when I awakened, I promised myself that before nightfall, I would confront Hawk and insist he talk to me; each night before I fell asleep I berated myself for chickening out.

Thom must have felt stranded, with a distracted, anxious mom and a withdrawn stepdad. Hawk had brought an elephant into our living room, but he didn't encourage me to feed or tend it. It just stood there, massive, restive. Previously, pot had gotten us through hard issues; we'd smoke and end up so mellow neither of us cared to pick at our wounds. Now, we had no mutual way to ease our discomfort.

One blazing afternoon I walked into the bedroom and found Hawk curled in a fetal position on our bed.

I sat down next to him. "Are you okay?" I asked. "Want to talk?" I dreaded and yearned for him to say yes, so we could crack open this ugly pustule which had turned our lives upside down.

He looked pale, his frown mark cut deeper, his mouth seemed thinned, pulled tight. There was no scent of pot around him; he had not been smoking.

"I'm just a little sad," he said. "That's all. I'll be fine."

He seemed grief-stricken to me, not "a little sad." How could he not know the depth of his own feelings when clearly they had knocked him flat? I traced the lines on his forehead.

"Tell me." If only he could let his feelings out, we might get somewhere.

"Nothing to tell. Just a little sad."

"Try, please."

"Sad. That's all." He curled up a little tighter, like a possum protecting its soft, inner parts.

I'd tried to get him to talk about his feelings on earlier occasions, and had finally given up, figuring if he wanted to come to me, he could. But this, this seemed so different. Maybe he didn't have a vocabulary for his own feelings. A thread of hope tugged in me. Vocabulary can be learned.

The next week I roared into my therapist's office, excited to explore this possibility. "What do you think?" I asked. "Can Hawk learn emotional language?"

Deborah pursed her lips and considered my question. "Can he?" she said. "I don't know. Perhaps, over time. Will he?" She paused again. "What do you think? What does your deepest intuition say?"

"I don't know," I said. "That's why I asked you."

"Skye," Deborah said, "you have a complex emotional language. Sit with your question for a few minutes."

We sat in silence. The pressure built in my chest, pounded in my ears. Finally, wracking sobs pushed their way out of my body. "I don't think so," I whispered. "It's never going to happen." After a few minutes, I blew my nose and mopped my eyes.

## The Answer—September, 1985

I trudged out to weed the carrot bed even though the sun was still high and hot. Eight months had passed since Hawk announced his "adopt or I'm gone" six-month deadline. I loathed approaching my fortieth birthday with life in such turmoil—a marriage cracking apart, an eleven-year-old child struggling to find his place in the world. As I yanked the abundant purslane—a therapeutic pursuit—I admitted I wasn't even able to support myself properly; my weaving business was going under, too. Hawk was bearing the financial brunt of our family. I was grateful for his support.

I reached over and picked a cherry tomato and popped it in my mouth, savoring the warm, tart burst of flavor. I yearned to be completely alone, to evaluate my life. I was convinced that, given enough quiet time, I could find the answer Hawk had asked for.

Lauren's husband, Blade, told me about a ten-day vision quest into the Inyo mountains in southeastern California. He had signed up to go. Excitement ripped through me. If I went, there would be no distractions; I couldn't alleviate my misery with food or companionship. I would have the opportunity to truly clear my mind. Thom could stay with Hawk and the rest of the farm community, with Ray helping on weekends.

"It's a long hike into the high desert," Matthew, our guide, said at the first preparatory meeting.

That sounded just right; the outside world of the quest would mirror the equally spare territory inside me.

"Paiute Canyon is bone dry," he went on. "We will pack in all our water. Remember, that's more than eight pounds a gallon." He paced in front of us, his wiry, rock-hard legs tanned from weeks outside. "Weigh your pack before you leave home. Keep it under thirty pounds.

You may take a journal, sleeping bag, and tarp. No tent. No music. No watches. No books. No entertainment of any kind. We quest at the dark of the moon." He whirled to stare at us. "Be sure and break in your boots."

I could feel the tension rise, but no one interrupted Matthew. He exuded confidence. We glanced at each other, evaluating what we saw. The skin on my arms jumped with goose bumps as his words sank in. I had assumed quests happened at full moon. My childhood terror of the dark still haunted me in nightmares. Who in her right mind would go out into the night desert without the companionship of the moon? This would be more intense than I thought—in addition to the problem I wanted to resolve, I'd have to cope with my fear.

"No food," Matthew said, "except a small amount of honey in case you get dizzy—Dana and I will handle the food for the communal days before and after your three days alone in the wilderness. You will take one book of matches to light a fire the last night of your quest." He paused and scanned the room, looking each participant in the eye. "This trip may not be for you. This is the time to back out." He let the silence hang as his gaze moved from person to person. No one shuffled with restlessness; no one stood up to leave, although the woman next to me picked her cuticles. When he got to me, I met his penetrating stare. I held my breath, imagined not going. No, I had to do this. I had to face myself.

"If you're in," he said, "it's time to formulate your question and set your intention. Do not leave without attending to that work. Remember. This quest is a rite of passage."

Eight of us—our guides, Matthew and Dana, and six participants—prepared to clamber into an extra-long brown Dodge van with packs and camping gear. I patted my pocket to make sure I had remembered matches and compass. Matthew packed food containers in the corners of the van first, and stuffed many gallons of water under the board supporting a large mattress that filled the back of the van. No seats. I crawled in next to Blade, a towering, lanky guy—and leaned against my pack. The other four crowded themselves and their gear in around us. The woman on my left stank of anxious sweat. I shifted my body to face a different direction. Oh my. Ten days of unwashed bodies.

We drove nine hours east and south through the California night, stopping only to pee by the side of the van—all scrabbling to find a small, private patch of dirt.

We arrived in Big Bear just as the coyotes sang in the nippy dawn. I breathed in the leaner, dry, high-altitude air, filled with the scent of pine and something else—granite, maybe, or icy water. We stopped long enough to check tires and fluids and load up on more water before we headed fifty miles cross-country over dirt and rocks. The lack of even a track to follow seemed foolish, crazy, and I felt anxious for my own safety. I didn't remember Matthew describing this terrain clearly to us. As the parent of a disabled child, I had no right to put myself at serious risk. Thom's well-being depended on me. And yet excitement burbled—anticipation and fear, both. Fear that I would somehow not meet up to our leaders' expectations, or worse, my own. Matthew and Dana had led many trips here; they must know their stuff.

Summer flash floods had driven boulders from the canyon ridges out onto the desert flats. Time after time, we stumbled down from the van—bruised from jolting across hardpan which threw us in the air, on top of each other and into the equipment—to wrestle boulders out of the way. I had no idea a vehicle could survive this kind of abuse. The trip pounded on for eight endless hours. Finally, I unfolded myself out of the back of the van for the last time and the others followed suit. We stood at the bottom of Paiute Canyon where it washed out on to the plain.

"We're headed up there," Matthew said. He pointed up the draw. "We'll break our way through those willows. Up above, as it gets drier and drier, the vegetation thins." Matthew was a master of understatement. The harshest details didn't seem to faze him. Although he was a slight man, he portrayed capable strength. Even the male questers did not challenge him.

I stretched my limbs, tied and double-knotted the laces of my second-hand, but still stiff mountain boots. I shouldered the unfamiliar weight of my twenty-eight pound pack. Dana handed three gallons of water to each of us, an additional twenty-four pounds. I had always thought of myself as athletic and tough, but as I began the trudge up the floor of the canyon with fifty-two pounds dragging on my shoulders, water bottles whacking my legs, I wished I had carved out the time to train. My calf muscles trembled, and my knees complained every step. The boots scoured my heels.

Three hours later, the pack had dug deep indentations into my shoulders. My lower back ached, and my face and arms bore lash welts from willow branches. My feet throbbed the most. Matthew called out, "We'll build camp straight ahead. Look for a circle of rocks."

He obviously knew this place well. As I dumped my pack on the ground, I moaned a sigh of relief. I sank down, unhooked the laces, and pulled the first boot off. Crimson stained my sock. Rolling it down, I gazed at two huge, gaping blisters. These were not like a fresh cut where the blood flow cleans the wound. Instead, I stared at murky purple lacerations. My own damn fault for not breaking in my boots. I hadn't been able to afford a new pair, and didn't find these used boots until a few days before the trip. A drop of sweat ran down my leg, and I watched it slide around my Achilles tendon toward the raw, open wounds, cringed at the antiseptic sting. I removed my other boot—same ugly sight—and felt around in my pack for the tube of antibiotic cream and spread it gingerly across the lesions, then bandaged both heels, worrying how this might affect the trip. There was no going home. Not wanting Matthew to ground me at base camp, I kept my secret in grim silence.

For four days, as a group, we prepared for our solitary time. We met in circle after breakfast and in the evening, opening and closing with prayers honoring the earth. I had plenty of alone time during the day to review my intentions for the trip. My willingness to adopt a child was not the only question I faced. Hawk's and my relationship had devolved into disconnected, though parallel, lives. My heart sank at the new suspicion that we'd never had much in common other than our love of the Ranch. Increasingly, our relationship seemed nothing more than a business arrangement. Our bed was lonely even though Hawk was there, or rather because he was there. We didn't talk much anymore. Neither of us knew how to reach across the widening gaps. How could we plan to adopt a child and parent together when we shared so little intimate ground? It echoed those months of interviews when Ray was adopting Thom—the responsible decision for Thom's sake, or so I thought at the time—but completely wrong for me. Yet surely Thom would benefit from having a young brother or sister. Our living situation was stable, and the other mothers provided generous, womanly support.

The camp bell rang for dinner. I jumped up, eager to eat. What I would give for a steak, but no chance of that. We were eating plain, vegetarian fare. As I walked toward the circle, questions still chewed at me. Could I love a child that was not my own? I struggled with parenting Thom; I wasn't sure I could bond as readily with a child I had not carried in my body, nestled near my heart for nine months. I had seen so many families skirmish with stepchildren, and adopting felt like a similar chunk of challenges. I thought about all the time I spent with Thom on his homework, trying to work around his dyslexia so he could get the concepts. The idea of being responsible for another child's well-being on top of Thom's challenges made me tired and resentful. The spare dinner, eaten in silence in the circle, did not cheer me as I hoped.

That evening, we revealed why we had come, passing a talking stick so each person had his or her turn to share without interruption. I had to squeeze back tears and force my words out. My problems sounded commonplace when spoken out loud—but for me, they were a roadbed as rocky as the landscape we had covered.

We went out alone the next day, each searching for the right spot to quest. My place failed to show itself and I returned to camp discouraged.

"You'll know," Matthew said, in the circle that evening. "You've got plenty of space, so range out a ways. You do not want to be in visual or sound contact with anyone; most likely you'll end up at least a mile apart." He stood and paced for a moment. "You will buddy up.

Each evening during the quest, one of you will hike to a spot you have picked together and pile rocks in a distinctive pattern. The next morning, your buddy will make the same journey, and change the rock cairn. That way, every twelve hours, one checks on the other. If you arrive and find the rock pile unchanged, head back to camp so we can form a search party."

Surprised murmurs popped up around the circle.

His gaze swept the group. "In other words, don't screw up and forget. It would be mighty embarrassing and potentially fatal."

I wouldn't forget. Touching the rocks my buddy had rearranged twelve hours before would be the closest human contact I would have. You can bet I'd put my hands on those stones and try to capture all traces of human touch.

I wanted to camp near a ridge. Not too high—lightning was common—but high enough to have a wide vista. The final day of preparation I climbed up and then up farther, until I got tired of winding through the scrub. I paused to survey the terrain. There! My spot jumped out, pulled me to it as though magnetized. I didn't understand why until I stood in the hillside indentation and gazed at the three hundred degree view.

I turned my head slowly, taking in the whole panorama—wide distances, granite outcroppings, and far, far, below, Paiute Canyon. A vista so wide, my own internal perspective must widen as well. And it was dead quiet. Finally. Quiet enough. Spookily quiet. It was going to be ominously dark up here, too. A chill scuttled through me.

The only plants that survived this high seemed to grow straight out of rock. They had so little support—virtually no soil, and little water for months on end. I sniffed the air, rich with the stew of sage, mesquite, and creosote. They did more than survive, they thrived in these difficult circumstances. I studied the plants more carefully. They sported woody protective stems, and each had a powerful scent, as though staking its own territory.

When I returned to camp in late afternoon, we met in our last circle. "Give me a general idea of where you have chosen your camp," Dana said. "We'll assign buddies according to location and, as you begin your quest, you'll head out together to pick the spot between your sites to build the cairns."

"Silence begins in the morning," Matthew said. "You'll have to take a final load of water up to your site early. Then your actual quest will begin. But before that, we have a long journey to make."

What? Shocked, I glanced up, hoping I had not heard correctly, but the other questers had stunned expressions too. I had assumed—depended upon—this last night being a time of prayer, quiet preparation, and rest. A time to firm up my courage and give my blisters a few more hours to heal.

Matthew continued. "Tonight, we will make a trek back to the van to pick up more water. As soon as it falls dark, we begin. We will walk single file, with no flashlights and no extraneous conversation. The only talking allowed is to warn the person following you what blocks the path. That might be 'rock to the right,' or 'branch, face high.'" He paused, and tipped his head back to think for a moment, scraping his toe against the stone shale. "Wear your hiking boots," he said. "This granite mountain shreds lighter shoes."

I groaned under my breath at the thought of lacing on my boots. And no flashlights? He must be nuts! During the dark of the moon? It had been a three-hour hike in broad daylight. The thought of finding my way down that draw in the dark unnerved me. I looked ruefully at my heels—still open, bloody wounds. I'd hoped they would have scabbed over, but the blisters were too deep. I spread more cream on them, a double layer of Band-Aids, then carefully pulled on my thickest socks. I waited until the last minute to don the boots.

Dana stayed in camp, Matthew led. We trudged off. The sharp pinch of the blisters finally spread to the familiar raw meat ache. The group's pace fell into a slow, timeless rhythm—for hours, murmured comments passed down the line prevented toe stubs, or twisted ankles. I developed skill at sensing the landscape around me, and caught willow branches before they smacked my face as we clambered through the dense stand at the bottom of the draw. My confidence grew. Blister pain didn't get worse than a deep ache. Dark, even at the dark of the moon, was not inky black. Eyes adjusted. Bushes and rocks stood out in stark relief. And the boogie man did not live out here in the wilderness after all.

But as I stumbled out on the flat at the bottom, my newfound courage flagged and I knew, just knew, we would never find the van, never find our stash of water. We'd die of thirst. Yet minutes later, there the van loomed, its motherly bulk a dark shadow in this stone and dust desert. I leaned into her and glugged some of our precious water. Never again would my childhood fear of the dark overwhelm me. I *could* get through whatever it dished out. That was worth a lot.

I decided not to pull off my boots and examine my blisters. There was nothing more to be done for them until I returned to camp. After only fifteen minutes, Matthew called to load up again. Some of the questers muttered about a longer rest, but he overlooked their comments; he knew exactly what he was doing. I had figured it out: for the final preparation, he was stripping us bare.

Because we had brought our empty packs, we could now carefully stash the water bottles, distributing the weight evenly. Only the constellations' movement and my increasing muscle exhaustion marked the passage of time as we trudged back up the mountain. We returned hours after midnight, but before visible traces of dawn. Exhausted but satisfied, I crept into my sleeping bag. I remember flinty ground, throbbing heels, restless sleep, and a spreading curiosity—and anxiety—about the upcoming three solitary days.

I had never been completely out of touch with other people. What if I disliked my own company and failed to decide about adopting? I might freak out and have to return to base camp. Maybe I was not up to this. Maybe I had been a fool to come, but I couldn't back out now. The silence seemed huge, made somehow larger by the steady breathing of my fellow questers. I wondered how Thom was doing, and the wonder turned to worry. I prayed Hawk was paying enough attention to him. Finally, to break my obsessing, I flopped over onto my back and stared at the bright, blinking, canopy of stars for a long time. They, not useless worry, would be my only companions in the dark.

The following morning, Matthew assigned my buddy—Blade—who helped me shoulder my pack, then the extra gallons of water. I did the same for him. In silence, we located and marked our spot with a diamond of rocks and, through hand signals, agreed he would construct his cairn in the morning; I would build mine in the evening. We hugged for a long moment. I leaned into him, breathed his scent, the balm of safety and friendship. Then we trudged off in separate directions. I didn't look back.

When I arrived at my sun-drenched spot, I busied myself making camp. I found the flattest area for my sleeping bag, and strung the tarp on creosote bushes to shield my sitting place from the piercing sun. I smoothed rocks and lumps away as best I could, and laid out my bag. I pawed through my pack and took out the items I had brought that were sacred to me: a rose quartz heart and a string of olivewood prayer beads which I laid on an altar rock. At the bottom of my pack, I found my small, soft stuffed dog, "Le Mutt." I perched him near my sleeping bag; he tumbled over. I stabilized his chin on a rock so his mournful little face peered at me—I have never been without a dog during challenging times, and I wasn't about to be now. He provided company. My guardian.

Finally there was nothing to do but face the questions. Anxious, I perched on a rock, wishing I had some task to do, some regular routine. Already, hunger pinched; dinner seemed a long, long time ago. I wrapped my arms around my knees, staring out at the wide sky. Out there, or inside me—somewhere—lay answers. Thom's well-being seemed as likely a place as any to delve into my inquiry. If he had a sibling, when he was eighteen, she would be only seven. Would he reach a point where he felt less able than the young child? Probably. Definitely. I wondered how he would handle it. It would be difficult for me, too. My attention would have to go to the baby, but that might be good for Thom. I could ask a lot more of him around the house. As it was, I protected him too much. He was old enough to see I needed help with a baby, and he still yearned to feel needed.

Writing always calms me, so I jotted my thoughts in my journal, then changed into cutoffs and carefully put on my tennis shoes, which didn't aggravate the blisters. I wandered around making the area mine, like an animal staking out territory. I looked for a private place for a bathroom, then chuckled at myself. Who would be watching?

But hunkering down out in the open, no trees to hide behind, went against my innate modesty. I discovered the most disconcerting part of this mountain—I couldn't bury my own excrement. There was no topsoil, only thin shale dust. Rocks would have to do, so I chose an indentation between two creosote bushes about fifty feet away, gathered as many small rocks as I could find, and piled them there, fastidious as a cat.

I tried to conjure another task, but couldn't. Used to being busy and tending to others, having nothing to do, no routines to divert my attention, made me uneasy. I wandered back and sat at my camp, hungry, but surprisingly, not lonely.

A day undivided by meals is a slow, slow day. I had planned to watch animals, but hadn't seen any. Instead, I noted the crawling passage of the sun and thunderheads building in the west. Those thunderheads got my attention. I stuffed my journal in a plastic bag, stashed Le Mutt, prayer beads, and sleeping bag in a protective sack, pocketed my matches, and waited. A few minutes later, I pulled Le Mutt out and nestled him inside my shirt next to my heart. In the oppressive heat of late afternoon, the storm struck. Rain lashed my camp. Lightning shot blue bolts behind the thunder blasts, no seconds to count in between. I huddled under my tarp, as small a target as I could make myself, miserable, afraid, alone. Oh, for the company of other humans.

The storm blew through and the sky cleared as dusk settled. I wondered if this had been enough rain to cause a flash flood through the canyon. Probably not. I thought about the other questers and hoped they fared as well as I. I felt proud my prize quest possessions were dry.

Time to hike to our buddy rock pile. I picked my way down the long hill and around to the far side. There I found our diamond marker, and in the center, I constructed a pyramid. Blade could not mistake the human touch.

That night, feeling vulnerable, I had difficulty falling asleep. I had not asked about native animals. There might be bears or poisonous snakes. I had heard stories of snakes crawling into sleeping bags and people awaking in the morning to a unique, horrifying bedmate.

Watching the Big and Little Dippers and the seven tiny stars of the Pleiades distracted me until I dozed. But I awakened to heavy breathing nearby. I lay paralyzed with fear. Large cat. Did pumas live around here? Hyper-alert, I held still. My bladder ached, but for safety's sake, I knew I must not move. I did not even dare reach for the comfort of Le Mutt.

A long time later, now fully awake and clear, I realized the heavy breathing—magnified by the sleeping bag over my head—was my own; *I* was the large, predatory cat. Embarrassed by the fabrications of my mind, I struggled out of my bag, put on my tennis shoes, and scrambled through the rock rubble to my privy, where I squatted in humble relief.

The second day I hunkered down and applied myself to hard-to-face lists. I wrote down every pitiful aspect about my life, my marriages, and my mothering. Certainly I had failed at marriage—either I picked badly for myself, or I suffered from some core flaw. Probably both. I made a promise, and wrote with all caps in my journal, I WILL STICK THIS MARRIAGE OUT, LEARN EVERY POSSIBLE LESSON, AND NEVER SUFFER THROUGH THESE PARTICULAR LESSONS AGAIN. NOT EVER.

I rewarded myself with a long hike along the ridgeline. Lightheadedness from hunger plagued me; afraid I might faint, I repeatedly sat down. Daylight dragged on and on. I hoped for time to pass. I fervently asked for an answer to my question of whether to adopt or not. I sucked on my water bottle and prayed for the waves of hunger cramping my belly to cease. Gazing out over the barren landscape—no people, no lights, no civilization—I imagined my problems could be happening at any time in the past few millennia. Then, over the edge of the hill, a fighter jet blasted so low I could read the tall numbers on its nose. The shockwave flattened me to the ground, but by the time my body reacted, the jet had blasted out of sight.

Silence.

Then its vast roar bellowed. My heart surged with adrenalin. I had been wrong. This was the twentieth century for sure, and I could not hide from the present—or my problems—anywhere.

I hiked slowly back to my meager camp, sank down on the dusty ground and, along with a solitary lizard on a rock, soaked up the hot sun. I dangled my hands between my knees and let myself sink into the moment. No past, no future, only the endless now. This baby Hawk wanted—a boy or a girl? A girl might be better for Thom, so he didn't compare himself every moment. Nursing Thom had been a highlight for me. I tried to imagine cuddling her, giving her a bottle, but couldn't conjure the image. I could see Hawk holding her up in the air, spinning her around, Thom giggling. But I could not find myself in the picture.

The late afternoon sun blazed in my eyes. I retrieved Le Mutt and set him on a rock. Writing in my journal didn't distract me enough, so I put it away and eased on my tennis shoes. The blisters were filming over; I had avoided wearing my boots since settling into my spot. Then I hiked down to the rock cairn, and sure enough, Blade had rearranged the rocks into the word "Hi." More communication was packed into that one word than Hawk had shared with me since that stunning day in Janice's office. Pebble by pebble I spelled out "FINE," and then hiked back to camp.

Sometime later—it felt like hours—the apricot sun slipped below the horizon, the sky purpled, and the temperature plummeted. I climbed into my sleeping bag and closed my eyes, trying to ignore the hard lumps and bumps beneath me.

Even later, I awakened and saw successive waves of fighter jets, dozens threading high across the night sky, contrails flaring behind. Panic gripped me. The cold war must have exploded into raging conflict. Marooned on a granite mountain with conflicts of my own, I had no clue about world events. Had San Francisco or Los Angeles been annihilated? Oh God. I prayed Thom was safe, sound asleep in his own bed.

After the Pleiades moved to the next quadrant of the sky, my grandiose worries settled into more personal agitation. I doubted I would get out of my family dilemma because of a worldwide dispute. A wave of hunger passed through me and, uncomfortable, I shifted in my sleeping bag. I thought about eating a spoonful of honey, but decided, since I wasn't dizzy, it would be cheating.

None of the choices I confronted appealed. Each had a huge downside. Becoming a single, divorced parent again would mean leaving Novato and moving out of Marin County. Rental prices had skyrocketed. I would have to sell my share of the Ranch and leave the first home I had ever owned. Thom would be forced to part from playmates and I would move away from friends of fifteen years. If I stayed, I faced living within a relationship where we couldn't seem to find real intimacy—and eighteen additional years of parenting. I would be almost sixty years old before my younger one left for college. Sixty years old! When, oh when, would there be time for me? I lay peering up at the wide, distinct splash of the Milky Way, and stared—far beyond personal concern—into the deep universe beyond.

Day Three began with preparations for staying up all night during the final stretch. What a relief to have a required task to divert my thoughts, fill the seemingly endless time. I gathered fist-sized rocks and marked off a circle six paces wide, large enough for a cozy fire in the center with space inside for me to lie down. It would be tricky to not fall asleep while prone, but I couldn't imagine sitting for eleven hours straight. One more day and I could eat again. The thought drove me to squeeze a drop of honey onto my finger. I sucked greedily, and then felt guilty. I wasn't really dizzy enough to warrant a drop. But I sucked another, and felt my body grab for its nourishment.

Matthew's instructions had been strict: enter the enclosure from the South at sunset. Do not leave until the sun rises over the horizon and casts its rays on your body. I steadied my compass, noted the four cardinal directions, and marked those with larger chunks of granite. I made sure to leave one stone unplaced—the largest, the south marker—which also served as the gate. I foraged for fuel in this sparse, rocky landscape, returning again and again to pile little twigs inside the circle. Feeding the fire would keep me awake.

The hunger pangs had ceased; my stomach felt as small and tight as an acorn. I carried my last gallon of water, my journal, and my sleeping bag inside the stone markers, then escaped through the open south gate, and set Le Mutt facing me on a rock outside. He must not be in the circle with me. I had to do this night alone. There was enough time left to seek inspiration from one last hike to the highest ridge. I examined my blisters before changing socks. The holes would take a long time to fill in, but they had stopped oozing, and I had avoided infection. As soon as I arrived home, I would dump those boots at the used store.

As I watched the sun dip toward the horizon, my spirits sank with it. Tomorrow morning my quest would be over, and I was no closer to answers. Why had I thought this experience would solve anything? But obedient to the instructions, I marched into the circle, said my prayers, and with a startling sense of claustrophobia, closed the south gate. As the sky darkened, I scanned the heavens for my evening's chosen companions, the Pleiades, and found them hovering near the horizon. By the time they crossed the heavens, I would leave, whether a decision had come or not.

We had been counseled to "cry for a vision." I wondered, what did it mean, really? Sing out loud? Pray fervently? My mother's bold voice rang in my head: do not draw attention to yourself. Do not make a display. Call for guidance. I could do that—internally, at least.

As the air chilled, I built my fire in the center—first a teepee of the smallest twigs on top of a bed of dried sage leaves, then pencil-sized sticks, the biggest fuel I had found. My hands trembled from hunger, and my first pass across the striker failed. I focused on stilling my fingers; on the third try, the match finally caught. "Blessed light," I said. The sound of my own voice seemed out of place in the night's silence. I touched the match to the sage, and at the first crackles, almost cried with gratitude. Small though the blaze was, it warmed me. I sent gratitude, along with prayers, out toward my son. "Thank you for coming into my life. Thank you for the depth of love you have called forth from me."

What was best for him? A brother or sister was practical, in the long run—familial companionship, particularly if I died young. But what was best for me? He needed a mother who made solid, positive choices. If I were miserable, he would be too. Prayerfully, I stirred the little blaze, added sticks, and blew my lack of clarity onto them. I get along with me just fine, I thought. I am a good friend to myself. But I sure am horrible at picking partners.

I opened myself up to the Pleiades as they inched their way up into the heavens. The Big Dipper slid toward the horizon. I worked my stiff hands to warm them. Then I paced and prayed to each direction: to the East for clarity of mind, South for innocence of heart, West for intuition and call of the deep, North for discerning wisdom. Fed the fire. Walked, breathing my question: adopt or not? Meditated cross-legged, paying attention to my breath. Fed the fire. Walked. Prayed again. Begged for answers.

Finally, my eyelids got heavy. I wrapped up in my sleeping bag and rested my head on my knees. I dozed. A bat whispered across my cheek and startled me awake. For a moment I wondered if I had imagined it, but the skin on my face tingled. Ashamed at my catnap, I watched the bat cartwheel into the dark, grateful for its presence. I knew, with their radar, bats don't run into objects. This felt like sacred intervention on my behalf.

I stood and set more sticks on the coals, which returned to life in flames. A moth hovered and dive-bombed toward the light. I waved it away, but it returned again and again, and finally, I watched—helpless—as it dove straight into the heart of the blaze. Its wings caught, curled, flamed like tissue paper. Then its furry body blackened, and it dropped, inert, into the embers. My chest tightened. That's what would happen to me, I thought. Self-immolation. Hawk has the fire to be a parent, I do not. I cannot live someone else's fire. Not at forty, not in addition to Thom.

Twice more, the bat dusted my face and kept me from nodding off. Each time, amazed and grateful, I prodded the embers back into life. My understanding and resolve deepened, my doubt dissolved. I had known from the first moment Hawk had said, "If Skye won't adopt a child with me, I'll have to leave her." I had known, but been unwilling to face the answer. My answer was no. It was so obvious. And Hawk would leave.

I sat for an hour or more, a universe of fresh grief birthing inside. Tears leaked down my cheeks, but I didn't weep. Finally, I had achieved adulthood. I could weigh difficult choices and set my feet down on the correct side of the line—for me. I waved away the acrid smoke—and I chose me.

The Pleiades eventually touched the far horizon, and soon after black lightened to gray; clouds dusted the skyline. I felt a welling of disappointment it wasn't a colorful, welcoming sunrise, and shed fresh tears. I did not want to leave the security of this circle, return to my daily life, face the repercussions of my adult decisions.

I squinted at the horizon. The faintest mauve edged the clouds. Mauve to purple, to magenta, then the whole sky crackled in peach and fire. I sat back on my haunches, astonished to see that clouds support brilliance rather than hide it. Surely this boded well. As the first rays blazed across the landscape, I turned toward the sun and welcomed the warmth that chased the chill from my body. Better than a lover, I thought.

In a peaceful state, I said my final prayers and opened the south gate. As a last act after packing up my camp, I dismantled my sacred circle, thanked the rocks one at a time for holding the space, and replaced them around the landscape. I took the final half-gallon, doused my head with achingly cold water, washed my indecision away along with the dust and grime, and toweled my head dry. Clean! I grinned with satisfaction. Then I hung Le Mutt so his face peered out of the back, and shouldered my pack. Despite three days of fasting, with firmer steps than before, I strode down the mountain.

I wasn't ready to give Hawk my answer. I needed to let it simmer inside for a while. He didn't ask, and made no move toward leaving.

# Chapter Nine

## Umbilical Cord—May, 1986

I shifted from one foot to the other with excitement as I waited for Mom at the Miami airport. I hadn't seen her in over a year. Smiling, she walked toward me. At seventy-two, she was straight-backed and vital, still sporting un-dyed, chestnut hair. She didn't seem to age. After a hug—warm for her—she looped her arm through mine. We walked and chatted about the trip arrangements.

She had invited me to spend ten days on a small ship cruising around the Galapagos Islands, then ten days in Ecuador, taking day trips out of Quito. Our family had a tradition not only of overseas travel, but of different generations exploring the world together. I had missed traveling with my grandmother—as the youngest grandchild, I was sixty-six years younger than she. By the time I was old enough to enjoy Europe, Nanon felt she was too elderly to handle a teenager. Mom chose me for this trip because of that loss earlier in life, and I was thrilled to go.

We had to hurry to catch our plane at the other end of the terminal. I noticed one tiny change in my mother—she no longer outdistanced me when we walked together. Finally, I could keep up. Just.

After we settled on the plane she asked, "How's my grandson?"

"Thom saw me off without tears," I said. "He hugged me tight and told me to have a wonderful time. 'Rest, Mom,' he said. 'You need it.' Can you believe that? From an eleven-year-old! I guess he's cut the umbilical cord."

She chuckled. "Don't be so sure."

I did need rest; my bones were tired. As the plane taxied, I fell quiet thinking about my son. Sometimes he astonished me with his insights about people's inner workings. He knew how much I did for him every day; he was aware of the angry fits he threw from time to time. Fifteen years later he admitted—and apologized for—being a tyrant as a child. Back then, at some level, he understood my need to unwind. But he did not know my being away from him brought its own kind of stress—an underlying, niggling, steady worry about his well-being.

After the plane reached cruising altitude, Mom set her hand on my arm. "And Hawk? I'm delighted he was willing to take over for you."

"He surprised me when he offered," I admitted. "I made it clear he couldn't just let the other moms at the Ranch step in. He said he wouldn't, that he and Thom would manage fine. I'm so grateful to him. School's in session, Thom's routines are in place, and he'll be with Ray on the weekends. They'll probably be okay; I worry too much."

She patted my arm. "You're a mom," she said. "Moms worry." Then we looked at each other and smiled. No need for words. I finally belonged to the Mom Clan.

One day, midway through the trip, we traveled by bus into the Ecuadorian highlands. I was quiet, staring out the open window at the lush countryside, sucking in the high altitude air, when Mom broke the silence. "When it is time for me to go, I want you to help me purchase the drugs so I can kill myself."

My head jerked toward her. Did she have cancer? Was I about to lose my remaining parent? My God, she just asked me to kill her! My heart thunked rapidly. I rubbed my arms, suddenly chilled. Her eyebrows were raised—a look I knew well, one that demanded a reply. Her blue eyes were clear and direct. I knew she did not want extraordinary means taken at the end of life—she threatened to haunt her children if we allowed doctors to hook her up to machines, or neglected to cremate her—but I hadn't realized she was considering suicide.

"My health's fine, don't worry. I'm talking about the eventuality, that's all."

"You scared me half to death." I rubbed my cheek, stalling for time. Something about this interchange felt familiar, but I couldn't latch on to what it was. I looked out the dusty bus window. A burro nibbled grass with a relaxation I couldn't imagine achieving again. Then I turned back to her. "When—if—that time comes, I'll sit with you. But buy the drugs, mix the smoothie, give it to you? No. I won't do that. That's counter to everything I believe in—we are here to learn lessons, and we're not finished until our bodies give out on their own."

"Hogwash!" she spat. Her brows crunched in a deep frown. She pinned me with her gaze. Usually her penetrating glance would drive me to look away. I met it head-on. "So you're forcing me to shoot myself," she snapped.

She caught me so off-guard that I laughed. "I'm not forcing you to do anything. You can buy the drugs yourself."

She narrowed her gaze. "I don't know where," she said.

This from my Phi Beta Kappa mother. She read voraciously on a broad variety of topics. I *knew* she knew where. "You can get the book from the Hemlock Society as easily as I can," I said. I had the fleeting thought she might have invited me on the trip for this purpose. "But that's not the point," I went on. "We kids will care for you, make you comfortable with Hospice, if need be. You don't have to commit suicide, for God's sake."

"That's *just* the point," she said. "When it's time, it's time. And it's not cancer I'm worried about. It's senility. I don't want to outlive my time like your grandmother."

Nanon had lived to ninety-eight, and suffered from senile dementia the last seven years of her life.

I tried rewording my thoughts. "You're our mother. We'll give back to you with the same loving attention you gave us. That's the natural way." Hoping I had convinced her, I took a deep breath and let it out quietly. I hoped this wouldn't be the main theme of the trip.

She grimaced and stared at her hands. "If that's the way you feel—if you won't help me—I'll have to ask your brother."

"I bet he'll respond the same way." Harry adored Mom. I couldn't fathom him agreeing to her plan.

"We'll see," she said, and with a circumspect, distant expression, turned her face toward the window and closed me out.

As the bus bumped along, my guilt compounded knots between my shoulder blades. Mom had done so much for me. In return, she wanted this one gift. I wasn't willing to give it. It's true I did not believe in suicide; it's also true that she was asking me to break the law: murder her, and then live with the emotional fallout, not to mention the possibility of life imprisonment. She would never ask a friend; she was far too private. I wondered why she chose me, instead of Harry or Maggie. Perhaps she saw how strong I had to be for Thom, and figured I had the "right stuff." Well, I didn't.

A few minutes later, she picked up chatting as though nothing had transpired between us. "I'm surprised by the amount of debris we see by the side of the road."

I heaved a sigh, aware only of similar rubble inside of me.

Mom never mentioned this conversation again—and taking the easy way out, I didn't either. But I thought about it daily for months, and then most days for years. As with Hawk, the request had been so huge, I didn't know how to approach a second conversation about it. I had no stepping stones. She blindsided me, just like Hawk had. In both cases, I had missed the clues. Perhaps I chose Hawk because his communication style was familiar. This kind of familiar didn't work for me anymore; I didn't want to have to decipher the people close to me. I wanted them to share freely on a regular basis.

I arrived home three weeks later, tanned from the walking tours, but sobered by my loss of innocence. In a subtle way, I would never be the same.

When I stepped into the house, Thom launched himself at me. "M-Moooommmm! Y-you're back! I had *no idea* how long three weeks was!" He hugged me so tightly I had difficulty breathing. Apparently that umbilical cord *was* still attached.

I thanked Hawk, who stood back with a crooked, happy smile. "It went okay," he said. "But it's hard work being a mom."

If you only knew, I thought. It's hard work being a daughter, too. I glanced at Thom. It must be as hard for him to be a son. I ruffled his thick, dark hair and planted a soft kiss on top of his head. Then I caught Hawk's gaze as he walked over to hug me, and thought, it's plain hard work being a family.

Three weeks later, Thom and I drove into San Francisco for his yearly cardiac checkup. This year they put gel on his chest and did an echocardiogram. "This tickles like crazy," Thom said. Once again, the report came back that his heart was stable.

## Caught Off-guard—November, 1986

Hawk, Thom, and I drove to Los Angeles to celebrate Thanksgiving with Hawk's extended family. Fourteen of us, four generations, gathered around my sister-in-law's beautifully appointed table. The congeniality warmed me. I loved these people, and in some ways felt closer to them than most of my own family.

Thom, sporting a new buzz haircut—all dressed up for the occasion, including a fancy patterned sweater—was having a good time with his cousins. The eldest of them, he smiled at their antics, and plunked down on the floor in his most characteristic position for relaxed play: butt on the floor, legs folded back, feet pointed to the sides like origami crane wings. A solid, three-point landing. He pushed a small Brio train up a "mountain" on the tracks, all the while making chugging noises. The smaller kids laughed and shoved each other to get closer. I loved that he could feel popular and shine in the moment; he so rarely had that experience. On the drive down, I'd encouraged him to be a role model for the younger children, particularly at the dinner table. Thom's sense of humor could be both slapstick and outrageous. I hoped he would contain it during the family holiday. So far, so good.

It wasn't Thom I should have worried about. At dinner, Hawk sat a few places from me. He was chatting with his brother. We'd had a pleasant meal, until the end of the main course when he announced loudly, "Well, Skye's frigid."

All conversation ceased. My face flared. I scrambled up, grabbing plates, carrying them to the kitchen, anything to get away. As I fled, conversation still had not resumed. I leaned against the sink, trying to get hold of my spinning thoughts, catch my frantic breath. How could he! My belly knotted, hard as the cabinet I leaned against. Outside the kitchen window, the autumn sunset illuminated the lurid brown smog.

My God, what a showstopper. *He still has no clue.* Not very interested in sex right now, correct. I could not gather up the energy, feel safe or inclined toward intimacy when he would not help resolve the huge gulf between us. The only disagreement he had ever managed to articulate, other than when I quit smoking pot, had to do with raising children. There had to be others. I could devise my own list, but what was the use? The man simply would not communicate his feelings. Maybe he was hoping this remark would drive me away. But why humiliate me in front of these people I loved? All he had to do was ask me to leave, and I'd go.

I shook my head to clear my thoughts and smacked on the water faucet to make it seem as though I had a task. I dawdled. Enough, I thought, as I listened to the comforting flow of water. I'll give this relationship one year. One year from today. If he won't talk, if we don't solve some of these problems by then, I'm *done*.

I knew I had to go back and face those people. Had they lost respect for me? What did they think of Hawk? I straightened and took a long, ragged inhale. Then stretching tall, teeth clenched, chin up, I marched into the dining room, scraped back my chair, and sat down. Somehow, we got through dessert. No one mentioned the incident to me. Not then, not ever.

After dinner, I said to Hawk, "It takes two, you know. This is not all mine." I did not divulge my one-year deadline. It remained something I could cling to. I needed a safety valve.

After New Year's 1987, we lugged our belongings from the chicken coop down the path and into the main house, a three-bedroom, sprawling, one-level home. In this communal family, it was our turn for the fancier digs.

I brought home a second dog, an Irish wolfhound pup I named Kyle. I had stuffed $20 bills into a sock for three years, saving for, and anticipating this moment. I dreamed of having an Irish wolfhound since the first time I saw a picture of one, when I was eleven. We all enjoyed the fast-growing, clumsy pup with huge paws and a tail that occasionally swept the coffee table clean.

Even with these changes, I was as resolved in my decision as I had been during the vision quest. A couple of months later, after dinner, Thom went out to play with the other children. I took Hawk aside.

"I can't adopt," I said. "I don't have the juice to parent again. I'm sorry."

His brows drew together and his shoulders sank. "I thought you'd say *yes*."

He whirled and left the room. I froze. The front door slammed, reverberations powering through the house. I heard his car sputter, cough, start. The gravel spat at the end of the drive as he wheeled onto Atherton Avenue. *He's gone. He won't be back.* I expected raw despair to descend, but it did not. I wondered whose door he would knock on to spend the night, where he would find comfort—then wondered why I didn't care more.

The house felt empty, but spacious, too. Not lonely. Only far too large. I had the urge to find Thom and wrap my arms around him, but then tears might come, and there was no point adding his worry to the mix. He would find out soon enough. The impending change loomed like a precipice—endless decisions: where to live, how to manage on an impossibly tight budget, how to tell my family I had failed yet again.

After 11 p.m.—much to my shock—Hawk returned. I didn't know whether to feel relieved or disappointed. I got ready for bed in silence—not an angry silence, but the gulf of knowing no words could solve or soothe. I assumed he would sleep in his office, but when he returned from the bathroom he crawled into bed with me. Startled, I rolled toward the outside, leaving him as much space as possible. I could not face touching.

We didn't speak much over the next few days. Hawk did not talk about his feelings although it was clear he intended to stay. I felt simultaneously relieved, anxious, and confused. I waited for a new lightning strike—as strong as the surges above Paiute Canyon—but it didn't come. Gradually, our daily patterns reemerged, and life went on. I could not imagine our marriage could thrive again, yet I had to stick it out. My previous divorces, the first ever in my family, were bad enough; I didn't have the guts to face failing a third time. Not until I was sure-beyond-sure I could not make this relationship work.

I thought I was seeking peace. In retrospect, I sought the path of least resistance by avoiding painful arguments or head-to-head conflict. Hawk walked out, and I did not have the gumption to pack up Thom and drive away. I hung on to the familiar and comfortable. I lived on ten gorgeous acres, picked dinner from an organic vegetable garden, and had five other adults willing to keep an eye on my son. I cringed at the challenge of being the sole household support—and raising my disabled child alone. I chose to remain in the marriage. But I knew I had lost trust in Hawk and respect for myself.

## Horizons—May, 1987

One cool spring morning after I took Thom to school, I had a sudden impulse to test drive mini-vans. Hawk and I had no plans to buy a car. I couldn't get him to discuss it, and he didn't seem to notice my car was too small for the pack of fast-growing boys I hoped would fill it. My wolfhound had to duck his head to avoid hitting the roof. I certainly could not afford a new vehicle on my own. But I was unreasonably restless.

I pulled my Mazda into the local Chrysler dealership. A van could seat seven—plenty of room for Thom and the friends I hoped he would make, plus the dogs. The first one I drove, a Dodge Caravan, felt like mine. I loved sitting up high and having a clear view of the road.

A week later, I was drawn back to the same car lot. The salesman combed over his few strands of hair and rubbed his hands. I walked toward the van. Its black-cherry metallic paint glowed. I peered inside. Boys could stretch their gangly legs. Their messy snacks would not harm the vinyl seats. Dogs could slurp the windows and drool. It seemed like a magical dream. I drove it one more time.

The salesman sucked his teeth, groveled, and when that didn't work, pressured me—but I picked up the slick brochure with the black cherry model displayed in blazing color and breezily told him I would think about it. I strode out the double doors.

Snipping the small picture from the brochure, I glued it to the front of my journal. Every day, I stared at it, imagining the van in our driveway. I did research, learned about the blue book values of cars, and found out from my brother it was possible to order a vehicle for only three percent over the dealer's cost. If the salesman whined, I would summon my courage, turn my back, and march away. When I was ready, some dealership would be hungry enough to take the deal. One way or another, I envisioned that time coming.

In June, my eighteen-year-old niece, Chandra, drove from Iowa after her high school graduation and moved in with us. This was an opportunity to get to know her better. I appreciated her youthful energy and pealing laughter in the house, and she served as a buffer when Hawk and I had little to say to each other.

## Big Shift—September, 1987

Trying to work off irritation, I vigorously dusted the bedside tables in the master bedroom. It had been ten months since Hawk's Thanksgiving blame-and-shame comment.

In couples therapy the week before he'd finally said, "Okay, I'm sorry. You're not frigid. I just got frustrated and lost it."

Finally. A tiny step. As I looked down and ran my thumb over a fingernail, I wondered what "lost it" meant. "I sure wish this apology had been made with your family present," I said.

He huffed out an irritated sigh.

A public apology would have eased my anguish and allowed me to save face in front of people who were important to me. Sure, he regretted bringing my rage down upon him in therapy—but the private apology could not undo my sense of humiliation.

But, even with weekly counseling, we shared less of our lives, not more. We ate together, but conversations were painfully superficial. We laughed less, and no longer teased each other. He didn't play with Thom as much. My three-and-a-half years of sobriety hadn't drawn us closer, but brought confusion and pain center-front. The previous night he had stalked out of a conversation with me, and, yet again, escaped his feelings by lighting up.

I had reached the end.

I picked up my journal and stared at the picture of the black cherry van. Moving, starting over. How many times had I done this? It seemed weird that I would be the one to leave, after his threat to do so. But he'd been at the Ranch first; I knew he'd insist on staying.

Single-parenting, again. I'd be forced to give up the weaving business as well; I couldn't live on what I made. I'd have to find a job, any job, to support Thom and me. I went to bed chewing on the questions. Worries woke me up at 2 a.m. with anxious adrenalin roaring. I dragged myself up, went into the other room and, with a pencil stub, scratched a list. The first three bulleted items: call Mom; call Barbara, our real estate agent; and talk to Hawk about his giving me a lump sum in cash for my share of the Ranch. I had to get my stake back. And I'd better call my mother before talking to Hawk; without her financial help, my exit plan had no reality.

I stuffed the list in the roll-top desk's secret drawer, and tiptoed quietly back to bed where I lay open-eyed and obsessing until 5 a.m.

When I was alone the next afternoon, I picked up the phone and dialed Mom. I cleared my throat a number of times, but couldn't relax. Finally her familiar voice answered, and I broke the news of another floundering marriage. I asked, yet again, for financial assistance.

"Sweetheart, I am sorry," she said.

I couldn't decipher her meaning. In the absence of clues, I fell back into old assumptions. Oh God, here comes the lecture, I thought, then the "No." I didn't know how I could leave if she were not willing to help.

"I don't think you have to feel like a failure. Most women of your generation have serial relationships. At least you married them." Her tone was as soft as when I'd been sick as a child. It was the kindest comment she'd ever made to me.

I laughed, but tears came. "I'm so sorry to have to ask again. I won't be able to stay here." I explained that moving back to less expensive Sonoma County was prudent, but even the rents there were beyond my means. Either I must move out of California altogether, or purchase a very modest house with a huge down payment so my mortgage would be under $400 a month.

"How will you manage parenting alone?" she asked.

"I handled it the year we lived in Petaluma when Thom was four," I said. "It will take getting used to—for both of us—but we'll manage."

"Are you sure you don't want to move back here?"

Loaded question.

"The services in California are better than anywhere else in the country. I can't deprive Thom of the best care."

That convinced her. She agreed to help with the down payment. By the time we finished our talk, I knew we had become more comfortable with each other. I had the growing trust she would reach out and offer help, and I had learned to receive more gracefully as well.

Feeling bolstered, I called Barbara. She had handled the complicated purchase of the Ranch—with its six owners—eight years before. I knew she would listen to my concerns and only show me houses I could afford. I asked her to search in Petaluma. "Please don't call with any listings until tomorrow. I have to get things straight on the home front."

"Right," she said. "I understand."

After I hung up, I slumped on the couch, afraid and overwhelmed. Thom would face a different school system, a new middle school, and strange kids—a rough adjustment. On top of settling in a new community, closing the weaving business, and searching for work, I faced educating new teachers, and unraveling the maze of a different county's health organizations. My heart pounded. So much to tackle. But better to confront these decisions alone than with a partner who, most of all, yearned to have his own children, and had difficulty talking about it. The thought galvanized me. Breaking up with Hawk would bring financial worries, yes, but coping with parenting issues would remain much the same. They would fall on my shoulders, as they always had. For better or for worse, Ray would continue to take Thom on the weekends. I could do this. I just had to find the brute courage to face Hawk.

After dinner, I walked into Hawk's office where he sat studying commodity charts. I shut the door and leaned against the wall. The curtains were still open, and the windows gaped, inky, deep holes. He glanced up.

"I'm leaving," I said. I looked away from those black windows. My palms were wet.

He frowned, confused. "Going where? Isn't it already after eight?"

I swallowed, hard. "Really leaving," I said. "Looking for a house in Petaluma for Thom and me."

He tossed his pencil down and pushed back from the desk. "Just like that? No warning?" He paced back and forth from the daybed to the reading chair.

"What do you mean, no warning? Lots of warning! More than two years in therapy. If I recall correctly, you announced back then that you were going to leave me." I wasn't able to quash my cynical tone.

"Yeah, but you never told me *you* might split. Damn! We just moved into this large house so we'd have plenty of room."

"Nine months ago. It's not working, Hawk. Not working for me."

He swerved and loomed directly in front of me. "When did you decide?"

I slid sideways, away from him. "Last Thanksgiving at your sister's house—right after you called me frigid—I made myself a promise I'd give the marriage one more year."

He slumped back down at his desk and opened his hands. "I apologized for all that."

"In private, yes. You never explained to your family. Your apology to me doesn't fix what's broken." It was my turn to pace. "We went over and over it in therapy." As I paced, my rubber-soled shoes squeaked on the cork floor.

He swung around, grabbed the window sill, and stared out into the dark. "Shit. You should have told me. You never said a word."

I moved toward him. "You're right, I didn't. I told myself that if we could not learn how to talk to each other, or resolve our differences about adoption, I'd leave you. I couldn't have gone forward otherwise. Our patterns haven't changed at all; certainly you can see that."

He stared at me.

"Anyway, it's done. *I'm* done. And I need to get my investment out of the Ranch," I said.

He snorted. "Not much chance of that. Like I have a big chunk of money to hand over."

"Hey," I said, "my down payment made purchasing this place possible. I want my money back. It will take me a while to find a house. You have a few weeks." I knew that someone in his family would step up for him just like my mom helped me.

Barbara and I drove up to Petaluma again and again. We walked through tiny tract houses, broken-down mother-in-law units, fixer-uppers of all kinds. I wanted four bedrooms, but knew I could only afford three. It looked like our weaving business would have to close. My production loom would require space, and Chandra was moving with us.

One unassuming flat-roofed beige house met the size requirement. It had a one car garage to boot, plus a large odd-shaped yard with a kennel. It sat at the end of a short cul-de-sac, half a block from Highway 101. I stood in the tiny front yard and listened to the steady roar of semis penetrating the neighborhood. This was a far cry from the Ranch which looked out on four hundred placid acres where horses and cows munched all day long. I shook my head. "I can't do it, Barbara," I said. "Too darn depressing."

We went back to the multiple listings, and I drove around Petaluma searching out "For Sale" signs. Finally, in late October, I phoned Barbara. "I can't drag this out anymore," I said. "If it's still available, I want to see that house with the kennel again. The one near the freeway. And I'd like to bring Thom this time."

"I suspected you'd return to it," she said. "I checked today. You'll make it work." Right before Thanksgiving, I signed the stack of papers on 11 Dean Court.

Leaving the Ranch must have been the biggest wrench of Thom's life, but he didn't have enough experience to foresee just how difficult the transition would be. When I asked him about it recently, he said, "W-what could I say? I-I was just a kid. It was a-awful tense with Hawk, and I was relieved to get away. B-but leaving the Ranch—that was hard."

A week later, Chandra and I yanked up the rank brown carpet in our new living room. Underneath lay ugly, brittle linoleum. We shoveled that off as well. As Thom watched us ripping the house apart, he giggled until he fell against the wall.

He left to explore. This was the first time we had lived in a neighborhood where he could walk to stores.

"Don't go too far," I hollered after him. "Not to Washington Square Mall, not yet."

I asked Chandra if she wanted the third bedroom, or preferred we convert the garage. She chose the garage, as it would give her more privacy.

We painted all weekend, and the fresh white and apricot raised my spirits. Thom served as the critical eye for the changes. He chose gray plaid for the curtains in his room. The new sea-green wall-to-wall carpet made it feel like home. We insulated, wall-boarded, and painted the garage, then put in a floor and rose-colored carpet for Chandra.

My home! An enclave of my family, living together. And best of all—with careful management—two weeks later, the black cherry Caravan I had dreamed about sat in the driveway, fully paid for, negotiated for only three percent over cost. I felt like a bulldozer. Even car salesmen had to give way.

# Chapter Ten

## Tie Your Camel—January, 1988

It had been forty days since Hawk and I split up, thirty-eight days since he had invited another woman into his house and his life. I found this out when a mutual friend called.

The same friend told me she wasn't simply a roommate; they were involved. I wondered if they had an affair prior to her moving in. A sense of failure flickered each time I thought of them sitting by the fireplace. I had so many questions that would never be answered.

When I put myself in Hawk's shoes, I couldn't deny him what he needed and wanted most. By moving first, I didn't have to experience the added grief and rejection of his leaving me. I knew splitting up was for the best; still, I was enraged by the circumstances.

Finally, I unpacked and flattened the last box. Exhausted but satisfied, I looked around the fresh inside of our tract house. I'd done the best I could. The clean smell of paint compensated for the house's basic nature—a plain, slapped together clone of the 1950s house next to it. But this was home. I slumped at the kitchen table and stared out the window at the van sitting sleek on the short concrete drive.

Unlike the spacious lane with acreage properties where I had grown up, this was a shabby, working-class neighborhood with debris at the bus stops. Well, I guess I'm a working-class mother now, I thought—I barely managed to pay my bills each month, and credit card debt mounted any time extra expenses came up.

Chandra paid rent, which helped. We never ate out, and rarely went to movies. Did the people here share the same values I had? I wasn't sure. I wanted this to be a safe neighborhood. I had to believe we were secure here, but at a gut level, I wasn't as relaxed or at ease as I had been from day one at the Ranch. I waved at neighborhood moms, but rather than smiling, they just stared in return. No one had knocked on our door to welcome us. Once again, Thom and I felt sidelined.

I tried to shove my worries down, but they popped back up like a noisy jack-in-the-box. This move had shaken Thom's world. I glanced out at our tiny front yard, isolated from other yards by tight little fences, and ached for the loose camaraderie of the Ranch—children bursting into our chicken coop to show Thom a thumbnail-sized tree frog, an injured sparrow, a grandmother zucchini. He had known some of them since pre-school years; they had accepted him prior to the age where children come to notice, and shun, differences.

I thought about taking him back to visit, but they weren't his age—while we lived there, all the kids functioned as a pack of siblings rather than friends. And returning was agonizing for me. I might have been the one to leave, but to see Hawk with his new honey neatly ensconced as though my life there hadn't mattered, made me hot with anger. Life at the Ranch had simply gone on without us.

I wasn't interested in Thom maintaining any connection with the special ed students from last year's class, either. It had never been a good fit for him. His language processing problems took him out of the regular classroom, but socially and emotionally the other students were not as skilled as he. I would remain in regular contact with the close women friends I had made during my seventeen years in Marin County. He was forced to start over here, as a budding teenager.

Aimlessly I walked around the house, glancing into each room. I knew from experience that the feeling of home—when each object in its place is familiar and comforting—takes a long time to settle over me. I peered into Thom's room with its single waterbed, small pine desk, and gray plaid curtains. A tiny room, compared to his previous one. I sat on the edge of his bed. The boy scent of well-used athletic shoes wafted over me.

After the initial shock of leaving, Thom didn't complain much. He didn't talk about the loss of the Ranch community either. I tried to draw his feelings out, but he stuffed them deep inside, steeled himself, and canted forward as though pushing through thick slurry.

And then teenage sarcasm stole the boy I knew. The long conversations in the car I had been able to count on to learn about school, friends, his inner life, vanished.

"How's it going?" I asked.

He sneered, turned his face to the window. "What do you think?" he muttered.

It was hard not to feel abandoned, yet I knew self-pity would only aggravate the situation. I grieved for the unaffected, unsuspicious child he had been. I did not give up—not ever—but I had to pay close attention to minute changes in his body language that might hint at a brief opening. I had suspected his teenage years would be hard for both of us, but I could not have foreseen how difficult. I swung between the poles of heart-breaking empathy and jaw-clenching frustration and, on occasion, rage. He knew how to shut me out, and wielded the skill with both precision and indifference.

Yet his slim, knobby frame seemed so vulnerable as he headed out the door to walk to his new school, I encased him in a prayer of protective light as he headed toward the freeway overpass. I did not know who or what he was going to meet each day, but I was desperate to believe this transition would be all right because we couldn't go back to the life we had before.

Two weeks later, a slight teenager showed up on our doorstep and knocked. "I'm Chris. Is Thom here?"

I felt a flood of gratitude. This slender, blond boy, with two legs and arms that worked, wanted *my* son to hang out with him. Maybe he had met Thom at school, or saw him walking home. I invited the boy in, but he flipped his blond bangs back and shook his head.

"No thanks, I'll wait," he said. "My shoes are caked with mud."

Chris gave me an immediate pinch of hope about our new life. Elated, I went down the hall to announce Thom's visitor. He seemed startled, then pleased, and grabbed his leather jacket.

I hurried back to the kitchen window at the front of the house so, when the boys left, I could surreptitiously watch their interaction. Our home anchored the end of the five-house cul-de-sac. Across the larger street lay a row of small houses, their back yards abutting the freeway.

I heard, then saw Thom clump toward the front door to greet Chris. I thought about offering them one of the chocolate chip cookies that scented the house, but I didn't want to insert myself. I imagined they might head around the side into our back yard, and squinted out the window to see. But the boys were not headed to the side gate. They met up with another lanky teen who towered six inches over them. Back at the Ranch I had known everyone Thom associated with, so letting him loose in the neighborhood with these kids, before I had met their parents, unsettled me.

The first weekend we slept in our new home, I suggested I might make visiting calls to meet—and check out—our neighbors. He said, "D-d-don't be nosey, Mom. They'll tease me." He was thirteen now, and deserved to be on his own more of the time. Since he had always showed caution and had a sensible streak, he had earned some basic teenage freedoms.

So I didn't call him back, and the boys strode down the street, Thom working hard to keep up. I wished they would slow down for him. Fresh concern threaded through my chest. Who were these kids, anyway?

The boys had crossed the far street, near the tree with an old high top sneaker dangling in it. I saw Thom had caught up with the other two. Good. I sighed and went to throw in a load of laundry. I'd find a way to check in with him tonight, see how his adventure went.

For a month or two all seemed good, even happy, with the boys. Either Chris or Dan would collect Thom after school, and I wouldn't see them for a couple of hours. It was a solace to have him out of the house instead of galumphing around complaining. Teens are supposed to hang out with other teens. He seemed to have a real social life, which made me happy for both of us.

One afternoon when he returned, he slammed the front door, and doggedly marched into his room. He avoided my gaze, not even "yo," or "what's for dinner?" I minded my own business and waited; he would come to me when he was ready.

He rewarded me a week later by finally spilling that day's events while I was sautéing onions for meatloaf. "Y-you know the pond across from the shopping center?" he asked.

"Where you fish with your friends?" The onion fumes had gotten to me. I grabbed a tissue to blot my eyes before continuing to stir.

Thom nodded, but seemed uncertain whether he wanted to continue. He looked sideways to see if I was listening. All my mother antennae stood at attention, and I stopped and turned down the heat.

"O-older guys showed up. They grabbed my arms and legs, yanked me off the ground, swung me back and forth," he said.

My hand jumped to my mouth. I wanted to wrap my arms around him, cuddle him, comfort him as I had when he was young.

"Like they were going to sling me into the water," he said. "D-Dan sided with *them*. Damn! I hate when guys do that shit." He jerked his gaze to meet mine full on. "S-sorry. When they do that *stuff*."

I thought back to that day—he hadn't come back wet, didn't appear to be injured, just upset. Calm settled on me. "Something similar happened to me too, around your age," I said. I leaned against the counter, spoon in my hand, drops of butter dripping. "Older kids hung me over a swimming pool. It's so scary to feel powerless."

He tilted his head, waiting for more.

"I think it must be a teenage initiation rite, more than anything," I said. "Teens test kids that are about to join their crowd."

"M-maybe," he said.

I resolved to pay better attention.

A few days later, I saw Dan and Chris snickering as Thom limped behind them, trying to keep up. I could tell they were making fun of him. A chill caught me. I had been wrong. Thom was right. They were teaming up against him, not planning to include him. The ease I had felt since the day Chris knocked on the door vanished as fast as mist off a mountain. I'd failed to hear what Thom had been trying to tell me, and had failed to protect him. I couldn't imagine how to control this situation. It had a power all its own. I had no one to turn to for assistance. But Thom himself had not asked for help. He had made it clear he wanted to handle the situation. All I could do was wait.

One Saturday two months later, I realized Thom had been holed up in his room since early afternoon. It was almost dinnertime. Usually he pestered me for snacks, sneaking slices of carrots, cucumbers, whatever I was chopping. Dan and Chris had been here briefly, full of whispers and laughing. Had Thom slipped out with them? No, he'd been home all afternoon. I tapped on his door.

"G-go away," he said. Then I heard sniffling. I hesitated, weighing my options. He had been so moody lately, edgy. I could march in, get hollered at, or take his words at face value.

I finally asked through the closed door, "Are you all right?"

"W-w-what do you think?" he snarled. "No!"

That settled it. I cracked the door open. Sniffles turned into hiccupping sobs. "D-don't ask," he whispered. He lay on the bed, blinking in my direction, but I don't think he really saw me. I walked in and he rolled toward the wall.

Something had happened, and I wasn't leaving until I found out what. I perched on the wooden frame of his waterbed and bided my time as he gathered himself. He turned back toward me. "Th-th…." He stopped, sighed, tried again. "Th-they barged in."

The chipper curiosity that buoyed him through each day had turned flat, imploded. As I waited for him to say more, I sorted, narrowed, honed what it was. I finally got it. Thom was wracked with shame.

His voice dropped to a whisper. "D-don't be mad, Mom. I was b-b-beating off. They caught me."

I tried not to show it, but this did startle me—Thom was a late developer, as I had been, and we'd had only cursory conversations about sex. But I jumped right in. "Don't ever feel bad about pleasuring yourself! You think they don't? All humans do that!" But even as I offered this perspective, I scrambled for words to eradicate the shame, terror, and misery those boys had injected. I got him calmed down, but I couldn't erase any of those horrible feelings. At fourteen, peer acceptance is everything.

The next morning, I called counselors around town and found a male therapist, a psychologist, who came highly recommended. At the end of the first appointment, he asked to speak to me in private. "Mrs. Arnold," he said, "Thom's not interested in talking about his feelings."

His assumption about my last name made we wonder what other assumptions he'd made. I didn't correct him, but I fumed. "Arnold" was Thom's last name; it hadn't been mine for eleven years.

"We sat in silence the whole time," he said. "You can bring a horse to water, but you cannot force him to drink."

Can't you be more original than that? I thought. "Obviously you two are not a good fit."

Thom pronounced the guy a "stupid dickhead," and rejected counseling for another decade. I look back at the mother I was then and wonder how I missed seeing—from the moment we arrived in Petaluma—that Thom needed the support and the outlet counseling provided. When I yanked him out of one world and forced him into another, he probably felt kicked out of the human race, and didn't know how to rejoin. I assumed if I were okay, if I were adjusting, he eventually would too. I had done my best, but my best had not been good enough. By not seeing his need for immediate support, I missed the slender window before he shut down.

The plans for our van had been a pipe dream. I had only driven teenagers in the car once. If my best had been good enough, I would have foregone the new van, used the money to pay for therapy, and perhaps eased years of anguish. I am so lucky that, in his misery, Thom did not completely close me out.

During one of those fleeting open moments, Thom and I talked about Chris and Dan. I didn't want him hanging out with them anymore, but they were the only boys his age in the neighborhood. I couldn't protect him from his peers forever. I feared if I forbade him to see them, I would isolate him completely.

One spring day a couple of months later, Thom stood at the doorway to his narrow bedroom. "Mom, I can't find my money anywhere," he said. "D-Dan stole it."

"Money?" I asked. "What money?"

He screwed his mouth into a pucker and stared at the floor. "C-couple of days ago, Dan snatched the wallet out of my jacket and was fiddling with it. I told him 'N-no, put it back!' All of Gram's Chr-Christmas money I had left," he muttered. "Forty dollars. W-when I turned around, he must've slipped the money out, 'cause when I went to Longs Drugs to buy candy, it was gone."

"Forty dollars?" I said, my voice rising. "That's serious."

"I kn-know!" he said.

I had allowed the apparently calm waters of the last couple of months to lull me. "We can't let it slide by, Thom. Forty dollars is a chunk—it could buy a pair of athletic shoes, a couple of pairs of pants."

"It-it's my money, remember?" His voice leapt from low to high register. "D-don't you do anything! S-sometimes they hang me upside down and sh-shake money out of my pockets. Then they grab it," he said. "My lunch money." He kicked the door frame. "Y-you step in now, it'll just get worse. They won't include me anymore." He kicked the frame again, harder this time. "I-I have to take care of this."

"Get worse?" My tone rose. He was right, but these twerps were using my son. No—bullying him, mistreating him. Taking what we could ill afford to lose. Stealing from Thom what he could never get back. Way more than money. This was too much.

"D-don't. I'll deal with it," he snapped. "D-don't you dare say a word."

He couldn't handle this situation; I wasn't sure anyone could. "I don't want Dan in this house anymore." My voice came out a whisper.

"I-I don't either." He looked downcast and disappointed as he dug his toe into the carpet, disturbing and ruffling the soft green pile.

I felt the walls of Thom's bedroom close in. "Come into the kitchen. I'd like to hear more." I put my hand on his shoulder as we walked down the hall.

I had so wanted these friendships to blossom, I'd let my guard down. Grief at my inept parenting choked me. There is an ancient Sufi saying, "Trust in God and tie your camel." I had floated on trust and my camel had wandered into the desert.

"What about Chris?" I asked, giving Thom a little space by putting away the dishes. "He seems polite enough."

Thom sat on the edge of a kitchen chair. "N-not really." His voice was almost a whisper. "Chris conned me into doing a wrestling move with him. 'P-p-pile driver.' He flipped me." He rubbed his neck and turned his head from side to side. "D-drove my head smack into the floor. I'm okay, but my neck could have snapped so easy. S-scared me, Mom."

I winced, and my handful of forks and spoons clattered onto the counter. My God, I could have lost him. Just that quickly. After all we'd been through. "He's no friend," I said. "Friends don't treat each other that way." My heart ached for my son, the feigned friendships, the obvious treachery, the sorrow of his learning this kind of lesson on his own. He was silent for a few minutes, but I could almost see thoughts buzzing around in his head. I kept busy, figuring something else was brewing. I shuddered at the thought of what might be next.

"O-okay," he said, gearing himself up, pushing off the chair so he stood in front of me. I think he needed to be as tall as I was in order to spit the words out. "Th-they took me to a drug house," he said finally. "D-down a couple of blocks."

I had to hold on to the counter for support, and my heart raced so fast I could barely speak. "In this neighborhood? You saw them do drugs?" I squeaked.

"Y-you bet. Six grownups. B-biker kind of guys." His shoulders slumped. He sank back onto the chair and hunched over. "D-Dan was buying pot," he said. He knew I would not let him go to Dan's house anymore. Or Chris's, for that matter.

"Was pot the only drug?" I asked, carefully neutral. I didn't know what to say; I only knew how important it was to keep him talking, not shut him down. If I seemed too interested, too pushy, the window into learning what went on in his life would slam. Once shut, it might be months before it reopened.

"P-pot. The room was real thick with smoke." His voice dropped barely above a whisper. "And something else—c-cocaine, I think," he said. "Th-th-they chopped some white stuff on mirrors and sniffed it through a rolled-up bill. A h-hundred dollar bill."

"Good Lord." I said, stiffening to attention. A one-hundred dollar bill—these people were selling cocaine! Great neighborhood I'd chosen. A drug ghetto. "Did they offer you drugs? Make you take any?"

He shook his head.

Okay, good. Cocaine and Northern California pot were far too expensive for addicted adults to share. Thank heavens they wanted it all for themselves. I revisited the urge to grab him and rail: why didn't you tell me sooner? But I knew why. What kid, desperate to belong, would rat on the closest thing he had to a friend?

"Thom…." My voice came out soft.

He chewed his lip; he knew a big blow was coming. We shared our own mother-son dialect.

"You can't spend time with them anymore," I whispered. "I'm so sorry. They are not your friends. Not really. It's not safe."

I couldn't see his eyes, but his lower lip trembled. "I-I-I've…" He got stuck, then started again, trying to start his words flowing. "G-got nobody to hang with. No one at all." I knew he wanted to throw himself into my arms, but he couldn't quite allow it. I reached out—inviting him in—but he shook his head. I wanted to weep, wrap my arms around myself, and rock.

I did confront their mothers. Neither asked me inside, but I made it clear I would not leave, so we spoke standing on their porches. Chris's mom helplessly shrugged her shoulders. I peered at the red rims of her eyes, noted how she avoided my gaze. The scent of pot wafted from her clothes. For a moment I felt as though I were looking in a mirror at my own past.

"I can't control him. Everyone around here does drugs," she said. "We don't even go in our back yard. Too many needles buried in the ground."

Needles. I shuddered, and promised myself we would get out of this neighborhood.

I found, after assessing the real estate market, prices had continued to skyrocket. I could not afford to move, but this no longer felt like home. After talking with Thom, I was sure he could tough it out a little longer.

I would have to be more vigilant. I wondered if the boys were stealing money from their parents, or worse, robbing houses or dealing drugs to younger children. Thank God, no matter how reckless they were, I knew I could trust my son. I could see his innate innocence, but wondered how much he had been unwilling to share.

Two decades later, Thom admitted to other acts the boys had perpetrated. When they hung him upside down to shake money from his pockets, the crown of his head had been only six inches from the sidewalk. They had taunted him, threatened to drop him and "wreck his brain some more." Once, Dan, using all the power in his six-foot frame, had slammed his hands over Thom's ears. Thom told me they rang for weeks.

The boys did not show up at our house for a month. My visits to their homes must have had some repercussions. Each time I thought about Dan or Chris, cold rage slalomed through me. I both hated and pitied them. Finally, one hot, late afternoon as I prepared dinner, I saw Chris sidle up to the door. I marched into the living room and stood on the threshold with my arms crossed. I felt like a cat that has blown up its fur.

"Is Thom home?" he asked, in a studied tone. He did not meet my gaze. The incessant whine of the freeway shrilled in the background.

"You are not welcome here," I said. "And if you do not know why, I'll be happy to remind you." He squinted at me with a knowing, calculated look. In silence, I stared him down. If he had tried to come in, I would have flattened him. He hesitated, shrugged, turned, and walked away.

They did teach Thom—they were a living example of how not to treat others. Those two boys harmed his ability to trust, and undermined my confidence in all teenagers other than my son.

## The Phone Call—June, 1988

Kathryn and I were shutting down our weaving business, and I'd accepted a job with my veterinarian as a receptionist and vet tech starting in two weeks. Every day was exhausting as we worked to empty our warehouse, advertised for a buyer for the huge dye pot, sold or found storage for five looms, and dealt with hundreds of skeins of yarn and stacks of yardage. This final process required us working at the warehouse seven days a week. Both of us were grieving, but our financial books exposed a bleak story. We weren't making it. Not even close.

Saturday afternoon, after sorting and packing over twenty boxes of yarn and fabric, I headed home. Thom had slept late, and I figured he'd go fishing, and be back before I was. But when I opened the door and called out, no answer. I didn't think much about it. Instead, I got started on a simple dinner—quesadillas, a staple for this tired single mother.

The phone rang. Still holding the knife, I picked up the receiver.

"This is Officer James from the Petaluma Police Department. May I speak with Ms. Blaine, please?"

The knife clattered on the counter top. "This is Skye Blaine," I said, dropping into a chair. My fist went to my chest, where my heart had leapt in fight or flight mode.

"I have your son, Thom, in custody. We arrested him for theft at Longs Drugs this afternoon."

My hands got clammy. *What the hell? I taught him better than this.* Fear and momma rage erupted simultaneously.

"You need to come down to the station. We'll talk more when you get here. Do you need directions?"

I squeaked out a "yes," and jotted instructions.

When I arrived at the station, my body was quivering—fear of authority, concern for how my son might have been treated, rage at youthful stupidity. I gave my name at the window and waited. Paced and stewed. An officer took me back to a small room, an interrogation room, I figured.

"I want to speak to you alone, before I release your son," he said. He pulled out a chair and sat down. "I believe he's a good kid. He made a bad mistake and got caught, but he's filled with remorse. That's a positive sign. We fingerprinted him and took mug shots—partly to give him a good scare. Of course he'll have to pay Longs $100 for the insult. I understand they took back the game." He stared at me. "I *highly* recommend you make him earn the money."

"You're damn right I will," I said. "And make sure his father doesn't let him off the hook, either."

When the officer brought Thom out, my son had difficulty meeting my gaze. His eyes were red-rimmed. No sign of bravado. "I-I-I'm sorry, Mom," he whispered. "I r-r-really blew it."

"That's for sure," I snapped.

As we drove home, I asked what happened.

"I-I stole a v-video game. Nintendo."

"Why would you do that? You don't even have a Nintendo set."

"Th-the kids at the B-Boys Club put me up to it; one k-kid has the set. The guy at the store who caught me took me upstairs—he sh-showed me the window where they can see *everything* that goes on. I-I had no idea. H-He asked me if I had any money, but I didn't. He called the p-police."

"You must have been frightened and ashamed. You know you'll have to go back to the store and apologize."

His eyes flew open wide. "I-I-I'm not ever going in Longs again! N-n-no way!"

"Oh yes, you are. You need to tell them face-to-face you're sorry, *and* pay them $100."

His eyes got big. "But I-I only have $20 right now. That's *all* my savings." He looked at me hopefully.

"Then you'll earn the rest doing chores."

He slumped farther down. "Maybe my dad'll bail me out."

"I'll make sure that doesn't happen. It's your responsibility. Did they handcuff you?"

"N-n-no, but I had to r-r-ride in the back of the police car."

"What was that like?"

"Em-embarrassing."

"I bet. I hope you've learned your lesson."

He nodded, staring at his knees.

"You're grounded, too."

"H-how long?"

"Until I'm convinced you can be a good citizen." I pulled into our driveway. "That could be a long, long while."

## God Box—July, 1988

It had been nine months since Hawk and I split up. No more strained silences; no more tiptoeing around. No more trying to hide a disintegrating marriage from my son. Thom and I had hard times, but at least I could be at one with myself. I stood up and stretched my hands high over my head. I loved living as a single mother.

I shut my bedroom door, sat cross-legged on the bed—it virtually filled the room—and wrote down all the qualities I had been stewing over for weeks. I didn't want to complicate my life, not now—no relationship until Thom was grown and on his own, if ever. I didn't pick compatible partners. Three failed marriages proved that. This list was to remind me, if I ever thought I was falling in love again, what was most important to me—and obviously unattainable—at least all in one person.

My true partner would:
>communicate feelings clearly
>be well-balanced and emotionally stable
>share a like-minded spiritual path
>be sexually compatible
>be financially responsible
>appreciate my friends and family
>love my animals as his own

I chewed on the end of my pencil and stared at the paisley bedspread. I couldn't think of anything else, so I pondered each item. Then I folded it up and put it in a carved box—the same box had held wedding rings from my marriages. Once again, it held what I needed to let go.

Four weeks later, I drove to the Joy Lake Retreat Center outside of Reno for a retreat, something I had not done since the vision quest. This time I did not have burning questions—I only wanted to spend time with my spiritual teacher and absorb the practices he offered. Ray agreed to have Thom at his house for three days.

I sucked in the dry, piney air and with the crude map the registrar gave me, went to locate my sleeping quarters. I caught a glimpse of the round yurts nestled together above Joy Lake, so I made my way up the narrow path. A slender, bearded man was walking toward me. My first thought—what a lovely man. My second thought—he must be in the couples workshop. Lucky woman. My third thought, as he drew near, was accompanied by a lurch in my heart rhythm—my heart knows this man; he's an old friend.

As we passed, I looked into his steady blue eyes bracketed with sprays of smile lines. We didn't speak. I went on to unpack and turn a cot, lamp, and side table into my home for the next three days. As I had on the vision quest, I set up an altar with my prayer beads, the rose quartz heart, and of course, Le Mutt. Feeling unsettled that a man could so easily knock me off my center, I went to sit by Joy Lake before dinner.

A few minutes later, he appeared, walking quietly toward me. This time we said hello. I felt tongue-tied and shy, retreated back into silence, and wondered what his lucky partner looked like.

After dinner, I grabbed my meditation pillow, and went up to the large meeting yurt for the first retreat gathering, taking a place near the front so I would have no distractions. I did not see this man, but felt him walk in and sit behind me. My back electrified. Finally I sneaked a look. He was here. Not in the couples retreat after all.

The next morning, as I was going down the path to breakfast, we met again. He pulled me into a warm hug. Owen—I learned his name at lunch that day—said I leaped into his arms. We have a shared memory: we felt as though we had come home.

On the second day, my teacher sent retreat participants on a walk around the lake. Owen's and my paths converged, and we strolled in silence—the deepest, most comfortable silence I could remember. We had no need or inclination to talk. No patter about sports, no flirting or covert glances. What a relief.

Over vegetarian lunch with him on the third day, I offered a little information about Thom and watched to see how he responded. I've seen many men unable to cope with even the idea of a disabled boy. I felt protective of my son, afraid to say too much. But his gaze did not waver; he did not turn away or stare at his cuticles. He listened with curiosity and interest. We traded phone numbers.

During our first telephone conversation, an excruciating three weeks after the retreat, I mentioned other details of my life: my twenty-year-old niece, my one-hundred-fifty pound Irish wolfhound, Kyle; Jesse, the new puppy I'd found at the Humane Society, and Francis, my black Persian kitten. "Be prepared," I said. "It's a menagerie." I worried about the unintentional flavor of that. It sounded chaotic.

"I'm ready to meet this menagerie," Owen said. "Tomorrow evening?"

My heart skittered—then kathunk-thunk-thunked—Owen, coming to my home. He lived in the country overlooking a pristine valley that hosted a pair of golden eagles. My house did not have what real estate agents refer to as "location." I was self-conscious about my neighborhood.

That night, I sloshed around on my waterbed, unable to sleep. What if I had misjudged him? Had my heart carried me away yet again? What if he didn't pay attention to Thom or ignored him in some subtle way? Kyle, ever-sensitive and aware, kept bumping my elbow to comfort me, occasionally stuck his big, cold nose in my ear. Finally he collapsed next to the bed and I heard his deep, cleansing groan. Soon he snuffled his doggie snores. I lay awake for hours.

The next afternoon, I told Thom that Owen was coming over. I was afraid to show my anticipation and delight, certain if I did, he would turn his teenage negativity on high. I kept my tone offhand. He gave a noncommittal shrug and walked away. "O-okay," he said, over his shoulder. But I knew he was curious. What kid wouldn't be? I prayed he wasn't thinking, oh shit, here we go again.

Thom peered out the window when the sporty Honda CRX pulled up in the driveway, then retreated to his room. Heaving a sigh of gratitude that I could come face to face with Owen alone, I opened the door. He took my hand, entwining our fingers. I leaned into him, listened to his beating heart. His arms around me still felt like home. Thank heavens he didn't ask me anything, or even speak. I couldn't have answered.

After a moment, I invited him in and called to Thom. He shook hands with Owen, who said, "How about a ride in my CRX?"

Smart move, I thought. He earned points on that one.

"Y-yeah," Thom answered, trying hard not to seem too interested. "I'd like that. R-right now?"

Oh God. Please let Owen pass this test.

Owen glanced at me, eyebrows raised.

"Sure," I said. "You two go, and I'll work on dinner. You can meet the rest of the crew later."

After they left, I sagged against the counter and blew out a loud breath of relief to have them both gone for a few minutes. I got busy chopping vegetables into shaky slices.

Thom came in grinning after the ride, and dinner seemed to go well. Chandra chattered about work. Afterward, Thom went to his room. Soon, the TV blared, a no-no before homework. He had me, and he knew it. I wasn't about to fight with him, not in front of Owen. This time, I let Thom win. Chandra retired to her space.

Owen sat on the couch, and Kyle stood, his head near Owen's shoulder, panting. Very affectionate, very embarrassing. Welcome to my home, I thought. This is the way it is. As we talked, Owen rubbed Kyle's ears with one hand and dragged a string along the couch for Francis with the other. Jesse curled in my lap, puppy-tired. We talked for three hours—no blaring TV sports, no pot or alcohol, just quiet background music and intimate sharing.

Owen left around 10 p.m. I turned off the lights and sat on the couch for a long time. The family interaction felt complicated, maybe too hard. Yet I did not know how I could ignore the sense of familiarity and comfort. He hadn't kissed me, and oh, I had wanted him to; maybe that was a sign that he wouldn't call again.

I asked Thom what he thought about Owen, anxious what his response might be. My meeting someone special wasn't supposed to happen for years, certainly not while Thom was in the awkward teenage phase.

"He's okay," he said. I couldn't get any more out of him, and I wasn't willing to press him for an answer. I prayed "he's okay" was a positive sign.

One day went by. I tried to concentrate on work and family. Then another agonizing day. Should I call? Even though I ached to talk with him, I decided against it. Owen had never had children of his own;

getting involved with a woman with a moody teenager—and a disabled one at that—took a special level of courage and intention. He needed space to sort this one out for himself.

On the third day, the telephone rang. I knew, just knew, it was Owen calling. With quivering knees, I picked up the phone.

Two months into the courtship, I remembered the list in my God box. I reread it carefully, pencil in hand. When I was done, I had checked off all seven items. Flooded with elation and shock, I stared at the list for a long time before I carefully refolded it and put it back in the box. I had believed I would not get entangled in a relationship again; the intent of the list—because it seemed impossible to fulfill—had been to keep me out of trouble, away from repeated misery. The timing was awkward, but my road map had apparently worked.

Three months after we met, Owen packed up his belongings from the rental that bordered pristine Audubon-protected acreage, and moved into our little home by the freeway. Thom sank more deeply into his teenage angst. Although he couldn't voice it, he was uncomfortable with a man in his mother's bed.

## Joining—May, 1989

May 7, 1989. Our wedding day. Owen and I, plus Thom and a few close friends and relatives, gathered in a cozy yurt at Ocean Song, high on a hill in Occidental looking toward the sea. Chandra made our wedding carrot cake. Threads of morning mist clung to the trees. The ceremony took place in a circle. At the end we shared a blessing dance, one of the Dances of Universal Peace. Each person faced another, singing "May the blessings of God rest upon you, may God's peace abide with you, may God's presence illuminate your heart, now and forevermore." We advanced slowly—an allemande left, similar to square dancing—and sang again with a new partner. I heard a strangled sound behind me, and saw Thom weeping. Was he upset? Happy? Overwhelmed? I shifted, about to drop out of the circle to comfort him, but Lauren signaled for me to remain. She slung an arm over his shoulder, and they walked outside. It took twenty minutes before he regained his composure and came back. She told me his heart, touched by the atmosphere, had fallen wide open.

## New Territory—June, 1989

We bought a 1906 home on an acre in Sebastopol a month after our marriage. It was seventeen miles northwest of Petaluma. Good riddance, Dean Court. Good riddance, Chris and Dan. Chandra moved out and found a small apartment.

In September, before school started—and with trepidation—I made an appointment at Analy High so Thom and I could get a sense of his new school. Another beginning. While a student showed Thom around, I had a few minutes with the special education teacher. I slid my fingers along one of the computer keyboards. An Apple computer for every student. This was terrific.

"Once special ed students enter the ninth grade, we really don't expect them to change," she said. Her tone seemed offhand, tired, even bored.

My head jerked up. Surely she was kidding. "What did you say?" I asked, "I don't think I heard you correctly."

She repeated the same statement, then softened it with, "Oh, you know, their attitudes shift at this age. They aren't much interested in school."

My fists curled karate-style. I shook them loose. How dare she envision no future for these kids? "I don't believe it," I said. "Please don't look at *my* son through that lens. He changes—and amazes me—all the time."

"Well," she said, swallowing what might have been a snort. "You know, parents always think the best of their kids." We faced off, staring at each other.

The room, only a moment ago so full of possibility, now lay beige and plain before me. The school room stench, too many years and too many teenagers, assaulted my nose. I felt the grit of dust on my finger that had swept across the keyboard with such hope a minute before.

"Don't you dare dismiss my son so easily," I retorted, frustrated that I was helpless to find more persuasive words.

Two years earlier, an acquaintance told me about a program for dyslexic kids in Santa Rosa—an expensive program of unique one-on-one after-school tutoring. Now we lived only seven miles away; previously, it would have been a lengthy commute. At that time, I refused to approach my mother, yet again, for money.

I drove home from the high school, intent on finding the program's business card even if I had to tear the house apart. Eventually, I discovered it in a hidden pocket in my purse. The next morning, I called the Excel Center.

Thom went with me to the appointment. After nine years of discouragement he didn't hold much hope, but he was willing to go. They interviewed us, asking a barrage of questions. Then we set up testing dates. First they had to determine *why* he had such difficulty reading. Although I would not let on to Thom, I, too, was afraid to hope. We'd had so many disappointments with tutors in the public school system. I wanted to prove to the Analy High teacher, and myself, that her limiting, negative attitude was a travesty.

After ten hours of testing, the Excel staff thought they'd found the source of Thom's decoding problems: he managed three- and four-letter words, but when he tried to read multi-syllable ones, could not retain the early syllables long enough to string the whole group together. He tested as a low second-grade reader. They were positive their methods could boost Thom's reading skills. I tried to push my hope down, cynically thinking they just wanted our business—but it burbled up anyway. The testing had been unlike any Thom had undergone. This might work.

"What are your goals for reading?" the head of Excel asked him.

Thom chewed his cheek as he considered. "I-I guess I'd like to be able to read a newspaper," he said. "Or-or Stephen King." He gave a quick glance to check her reaction.

"Great goal. We'll aim for Stephen King," she said.

I called my mother—with high excitement—and asked if she would take on this expense. I had no doubt she would be thrilled to help Thom read. I was right.

Marlene was assigned as Thom's tutor. In her approach, she used all the modalities including inch-square blocks with letters on them, sound, visuals, and texture. Best of all, she used humor. Often I would walk up the stairs to their second floor offices and hear Thom's loud cackle from down the hall. My God, he was having fun!

He took to calling Marlene "Grandma," which struck me as strange. She was only thirty-five and looked twenty-something. Her personality was diametrically different from his own grandmother. Mom had never bonded with Thom one-on-one, which saddened me. Maybe deep inside, he wished he had a grandmother who was as much fun as Marlene. Or perhaps he had a crush on her and unconsciously wanted to manufacture a grandmother's distance between them. Whatever it was, she withstood Thom's teasing and threw it back, full tilt.

One afternoon, as we walked toward the stairs leading down from Excel's offices, I said to Thom, "When you're an old man—say eighty—I bet you'll still be chuckling about Marlene."

"I-I don't plan to live that long," he said. "D-don't want to."

I gaped at him, folded my fist over my heart. I had never imagined a fifteen-year-old would not desire a long life.

He saw my reaction and said, "G-get over it, Mom. Would you want to live to eighty in a body like mine?"

A wide canyon opened inside me. My child, whom I thought I knew so well, lived in a different universe. From then on, I looked at him with fresh respect. He wasn't hanging on. I was. I realized my wishes, my goals for him, were not pertinent. He was a young man walking his own path, and it was not my place to force my desires or hopes on him. Our relationship became easier for us after I learned this lesson. Not easy, just easier. In day-to-day situations, I let go faster.

A year later, tired from a concentrated day of work, I drove to Santa Rosa to pick him up from Excel as I did every Monday, Wednesday, and Friday. A new Barbara Kingsolver novel lay on the passenger seat, something to read in case his session ran late. Pelting rain marked wintertime. Thom slid into the car, spraying rain from his curly, shoulder-length hair, and I snatched up the library book to keep it from getting wet. "Here," I said, handing him a towel.

"W-what ya' reading?" He reached for the book. "*Animal Dreams*. Interesting title. Any good?"

I pulled out into the street. "Don't know yet. I've only read the first few pages," I said.

He flicked it open and, from the middle, began to read out loud. He read with flow and ease, clearly comprehending the content. Tears stung my eyes. I quickly maneuvered into an empty parking place because I couldn't see well enough to drive safely. Through my tears I could see his wide smile, his pride of accomplishment. His eyes filled too. "I-I know, Mom, isn't it something? All this hard work paid off. I-I can read!" He sat next to me patting my shoulder. "It's okay," he said. "Oh, Mom, it's okay."

I broke down and wept hard, leaning against the cool steering wheel.

# Chapter Eleven

### Compatriots, September, 1989

I picked up the ringing phone. It was Sue, the Analy High nurse. "Thom tells me he has these nose bleed fountains often. I've put him flat, and he knows to put pressure for a full five minutes, but I thought I'd better notify you."

"Thanks," I said, happily. Finally, here was a school nurse with a warm, friendly tone. "Yes, he gets them a lot."

"I gave him a T-shirt I keep in the office," she said, "but if you could bring a couple of extras, he'll have a change of clothes here and won't have to walk around school looking like he lurched out of an ax-murder movie." She giggled. "Although, he might like that."

I laughed too. "Great idea," I said. "I'll drop a few by today."

We agreed to meet after school, and Sue gave me directions to her office. When I walked in, I knew who she was without even asking—I saw her smile lines first, her concern and compassion as she spoke to an overweight girl—nothing dried up or burnt out about her.

"I like Thom," she said, after the student left. "I've gotten to know him because he comes in to chat with me when he needs a break from the population out there." Her arm swept wide, indicating the whole school. "As you can imagine, it's not so easy for him. New kid, limps, special ed."

"I worry." I sighed, setting his T-shirts on her desk, and slumped into a chair. "He's got learning challenges, but he's bored stiff. Special ed doesn't meet his needs at all. Even his teacher puts me off." I repeated what the woman said to me about kids this age not changing academically.

Sue frowned, and planted her hands on her hips. "I hope she didn't say that in front of Thom. I don't think he will ever stop growing and changing, and he doesn't need—or deserve—her negative prognosis."

"He was off touring the school," I said. "But I wouldn't put it past her to work it into a conversation."

"The kids report stuff to me. From what they say, that woman needs to be slid smack into retirement," she said. "I do speak up around here. Doesn't make me real popular with the higher-ups."

"You've got my vote," I said. "Sue…." I hesitated. "My main worry is Thom hasn't made friends yet."

"He's been hanging out with one boy," she said.

"He has?" I paced across the room, not sure if the flood of energy in my body was relief or anxiety. Bleak images of Chris and Dan streaked through my mind. "Real short kid? I might have seen them together outside of the comic store the other day. Thom's never mentioned him, though."

"Jason. His friends call him Jay. Yeah, scoliosis, that's why he's so short. He's nice enough, although Thom's got more on the ball. Jay's nineteen, still trying to finish high school. He has serious physical disabilities and health problems." She paused, and caught my eye. "Let Thom tell you about the friendship when he's ready. Don't spill the beans."

Finally, a real ally within the school system. I wanted to move into her office. Base camp, right here.

"Thanks for letting me know." I shook my head. "Thom's avoided handicapped kids ever since he was mainstreamed. I kind of understand. For his first six years, the disabled kids were always corralled together—but his universe would be larger if it included everyone."

"We'd all be better off if we followed that advice," she said. "Stay in touch, okay?"

A few days later, as school was letting out, I headed to the health food store, looking for Thom. I finally saw him with Jason, in animated conversation. Thom, still so darn skinny, limped down the street, left shoulder dropping low, left wrist folded, hand up, pressed to the back of his hip. He was leaning down close to his friend to hear what he said. Jason was a full foot shorter, frail and clearly stunted, yet thick-chested.

Later, I saw how the scoliosis had bent, spiraled, and compacted his undersized body. Because of a severe heart defect, the doctors did not believe he could survive surgery to straighten his spine. Thom and I still faced our share of challenges, but at this point, none were life-threatening. We had come so far. I no longer woke up fearful, wondering if he was still alive as I had when he was an infant. We were darn lucky.

The first time I met Jason's mom, she came to our house. We talked while the boys holed up in Thom's room and listened to a new Metallica CD. Betty was a direct, plain woman, and she didn't mince words. As soon as she sat down she said, "I worry half to death that Thom will fall at our house, break an arm, or a leg. Or worse, crack his head open. I'd feel so responsible."

"He's fallen a lot in his life and rarely even bruised," I said. "You know, I worry about Jason, too. I get freaked out by the color of his lips—so blue! He won't keel over of a heart attack, will he?"

She laughed, and we passed knowing glances, the embattled parent look. "No, he has chronic heart problems but, apparently, a heart attack isn't what would happen," she said. "Cardiac failure is more likely. He's already outlived the doctors' predictions," she added softly, tapping her thumbs together.

"Really? Oh my, I didn't realize…." My voice trailed off. Conflicting emotions flew through me—sorrow for their situation, a rush of concern that my son might lose his best friend, and relief that I didn't face what she did.

"Don't feel bad; there's nothing to be done," Betty said. "Except love the kid. I have a daughter, too, younger—and healthy, thank heavens. Jason takes so much energy; it's been hard on her. And it's real tough on his dad."

"Dads have a difficult time," I said. "It's hard on Ray, too."

"Your husband?"

"Ex," I said, and felt a wave of tiredness even thinking about my next interaction with Ray. "Thom sees him on the weekends."

She looked around the living room. "But you're married now."

"Yes."

Her glance said so much. She was right; few single moms parenting a disabled child live in a lovely old home on an acre in Sebastopol, California. "We're the lucky ones, with men that stick around. I'm real grateful to have Bud. He's good to Jay. Of course the kid drives him haywire-crazy, too."

"Same here. Most of the time I feel like I'm standing in the middle trying to arbitrate. Or translate. The other night, Owen lobbed a tube of toothpaste down the hall after Thom."

She giggled. "Toothpaste?"

"Nearest handy thing, I guess. He's never thrown anything before. Doubt if he will again; scared the shit out of both of them. Thom was in a real ugly mood. Unreachable."

"Jay gets that way, too. I think half the problem is that they have so few friends. I'm glad for our boys' friendship."

"Me too. Very grateful." My words caught in my throat. "It's made a huge difference."

The boys piled out of Thom's room. Jason was wheezing a bit.

"Catch your breath," Betty cautioned.

Jay stood still for a moment, leaned his palms against his thighs, and took a couple of slow breaths. "Will you drive us to town?" he asked when he could speak. "Thom will walk home with me after."

She glanced at me. I nodded and turned to my son. "Please be back by five-thirty, for dinner."

"I'll run him home," Betty said.

The boys were inseparable, rolling in and out of our two houses with equal comfort. I began spending time with Betty on the afternoons when I went to collect Thom at their house. The first time I walked in, she said in a matter-of-fact tone, "Nothin' fancy here. Hope you don't mind. Sit down if you like; the boys are still out and about."

I sat down on a chrome kitchen chair with torn vinyl pads. The scent of chicken soup wafted through the room. She set a cup of hot, black instant coffee in front of me, and placed Coffeemate and sugar nearby.

"Thom has more leg surgery coming up," I said.

"When?"

"After school's out. To give him the summer to heal. I dread it."

"I bet. What are they going to do?"

"He sprains his ankle a lot because he toes in badly. Then he can't walk at all, because he doesn't have the left-side coordination to manage crutches. The doctors are talking about turning his leg around so his foot points forward again."

"Yikes. I won't even ask how they do that."

"I'm not sure myself, but I hope Jay will keep coming over. It would cheer Thom a lot."

"I'm sure he'll want to." She lifted her gaze toward the late afternoon sunlight that spilled in through the worn chintz curtains.

## Paper Clip—February, 1990

Thom stamped in from school, threw his door open, then slammed it shut. The house reverberated. It happened so often, I wondered if, one day, the foundation might fold in on itself, and our home implode. I leaned my hands on my desk and shook my head. I thought about calling Sue to see if she knew what had happened. Something had gone down with other students. I glanced at the clock. Too late. No home number, and it wouldn't feel appropriate to call her there anyway. She certainly put her time in at school.

I heard his backpack thunk on the floor, then rhythmic hard smacks, and "Fuck you!" shouted again and again. I detested that expression—I made sure he suffered consequences when he directed it at us—but if he vented behind a closed door, I let it go. When he was most upset, he beat a piece of hard rubber hose on an outdated telephone book. Today he pounded for a full fifteen minutes. I sighed. I didn't have a clue how to reach him when he hurt this badly.

Later, stony-faced, eyes like dark bullets and frown marks carved deep, he stormed the kitchen for a snack. I did not ask what had happened. I knew better than to intervene; he would turn his powerful sarcasm on me. He smashed crackers trying to spread peanut butter on them, finally swept the mess into a bowl, sloshed milk on it, and slurped it with a spoon. He ripped a banana out of its skin and stuffed that in the bowl too. I caught the waft of fruity scent, and thought of the easier years when I had added them to his Star Wars lunch pail.

At dinner, when Owen saw Thom clump into the kitchen, shoulders hunched, and his hair over his face, he raised his eyebrows but didn't try to engage him. Owen had been verbally bitten often enough; he knew when to hold his tongue. Sometimes our home was a bitter winter encampment. I wasn't afraid of Thom; did not worry he might harm us, nor was I concerned about his harming himself. He had fought for life, choosing life more than once. But the loss of his sweet innocence, torn away by cruelty, frightened me. I didn't know if he would be able to find his way back to himself. Other parents said their kids went through the same agonizing experiences, but I wondered.

Thom shoveled in his dinner, head about four inches from his plate. I opened my mouth to correct his manners and shut it again. Best to pick my battles. He offered monosyllabic responses to my questions about Jay, but did not generate any conversation. It was not until Owen and I finished the dishes and headed for the living room that Thom asked me into his bedroom. Since we had moved the summer before, invitations to his private space had been as rare as shooting stars. I stood in the doorway. A catastrophe. Huge piles on the floor: clean and dirty clothing mixed with books, school supplies, an occasional comic, parts of models. His internal state must be in equivalent chaos.

"C-c-come on, come in and shut the door," he snapped. "I need privacy."

I crossed the threshold and tiptoed around the radioactive piles.

"I-I-I need to know what to do," he said, "other than tromp on kids or smack them with my karate elbow." He rubbed his hand through his shoulder-length Afro as though combing for something. "Jeez! T-two bullies pitched paper clips into my hair all through s-study hall," he muttered. "When the period ended, I went to see Sue in her office, and s-she helped me pick them out. Th-the cretins were snickering in the hall the whole time. S-s-so damn humiliating."

I listened until he'd spewed out his misery. He looked at me expectantly, as though I might have a solution. I sighed. "I'm so sorry," I said. "You don't deserve this."

"D-damn right I don't!" he said. "Wh-what gives them the right?" He knew better than to use "fucking right" in my presence.

"They're losers," I said. "Best medicine is to ignore them."

"Y-yeah, I did that." His knuckles blanched from fisting them so hard.

"That's my suggestion," I said. My shoulders rose toward my ears, and I turned my palms up, praying for a different, inventive solution. I ached over my inability to ease his distress. "If you react, they'll bug you forever. If you ignore them, eventually they'll stop."

"Is that the best you've got?" he asked. His eyes were filled with disappointment and hurt.

"You could report them." I hesitated, then added, "You could cut your hair."

"W-wouldn't make much difference," he said. "Th-they'd find some other way to torment me." His voice came out a low growl. "And you know th-that reporting them would make it worse."

I nodded. "Sometimes I don't have much of an answer," I said, "other than to commiserate and love you. We can hope one day they'll grow up and turn into decent men."

"I doubt it." He still had his fingers deep in his hair. "H-h-here's another one." His eyes filled with tears, but he blinked them away. "Help me get it out?"

I knew how hard it was for him to ask. Without two-handed coordination, he had to rely on assistance. His left hand jerked behind his back, and he pinned it against his hip so he wouldn't whack me.

His energy had shifted. When I could get him to spill his misery, the rage abated. "Of course," I said. Finally, something I could do. He pointed to the spot. With care, with all my love in my fingers, I unwound the paper clip from his wiry hair and dropped the offending object into his palm. "Living proof. I'm tempted to walk into the principal's office myself."

"Th-th-that would be the vice-principal. D-don't do it. I have to stand up for myself. All I want is to mash those assholes flat, g-grind them into the dirt. B-but Mr. Ito would have banned me from the mats forever." He leaned back against the wall and smacked his hand against it for effect. "It might be worth it. I-I can't even s-spit my words out fast enough at them because I can't get my sentences going."

Thom hadn't taken karate lessons since we moved away from Novato, but Mr. Ito's edicts still rang in his head, thank heavens. This was about more than paper clips. Changing schools during teenage years is difficult for any student. Thom's heavy limp and stuttering, plus being in special ed, made him the steady butt of pranks. These kids had not grown up with him; he was a new, unusual element in their lives. Teens focus on what's different. I wondered if the bullies bothered Thom and Jay when they were together. I suspected that lost in their own world, they weren't targeted or, because they had each other, no longer cared.

Thom didn't make it easier for himself either. His enormous head of hair attracted attention. When his hair was not covering his face, his well-formed mouth drew into a flat slash, and his frown lines were deep, permanent crevices. The depth of his misery, like a sinkhole, either drew unwanted attention or else people steered clear.

From my vantage point, hair was one safe way for him to rebel. All teens needed outlets. I was so grateful he had not gotten involved with drugs that his mane of hair was easy to accept. At least he washed it every day.

"M-my dad? Should I call him?"

"I wouldn't. He'll get so enraged he might march into school and cause a worse scene."

"Y-yeah, you're right. D-damn." He smashed his hand hard against the wall again, and I winced, feeling the pain shoot up my own arm.

"D-dads should help, not make the problem worse," Thom muttered. "He's no help at all."

"I know; I'm sorry," I whispered. Ray's rage, Hawk so shut down—without good role models, Thom had not learned to turn to older men for guidance, and didn't let his stepfather parent him. Soon after meeting Owen, he had informed him that he already had a dad, and one was enough.

I was nothing but an ocean of "I'm sorry." I felt I was failing Thom, a small, sinking boat in that same storm-tossed ocean. He needed a bucket to bail. I'd do whatever I had to. I'd find those buckets, jump in, and bail with him.

## The Nail—June, 1990

While Thom got dressed again, the orthopedic surgeon at Stanford Children's Hospital signaled for me to come over, tore off a piece of paper from the examining table roll, and enthusiastically sketched his plan for Thom's left leg. "We'll break the bone here." Dr. Travis pointed to the femur he had drawn. "De-rotate the leg so his foot points forward again, and then run a nail down the length of the bone and secure it with screws, here." He pointed to the knee and the hip. "His ankle should no longer be at risk."

"Nail?" I asked, my voice quavering into a squeak.

"Pin. You know, like this." With a smile, he reached into a drawer and handed me a stainless steel rod about sixteen inches long and three-eighths of an inch in diameter.

My hand, and my heart, sank from the cold weight. I hefted it. This was a serious piece of hardware.

"He should be up and walking soon," he said. "We'll take the nail out about a year after that."

Did I have enough strength to face this surgery? Did Thom?

Daily life was already hard enough. Isolated and angry, Thom took out his rage where he felt safe—at home, on Owen and me. He took it out less on Ray; his rage could inflame his dad's, and neither of them could handle the conflagration that ensued. Thank God for Jay. He provided the only respite in Thom's life.

I looked at Dr. Travis. My shoulders slumped. No matter what the doctors said, this surgery would bring huge new stresses. I prayed it would be worth it in the end. "This should prevent sprains? They've happened so many times," I said.

He nodded. "That's our goal. It's important he doesn't break that ankle. Did you give blood? We don't expect to need it, but we ask the parents to contribute, in case."

I nodded. Donating blood was a life-affirming action I could take. Over the years, I'd donated close to six quarts—enough to fill more than an average adult body.

Thom limped back into the room. "W-whoa," he said, his voice cracking from low to high. He took the rod from my hand and balanced it, feeling its weight. "Heavy duty. W-will I set off the sensors at the airport?"

"You bet!" the surgeon replied.

"Cool." Thom said. "W-wish Jay could see this."

"He can," Dr. Travis said. "After the nail's done its work, we pull it out."

I shuddered. Yet another surgery. This would rock the family big time.

That night, relieved Thom had retreated to his room, I sat down with a careworn Owen. Rap music blasted through the closed door, but at least we had privacy.

"This summer," I said, simply. "The surgery has to happen then. God, what a dreadful summer for a fifteen-year-old."

He nodded, and put his arms around me. "We'll get through it," he said. "Somehow. Together."

I believed he was right. We most likely would survive it as a family, but I had so many regrets. Owen had deep worry lines, new since we met. He bore our hardships with a great deal of grace, but the burdens I brought to our marriage were not only heavy, they were unwieldy and unpredictable. I don't believe he—or anyone—could have accurately pictured what it would be like to shoulder these challenges. I couldn't lighten them for him.

## Aftermath—June, 1990

After Thom was wheeled into the recovery room, Dr. Travis pulled me aside and promised me Thom would walk soon. It was a hopeful lie, even an invocation, but a lie nonetheless. Thom's leg cramps, erupting the moment he awoke from surgery, were so severe that Dr. Travis, afraid the spasms might shatter the pinned leg, casted him—a bitter reminder of the experience ten years before, but with the misery quotient ratcheted up. Instead of a long leg cast, this one went from his toes halfway up his chest. The next morning, Thom lay in bed, hollow-eyed. "S-s-shit," he said, "It was tough enough before. N-now I'm on the rack. In jail."

A week later, they sent him home. "He'll be in the textbooks," Dr. Travis said. "No idea how long he'll be confined to the cast. His progress will dictate that." Because of the cast—Thom couldn't fold his body into a sitting position—he had to travel flat in an ambulance. I followed in my car. On both Thom's and my behalf, I railed at God the whole way. What was the use of prayer? A stupid balm to make me feel better. Thom was the one who needed the help! I saw no point in trusting God—again and again—when we repeatedly got hit with devastating outcomes. This surgery was supposed to have gone well. Some damn thing was supposed to go well for my kid.

I finally understood doctors don't know much, no matter how many advanced degrees they have or how confidently they act. Once again, they had thrown up their hands and thrust Thom back into mine. I corrected myself. Into ours. Owen, Thom, and I were a family now—although new, and mostly untested. Day-to-day life already presented a significant load—Thom's disabilities and unpleasant teenage disposition, aggravated by Ray's rage that leaked all over us on a fairly regular basis. Now, we faced nursing Thom through the aftermath of this surgery, and another one next year, to pull the rod out. But if—and it was a big if—we managed to stand strong under this weight, we would come out of this a fortress. A fortress of love.

Thom lay confined in a rented hospital bed—at least his room was right off the living room, so he could feel part of the family. I figured this would feel familiar to us after the surgery ten years before, but I discovered I was stumbling in a complex maze without a guide. Valium barely eased his agonizing spasms. I could see the rhythmic cramping of his toes and knew those cramps ran all the way up through the cast to his hip, which had plates and screws in it. My body cringed in response.

I took the brunt as Thom wielded his now-extensive four-letter vocabulary. Again he wept softly much of the time, that side effect of Valium. He was forced to rely on me as his nurse for intimate tasks no mother should have to perform for her teenage son: holding the urinal, steadying the bedpan. I saw my son's genitals for the first time in years—unavoidable—and such a violation of his privacy.

"Geez, Thom, I'm so sorry," I said, when the sheet slid to the floor. He grabbed for it, but missed.

"F-forget it," he said, turning away, his expression shut down. "D-do what you have to do."

After he fell asleep in the evening, I sat with my head in my hands, angry at Thom for no reason other than that he was incapacitated, angry at myself for my frustration and impatience, and very angry at God. This wasn't fair. Our life wasn't supposed to be like this. No child should have this much misery. I wondered whether this experience would blacken our connection, if we would ever be easy together again. Owen served as my ballast, a steady force for peace. He wouldn't respond to my railings with words, only with a tender hug, a quiet touch, or a shoulder rub. I have often wondered why he didn't bolt from our lives during this period.

Every few days, Jay came by—those were the good days. Then delighted cackles erupted from Thom's room. I don't know who was happier, Thom or me.

His dad came to visit one day during the body-cast period. By now, the cramping had eased by half, but Thom, still immobilized and cranky, hollered at his dad when Ray tried to adjust the pillow behind his head.

"Fuck you!" Ray yelled, and stalked out of the house. I heard Ray all the way in the kitchen. I shook my head in disgust. Two teenagers.

That kind of behavior was age-appropriate for one of them, but the other should darn well grow up. After a visit with Ray, Thom's moods were always edgy, darker, closed-in. I went into Thom's room to see how he had weathered his dad's outburst. His one good hand, planted over his pulled-down mouth, quivered. His eyes were pressed shut, and tears leaked down his cheeks. He broke into hard sobs. Valium was not the cause of this. The nippy attitude was gone—but so was his courage, courage he could ill afford to lose. My own courage was deeply shaken.

"It hurts so much, Mom," he said. "S-something's wrong. D-D-Dad doesn't believe me."

"I believe you," I said. Inside, I was cussing Ray out—with every expletive Thom had added to my vocabulary. The forbearance I had for Ray's angry explosions snapped that day. I sat on the bed and smoothed Thom's forehead. "And we'll get to the bottom of this. Your dad is way out of line. Show me again where the worst pain is."

Still sobbing, Thom pulled his hand from his mouth and pointed specifically to his ankle. "R-right there, Mom. Th-this isn't cramps."

In a moment of clarity, the raw-meat blisters I had suffered on my vision quest flashed into my mind. Thom knew his own body. The powerful spasms must have rubbed blisters inside his cast. Anxious, crazy to get him medical intervention, I phoned Owen, but he had left work. Thom only weighed 115 pounds, but with the additional weight of the cast he was too heavy for me to carry, even fireman-style on my back.

The moment Owen arrived, we carried Thom to the car and drove him to the emergency room. At first, the doctor on call wasn't convinced, but I powered on. I had regained some measure of faith in our process. Thom might complain, but he did not exaggerate or fake symptoms. I demanded the doctor saw a chunk from the cast behind Thom's heel. When he finally carved out the square of material—muttering the whole time about losing the strength and integrity of the cast—he exposed huge, murky holes in Thom's ankle. Shock and relief flooded me. The blisters were ugly, but not infected. We got to them in time. The sharp intakes of breath from the medical staff said it all; Thom was redeemed, and so was I. When we returned on two more occasions for the emergency room staff to saw more holes in the plaster to expose fresh wounds, Thom and I were treated with quiet respect—a new experience for us in the medical community, and long overdue.

At some point during that long, hot summer we returned to Stanford, and Dr. Travis cut off the body portion of the cast, leaving only a long leg version. I had to step back and fan the air to clear away the stench of old sweat and moldering cotton batting. Now Thom could sit up and, leaning heavily on my shoulder, hop to the bathroom. Soon, he was able to get there with a walker. Hallelujah! We were no longer tethered like two people in a three-legged race.

I continued to lie awake at night, frightened that he might not walk independently again, but I was equally frightened to voice that doubt to anyone, not even Owen. Voicing might make it so. I'm sure Thom obsessed about this too. That was why, in September, Thom refused to return to school in an electric wheelchair. He believed if he gave in to the chair, he would never get out. I called Sue. She suggested tutoring. With the help of the school's tutor, he was home-schooled.

"I'm here to help," she chirped that first day. "We'll have fun together."

He rolled his eyes. "Right," he muttered.

She came to the house three times a week, working with Thom for a couple of hours. I could hear his irritated stutter, books landing on the floor. One day in early October, she marched out of his room. "I'm finished. Can you believe he just called me a bitch? For no reason! He's out of control."

After she left, I stormed into his room and put my heavy mother foot down. I had nothing more to give, no internal resources to lean on. "Back to school," I said, my voice stern. "Wheelchair or not."

"F-fine," he snapped, turning his head away. "I don't give a shit."

By November he could manage a walker and, in January, seven months later than expected, he could limp unencumbered once again. His foot did point more or less forward. But now his leg made a weird circle in the air when he swung it ahead to plant it on the ground. Thom and I could finally agree on something: this modest gain had not been worth the months of misery.

Life returned to a new normal. Thom wasn't the same as before. He had a more stoic level of grit and, unfortunately, a deeper, more permanent cynicism. As his teenage hormones rose and fell in waves, different styles of music issued from his boom box—most weeks, the nasty rap band 2 Live Crew, sometimes Metallica. Occasionally, on the better days, I was serenaded by Mozart.

There were the usual bouts of bloody noses. I folded the stack of washcloths that we used for sopping up, then paused to finger them. Permanent stains, everywhere. But my son could walk again. He could walk into his future, whatever that might bring—and relieved, I could stand back the proper distance for the mother of a sixteen-year-old, and say thankful prayers that we each had regained our independence.

And Jay, always Jay.

# Chapter Twelve

## Loss—April, 1991

In April, we visited Jay at Moffitt Hospital. He looked blue and small under the covers. Although he didn't have the strength to talk much, he seemed cheered by Thom's visit. He perked up once when Thom showed him a new Batman comic.

On the way home, I glanced at Thom after we passed over the Golden Gate Bridge. Daffodils blossomed by the road, but he didn't see them. Fists hard in his lap, lips pressed so flat together that no blood could flow, he sat rigid, a fortress of teenage misery and fear. Any attempt on my part to start a conversation led to monosyllabic responses, and finally, "F-fuck—lay off, Mom." I fell silent and concentrated on driving. This was not the time to push.

When Betty and I first met, she'd said Jay had already outlived the doctors' expectations and yet, knowing him, I could not accept the inevitability of his death. His buoyant sense of humor, laughing off his trials—surely he would not succumb, at least not until mid-life. Not Thom's best, and only, friend, and not now, during these dreadful teenage years when they needed each other for support.

During this visit, the true threat trickled past my defenses and for the first time I pictured a world in which Jay might die. His illness frightened me, and terrified me for my son.

The next day after school, Thom seemed glum, but not so rigid. His body seemed softer, more vulnerable. I learned over the years he couldn't remain in profound deep freeze for long. Maybe now I could broach Jay's declining health. I asked Thom to sit down. "Jay's awfully ill; you know that, right?"

"Duh, Mom. He's been in bed for weeks. Is-is this a lecture?" He screwed his face into that black expression—the one he saved for me—the deep furrow, eyes blazing under the hood of his brows. With this mask, he blockaded himself, reminding me of a porcupine rolled into a defensive ball, quills on edge. I had to tread carefully, ease into this. Any wrong comment would drive him away from me and deeper into himself.

"No lecture, I promise. He might get better; I sure hope so. But he might not, and I don't want you to be caught by surprise."

His shoulders dropped. "I-I know," he muttered. The blazing eyes were gone. In their place lay honest-to-goodness, gut-level fear. "I j-just try not to think about it."

I wondered what Thom and Jay had talked about the day before. I would never know.

"You try not to think about it, but you worry about his worsening health all the time, don't you?"

He met my eyes and nodded. Deep anguish pooled there. I moved closer and put my arm around his shoulders; he leaned into me. I did not need to drag out the conversation. He knew I understood and would support him.

The next weekend, Thom and his dad went to a comic-book signing at a specialty bookstore. Thom waited in line and, with his allowance, paid for a Batman series comic and had the artist sign it for Jay. The next day after school when Thom did not return to our house until almost dinnertime, I figured he had gone to Jay's.

"J-Jay didn't want to see me," he said.

Strangely, Thom didn't seem depressed by this; his voice lilted, a normalcy I hadn't heard in many weeks. He clunked down on the kitchen chair.

"F-from the bedroom I heard him say, 'N-not today; I'm too tired.' S-so I just barged in!" he said, with a wide smile. "H-handed him the comic without a word. He scanned the front, saw the artist's signature. Y-you should have seen his face! L-like, he just melted on the spot."

Miraculously, Jay recovered, even returned to school. But Betty told me each time he got that sick, he had a harder time getting his strength back and didn't quite reach the level where he'd been before. Then, near the end of the school year, he had a couple of energetic weeks. He even visited our house, although I noticed that instead of walking, Betty drove him. His color had pinked up, and he didn't seem to be wheezing so badly. Thom's grin came back. I didn't lie awake at night gnawing on worries.

"Maybe Jay's beaten the odds," I said to my older sister. Maggie had divorced and come from Iowa to live with us a few weeks before.

Jay was so much better that when my mother invited Owen and me on a week's cruise up the Columbia into the Snake River gorge, it seemed like the perfect time for a getaway. Owen and I had never been to Oregon, and Maggie was happy to keep an eye on Thom.

The third night on board the ship, the purser's office paged me. A call on a cruise ship can never be good. I thought of the page my mother got at the zoo when my father died. I briefly prayed for us all—for well-being, for courage. Then, trying to even my breath, I walked fast down the hall. The uniformed woman handed me the telephone. As I waited for her to leave, I pressed the receiver to my heart. When I put it to my ear, I heard Thom's voice and the ship's engine noise vanished. My son was all right. This must be about Jay.

"S-s-sit down, Mom," he said in a measured voice. He waited. I leaned against the desk. "You sitting yet?"

"I'm sitting," I said, my heart thudding. Jay must be worse.

"J-Jason died tonight." His voice slowed, as though it were settling into wet concrete. "An hour ago."

Now I sank into the desk chair. My dear child, only sixteen, shouldn't have to suffer the awful loss of a best friend. His only friend.

"Oh Thom." My heart battered my chest. "I'm so sorry. Tell me. He seemed to be doing so much better."

"I-I just got off the phone with his mom. L-last night, she was helping him into the bath, and he said that he really loved her. T-that freaked her out, because he doesn't go for that gushy stuff." Thom gave a big sigh, then his voice broke and settled into its deepest range.

"Y-you know Jay—not the sentimental type. Then tonight, he told her his heart was hurting, so she rubbed his chest. Sh-she does that a lot." Thom took a ragged breath. "R-right then—in her arms—he had a heart attack. Sh-she said he was gone real fast." He was snuffling now.

I waited until his breathing calmed. My chest ached, and it was hard to speak through the rock in my throat. "I think we should come home early," I said. "When's the funeral?"

"On-on Friday. D-Dad said he'd take me." He fell silent for a moment. "Don't come home, Mom. Th-there isn't one thing you can do to make this okay. Aunt Maggie's being real supportive." He cleared his throat. "It-it helps me to know that you're having fun."

"Hang on a minute." I couldn't speak. How could he be thinking of me at a time like this? Hot tears spilled down my cheeks. I mopped at them, took a slow breath, then returned to the phone. "I'll sleep on this, and talk to Grandma, see how she feels. You don't have to go to school tomorrow. Just have Maggie call in. She can talk to Sue."

"Th-that's what Maggie said, too."

"Thank you for calling, sweetheart. I sure needed to know this. I'll call first thing in the morning, okay? If you get restless tomorrow, you might walk down to Bud and Betty's."

"D-do you think they'd want to see me?" he asked, his voice a whisper.

"You'd brighten their day."

"I-I don't know," he said doubtfully. "S-seeing me might make them miss Jay more."

"It might, but I don't think they could miss him any more than they do right now. They have a huge hole in their family. You loved Jay; you were his best friend, and you hung at their house a lot. You're part of them." I thought for a moment and added, "His sister could use a visit, too."

Over the phone line, I could hear his feet shuffle as he thought about that.

"Y-yeah," he said, a little doubtfully, "I g-guess you're right."

"Thom? Ask Maggie to order a bouquet with a note from all of us and have it delivered to their home. Any special kind of flowers you'd like to send?"

"Y-you pick, Mom. Or Aunt Maggie can. I'll walk down to school and talk to Sue tomorrow," he added. "Sh-she always knows what to say to me."

"Good idea," I said. God bless her warmth and compassion toward my son.

Owen and I ended up staying on the ship. Mom had so looked forward to this trip she'd planned, I couldn't disappoint her. But I felt shredded between making nice with the people on the cruise and my unceasing concern for Thom. Each day—greedy—I called him to hear his voice, so cracked open, so alive. And each day, when we stopped for field trips, I gathered bouquets of wildflowers in remembrance of Jason and left them near ancient pictographs carved in the rocks above the Columbia River. I offered prayers for him, his family, and my son.

After we flew home, I set my luggage on the floor of a too-quiet house, and found a note from Maggie—she and Thom had gone to the grocery store. Owen picked up my suitcase and headed toward the bedroom. "Hon, you go on and see Betty," he said, over his shoulder. I called her.

"Betty, it's Skye. Would it be all right if I came to visit?"

"Sure. We're not up to much. I can hardly gather my energy to cook. Not that I need to; people stuffed our freezer with food." She sighed. "Come on down now, if you want. That'd be real nice."

Instead of driving, I trudged the same back roads the boys used to take. Near Jay's house, I paused and ran my hands along the picket fence by the gravel alleyway, imagined how they had pitched rocks into the empty lot, shared private thoughts in this quiet place. My throat thickened. It dawned on me that Jay would never get to heft the weight of the rod when they finally pulled it out of Thom's leg. So many shared moments, missed. The fresh weight of Jay's death pressed down.

Betty must have been watching for me, because she opened the door before I knocked. I took my usual seat in the kitchen. The generous scent of cut flowers filled the room.

"Thom stopped by. I'm awfully glad he did. I can't imagine this house without him clunking around, laughing his crazy laugh." She teared up then, and grazed a finger against a pink star lily in the bouquet on the table. "Thanks for these," she said softly.

"I felt so bad we were out of town." I reached across to touch her hand. "Betty, I'm so sorry. I can hardly imagine life without Jay in it."

"I know," she said, blinking quickly. "Me either. He took so much of my energy. But he's at peace now—finally—and Karen needs my attention. She hasn't shown any grief yet." Betty rested her head in her hands for a moment before looking up again. "I'm real worried about her. Not one tear. She acts like nothing happened."

I wanted to wrap my arms around Betty, but didn't dare. Our friendship didn't extend that far, and it wasn't my right to crack her open, as hugs often do. "That's her defense. In *her* time, the grief will come."

"I hope so; sure don't want her doing anything stupid."

"What kind of stupid are you worried about?"

"Acting out. Trying to get attention from boys. Getting pregnant, you know...." She trailed off.

No matter what stupid action Thom might take, he couldn't get pregnant. What a relief.

"She's dressing so racy these days; won't listen to me," Betty went on. "Gets on Bud's nerves real bad. We're kind of a mess around here."

"Of course you are. You have to expect that."

"Say, one thing happened at the wake that you need to hear from me."

"What's that?"

"Bud raised a toast with Jay's peppermint schnapps, and we let Thom have a swig or two."

Inwardly, I cringed. Damn. All I could think of was how Thom had sucked away on the whiskey nipple as an infant.

"Jay had his own bottle of schnapps? You must have known he wasn't going to make it to twenty-one."

"I knew. Anyway, it was the only adult thing he wanted. He was close enough; twenty. We didn't let him keep it in his room." She cradled her arms around herself, then glanced up at me, her brow knitted. "He died in my arms."

I nodded slowly. "Thom told me. I guess if a son has to die, that's the proper place." I could imagine only too easily what that must have been like—the nightmarish disbelief, the powerlessness.

A long silence. Tears flooded her eyes. "We didn't even call 911. I couldn't stand the thought of them shocking him with those paddles. Why resuscitate him so he could go through it all over again?" She wiped her hand slowly across her eyes, a weary gesture.

"I wouldn't have made him suffer either, Betty. Enough is enough."

"Send Thom around from time to time, you hear?" Her voice broke.

"I'll do that," I promised, even though I knew it was not a promise I should make. Thom would button up these memories and store them securely in a private heart place. Probably he would have trouble returning here.

I could see Betty knew this too. We looked steadily at each other. I took a last long inhale of the fragrant star lily, and slipped out the way I had slipped in, through Jason's back door.

## Open Sesame—September, 1991

On a September morning before taking Thom to school, I stirred oatmeal and marveled that he was clomping around our house again, like the days before leg surgery. The sound that used to aggravate me was now comforting. He no longer shouted from his room like he had during the body-cast days; now he came to find me in the kitchen before opening a conversation.

We greeted each other with smiles.

"Ready to go?" I asked.

His grin broadened as he handed me a piece of paper. "Here, s-sign, please."

"What's up?" I glanced at the paper. A permission sheet for Driver's Ed class. "Oh my God," I said—a poor opener for the conversation to come.

He looked down at me, his eyes charged with an electric desire I had not seen since his karate days. "I-I want to take this class, Mom. It-it's just a class; they d-don't put us behind the steering wheel."

"Well...." Doubt clouded my tone; my mind leaped forward into the rat's nest of difficult questions: What about a car? Adapting a car? Lessons? Insurance for disabled kids? Sleepless nights?

"J-jeez." His voice was filled with angst and irritability. His left leg gave way, and he smacked his hand to the wall for balance, then leaned against it for support. "I-I can barely walk; I can't even ride a bike. I-I thought you would be happy if I learned how to drive."

"You're right." I huffed a loud sigh. "Okay. I worry, that's all."

"Y-yeah, you're a mom. That's your job."

"We have to take this one step at a time." I chewed my cheek as I thought. "There are tons of questions."

"W-w-will you just sign? This class teaches us about safety, for God's sake."

I let him fidget for a couple of minutes while I read the sheet carefully. He was right. It spoke only about safety. I reached for a pen and signed at the bottom.

"T-thanks." He grabbed the form, and headed back down the hall before I could change my mind.

A couple of minutes later, he reappeared, backpack slung over his right shoulder.

"Let's go." The words floated down the hall behind him. I glanced at the clock. Unbelievable. Ready, ten minutes early.

After I delivered Thom to school, I called Owen at work. "We need to talk in private," I said. "Want to have lunch together at East West?"

"What's up?"

"Driver's ed."

"Driver's what?" Pause. "Oh my God."

"My words exactly, and they didn't go over well."

We agreed over lunch at the café that Thom needed to have a chance to develop this level of independence. Our agreement did not come without reservations and a plan of action. Yes, he could take the class. If he did well, we would consider driving lessons. I wanted these lessons to be provided by a professional company with instructors who could assess his peripheral vision, reflexes, overall ability to focus on the road and all the additional distractions: traffic lights, other automobiles, pedestrians, and children playing nearby.

Owen said, "I don't think either the Caravan or the CRX is appropriate for him to drive—the Caravan is too large, and the Honda's a stick shift. He needs a compact, automatic sedan."

"Yes, and it'll need adapting, as well."

"In that case, when the time comes, we'll sell my CRX."

I stared at him.

"Why are you surprised?"

I couldn't formulate a response immediately. Owen had told me when we first met the CRX was his dream car—the first car he purchased just because he loved to drive it. Not a practical decision, he said, but an important one. "Usually I'm too darn practical," he added.

Finally, I croaked, "You would do that?" Owen was such a generous person that he'd paid off my debts before we got married, but this—his CRX.

"Yes."

"Thanks." I reached across the table and took his hand. That he would give up his car for a surly teenage stepson flooded me with gratitude.

"Let's not tell him too much, too soon," Owen said. "I think we'd better dole this out, reward him as he proves he's doing his part."

I agreed. Thom had no idea how lucky he was. Finally, he had an older male in his life so different from Ray. I prayed one day my son would figure this out.

Thom not only got an A in his driver's education course, he developed the habit of correcting me when I drove.

"W-watch out for the wolf pack ahead," he said, one day on the freeway.

"Wolf pack?" I peered at the traffic, trying to figure out what he meant.

"Th-that clump of cars. Watch out! W-we saw videos on wolf packs in class. Th-they're real dangerous."

Thom succeeded on their detailed assessment. I asked them to test my reflexes as well, and my scores were not as high as his. He chortled. He took the written test for his learner's permit and passed that as well.

I sat him down at the kitchen table for a mother-son talk. "We appreciate that you take driving so seriously. Owen and I will find you a used car, and have it adapted. We'll pay for the insurance—you know how high it is for teenage boys." I shifted so I could look directly at him. "But this is a one-time deal. You have an accident that is deemed your fault, and you'll have to earn the money for insurance the next time. Trust me, it'd rocket up." This was standard-operating-procedure among the parents of teens that I knew. The kids had to earn the privilege back.

He chewed his lip. "F-fair enough. Hey, thanks."

I was pleased to see he was serious about the responsibility.

Owen sold the CRX. We purchased a late-model Toyota sedan, then adapted it with a knob on the steering wheel and turn signals rigged for Thom's right hand.

Formal driving lessons came next; we were relieved not to have the task of teaching him. I allowed him to ferry me around from time to time, but I was a difficult passenger. His inexperience behind the wheel terrified me. When I flattened against the seat with a pounding heart—and sweaty palms—it made Thom jumpy. I blessed my poor dad! I knew now what he had endured teaching three kids to drive.

Finally Thom's teacher said, "He's ready to take his test. He's solid." She sounded well-pleased. "Equal to any student I've taught. He doesn't fool around."

Better not, I thought. I was proud of his accomplishment, but I caught myself musing that people might assume an accident was his fault because of his physical disabilities.

When he returned home from the examination, Thom's grin could have lit that moonless night on my vision quest. With a flourish, he handed me his test. I stared at it. One hundred percent, higher than my first score at his age. "Great job!" I beamed back at him. I was happy for his accomplishment, but cold prickles swept down my body. I can't keep him safe any longer, I thought. "Want a root beer float to celebrate?" I asked, as I headed toward the refrigerator.

## Winds of Change—December, 1991

This particular New Year's Eve held more significance—Owen had lost his job, and we had to decide where to resettle. The cost of living needed to be more manageable than the Bay Area.

He and I had a tradition of nestling at home for a quiet closure to the year. This year Maggie joined in, as did my wise-advisor friend, Susan. We cast the Tarot, Runes, the I Ching, or drew angel cards to sense the flavor of the year to come.

Thom appreciated the idea of getting to leave Analy High, but the reality of moving out of California hadn't sunk in yet—not enough to persuade him to join anything that smacked of a family meeting. He grabbed his Stephen King book and headed for his bedroom.

"C-call me if it gets interesting," he said.

Owen and I wanted a climate with more rain, but on the West Coast because of its open spaces and forward thinking. Maggie had never taken to California, so she was cheered by the idea of leaving. The Bay Area had been my home for twenty-two years—the idea of leaving Susan and other dear friends was daunting, but resettling at age forty-five seemed a far better plan than waiting until we were even older. California's cost of living was rising fast, and so was the population—by our retirement age, Sebastopol would no longer be affordable.

I spread maps on the floor: Northern California, Oregon, and Washington.

"We need a large enough population to support my new drafting business," I said, "and Thom's special services. Hospital, good cardiologist—maybe a brace-maker. And I'd like the intellectual atmosphere of a university." I stretched out on the floor to ease my back. This might be a long night. Susan curled in a chair.

"I like that," Maggie said. "A university changes the tone of a community. The town has to be big enough for me to find work as a therapist."

Owen nodded. "And some kind of engineering work for me. So a town at least the size of Santa Rosa seems right." He ran his finger out of California and on to Oregon. "I wonder about Eugene," he said. He flipped the map over to check the population. "With the addition of

Springfield—smaller, but looks like it's just across the river—the two have a population larger than Santa Rosa. And the University of Oregon is there."

Over the next couple of hours we discussed and ruled out the larger environs, Seattle and Portland, and decided Owen and I would visit Eugene. I invited Thom to check out the map, showing him Eugene's location. He shrugged, but brightened when he realized he would be with only his aunt and the beasties while we were gone. Maggie would let him chauffeur her around. When we returned, she could go for a similar visit to get a sense of the town. We were feeling more upbeat about the future.

Susan had grown quiet. I felt her staring at me.

"This is really going to happen," she said. "That's a sobering thought."

We hugged. It felt grave. Nothing definite had been decided, yet the separation had already begun.

We left on our exploratory trip to Eugene on the last day of January. What a relief to get out of the flat inversion layer of the Central Valley and climb into the foothills north of Redding. As we approached the high plateau to the Oregon border, seven full rainbows—one after the other and two of them double—welcomed us, led us along their rainbow bridges. With such good omens, we were willing to embrace this new possibility.

Tired after the drive, we entered Eugene at the top of a long hill, and paused so I could photograph a deep orange and fuchsia sunset. Another great omen. The prospect of a new place could mean a fresh start for Thom, for the whole family. I could hardly wait for morning.

# Chapter Thirteen

### Flattened—October, 1992

A hundred-year-old oak towers over the plot for our manufactured home. A huge branch hangs too low to clear the roof, and we have to saw it off before our new home can be delivered. The leaves are flecked with autumn hues.

Owen and I peer up at the branch's foot-wide girth, noting how it divides into two long, sweeping parts. "Chain saw?" I ask.

"String saw," he says. "We need to stay on the ground. Too dangerous on a ladder."

We set to work. "Pull!" Owen yells. I strain on my end of the long flexible wire.

"Pull!" I call in return. The string saw crunches through the hardwood as, sweat pouring, we find a satisfying rhythm. After being apart for nine months, it is a delicious relief to be laboring next to my husband again. Owen roomed with Maggie in Eugene for a few months, then in May moved twenty miles southeast to this rural environmental community in Dexter, Oregon. Thom and I arrived ten days ago after finally selling our old house. Thom is off working elsewhere on the property, probably weeding in the large communal vegetable gardens. Eighteen now, he has freedom here—his own one-room cabin and ninety acres.

The saw chews steadily. The branch cracks sooner than I expect. Adrenalin pumping, I run, trip on a ridge of dirt—dirt I shoved there with the tractor the day before. I barely see the raw branch end before it strikes, a battering ram against my ribs.

Slammed to the ground, I scream, "I'm hit!" But the words come out barely louder than a whisper. Each breath is agonizing.

Owen's aching question arcs across the plot. "Skye? Where are you?" Then he races to me, his arms, carefully, oh so gently, slide under my head. The clear autumn sun shines into my eyes, and leaf patterns dance high up in the sky. I smell the pungent, fresh dirt and feel rocks poke up under me. I look at the ragged butt of the branch at rest near my head. We are both broken. The tree will survive. Will I?

Owen's brows pull together; he looks so worried. Softly he asks, "Do we need help?"

"Yes," I whisper. I know I am torn inside.

"Can I leave you?"

I feel him coiling to run for help. "No!" I beg. "Don't leave."

"I'm going to shout." His strong male cry, "Help!" unmistakable in its urgency, sirens on the air. His hands, so dear to me, have so many jobs to do—block the bright rays, cradle my body, offer solace and strength. I have a sudden rush of fear for my son. I grab Owen's arm. "Am I going to die?"

"No," he strokes my forehead. "No way."

Dianne appears; she crouches near me. She is calm and balanced in any situation. "Are you all right? Can you walk?"

"No." Breath is so hard to find. My voice a faint thread, I struggle to tell her how it is inside. I ache all the way through my body, a penetrating, punishing hurt where there should be none. "Bleeding, inside. I need medical help." Life is an edge I cling to with breath. I reach for that next cruel inhalation.

More people from Lost Valley come at a run. They seem so tall as I stare up at them. I see their confusion. They don't know what to do. I shift my body against the agony inside. One woman asks all the important questions. "Can you wiggle your toes and fingers?"

I try. "Yes."

"Pupils are equal and reactive. I don't see any exterior bleeding. Does your spine hurt?"

I take my awareness inside. My rib cage feels shattered and rearranged, my insides torn, and I am freezing cold. "Shocky," I whisper. "Spine seems okay."

The need for teamwork gathers the people together. Yes, there is a stretcher on the property.

"Get the van."

"Quicker to take her in to emergency than wait for an ambulance."

"You two, go get the cot and blanket."

So smoothly they communicate with one another. No disagreements, no dissension, it feels like a safety net, and relief floods through me. The stretcher appears. Owen keeps touching me, loving me; he strokes my hair, holds his hat to shield the bright afternoon sun from my eyes.

Where is Thom? He could be anywhere. I don't want him to see me like this; I'm supposed to be the strong one. His struggle is hard enough, and now he's pushing away, trying to separate. I fight the desire to close my eyes, slip away from the aching stabs. If I let myself go, I may not find my way back.

Four people make a web of their hands, a trust lift, and transfer me gently to the canvas, tuck a blanket around. Nausea pulses through me. The light shafts through the trees, the tender rocking of the stretcher, the voices of my rescuers, these are my companions. They talk themselves to the back door of the van. I flush hot, cold, and hot again as they slide me in—how slowly each moment passes as I seek breath.

"I'll drive." Owen's voice is firm. "Dianne, will you ride with Skye in the back?" I want Owen with me, but he is such a steady, safe driver. Dianne crawls in next to me. If I am to die, thank God I won't die alone.

The smallest motions—gravel on the driveway, gentle pressure on the brakes and accelerator—send excruciating waves through my body. Tears start. No—weeping ignites the pain. Dianne holds my hand; uncontrolled shivering amps my nausea. I keep my focus on breathing to quiet my belly. Finally I feel the change from smooth freeway to stop-and-start town driving. They discuss the clearest approach to the

Sacred Heart emergency room. I ponder death and life—the margin is much subtler than I ever knew.

The hatch opens. Time shifts.

Unfamiliar voices, then new hands placed me on a gurney, wheeled me through doors, down a hall, through dizzying lights, confusion. A curtain rippled closed between me and another gurney.

"I-I-I still need a mom." Thom's deep teenage voice cracked in that way that embarrassed him. "Are you going to die?"

I rolled my head an inch at a time toward the voice, dismayed to see my son standing a little way off from my gurney. My sister, too. Why did she bring him? Thom limped closer. The dark quarter-moons under his eyes mirrored the terror I heard in his tone. The mother in me tried to ease his fear.

"No, Thom, I'm not going to die." I wasn't sure this was the truth, but saying it might help make it so.

A surgeon arrived. The nurse showed him the urine bag filled with my blood, and my belly clamped down with fear. The surgeon's eyebrows bounced up.

I struggled to focus my gaze on him, not on the scary bag. "Do a good job," I said. "I still have a lot of work to do."

The doctor took in Thom's gimpy body—how his left shoulder dragged down, his spastic arm—then he turned to me. "I'll do my best," he said. "You were using a string saw? We docs call them 'widow-makers.' You were lucky to get here alive."

Thom flinched. His face blanched. His Adam's apple bobbled up and down. My heart contracted in empathy.

The gurney shot through long, gray tunnels to the CAT scan. I felt dizzy and sick as the ceiling swept by. An orderly calmly supported my head while my lunch, five hours old, came up. The act of throwing up with severe internal injuries was agonizing. It terrified me too. Would it make the bleeding worse? I had to live. I could not leave my son without a mother. He wasn't launched yet.

The scan itself: the hollow surround, thunderous metal clangs. Then the words, "It's her spleen—she'll bleed out. Surgery, stat!"

They really do say "stat," I thought. The doctors were in charge now. I closed my eyes and allowed myself to drift away.

Shivering. Reaching for consciousness, too hard. Fuzzy, fat tongue, tastes of metal. An unrelenting, penetrating ache weighs down my belly. Each breath sends a sharp spear through my left side.

"Skye?"

Finally, Owen. Tears have to serve as words; I struggle to break through the dense layer of anesthetic fog.

"We need the nurse. Hang on," he says.

"Don't go!" My words make no sound.

"Something's wrong—check her. Please."

Who is Owen speaking to?

The cuff squeezes my arm. Again. Then again. A woman's voice, "I can't get a read. Her pressure's too low. I'll call her surgeon." Sounds fade.

I forced my eyes open. A small, deep-red bag hung above my bed. Blood. Nourishment. I found the strength to shift my head, and looked around. How strange, not the recovery room anymore. Where did it go? Light poured through the window of a small, triangular hospital room. Morning? I must have survived.

Owen rose and came to my side. He rested his hand on my forehead, a calming, cool touch. "Welcome back, love," he said.

The surgeon walked in, and Owen made room. "Close call," he said. "Broken ribs, battered kidney, torn spleen. Most people die from spleen injuries. You were very, very lucky." He lifted the dressings. "Looks good. I'll stop in later. Is the blood helping?" I nodded. He smiled, waved, and left.

Owen returned to my side. "Where's Thom? Is he okay?" My voice, a dry croak, sounded like a teenage boy's.

Owen watched deep red drops as they left the bag and slid down the line toward my arm. He smoothed my hair. "Eighteen, but he's not fully cooked yet, is he?" Smile lines crinkled around his eyes. "Dianne took him home last night. Poor kid, he looked like he could use a transfusion, too. But the tables are turned—now you need his strength."

I feared my son didn't have enough strength to give anyone else. Not yet. Maybe he could donate blood. I was pretty sure I was going to need it.

Concerns about how we would move our belongings from California, the placement of the manufactured home, fell away. My priorities clarified, simplified. I faced only one task—healing.

## Aborted Flight—November, 1992

I rested in a lawn chair, enjoying the sun on my face—a last warm day in mid-November.

"M-Mom? Oh, you're still sitting here." Thom's voice stayed in its mature register.

I laughed, then winced and held my ribs. "Not used to having a tortoise for a mom, are you?"

He shifted from one foot to the other. "I-I want to drive to Eugene. The weather's perfect. O-okay?" His eyes were bright, alive, excited.

A treacherous stretch of two-lane road connected our rural home to Eugene—a hilly, winding, eighteen-mile drive.

"How come today?" I was stalling for time. I had not wanted this moment to ever come.

"G-garden work slacked off. I want to check out the university."

I released my breath. Might as well. I had to let him go sometime. "Well, okay," I said, hesitant. "Be back before dark."

"Sure! Th-thanks!" His wide smile as I handed him the keys held such joy.

For the first time in his life, autonomy—his own one-room cabin, now a trip alone behind the wheel. I did not have the wherewithal to argue or refuse—I had returned home after three weeks recuperating at my sister's apartment, and was still on heavy narcotics. I had to creep everywhere I went, stopping along the way to breathe. He caught me in an exhausted moment.

All afternoon, I couldn't settle down. Our new phone line wasn't installed, so Thom couldn't call. My body, sensitized from surgery and anesthesia, was uneasy in that mother-way that kept me padding slowly from one room to another. I repeatedly glanced at the clock, wondering where Thom was, what he was doing. Finally, I gave up trying to focus on any task, and sat outside again in the thin autumnal sunshine.

Later, at dinner, even the scent of lasagna revolted me. As dusk fell, my disquiet erupted. "Where is he?"

Owen's look told me I sounded as fretful as I felt. "He'll be back. He lost track of time, that's all."

At 6:30 p.m. a community member knocked on our door. "We got a call at the kitchen in the lodge from the Eugene police. Thom's all right," he said, "but he's been in a car accident." My skin crackled and I grabbed for air. Deep breaths still hurt, so I hugged myself to give the incision—and my broken ribs—support. My heart thudded against my breast bone, rang in my ears.

"Did he hit another car? What about the other people?" I asked.

"Everyone is okay, just shaken up," he said. "Your car is not drivable; someone needs to go to town. The police are on the scene and, apparently, Thom's real upset."

My hands quivered so hard I shoved them deep in my jean pockets. Questions jammed my mind. Thom didn't have an Oregon license yet; his was still from California. Would the police take it away? Would he be deemed unfit to drive because of his disabilities? Would there be a huge lawsuit?

"I'll go," Owen said.

"I want to go, too," The words tumbled from my mouth. "I have to go."

"Are you sure?" he asked. "Sitting in the car all that way?"

"I need to. I can doze."

He slipped his arm around me. I knew he could feel me shaking. "Okay," he said softly. "Okay, we'll go together."

I couldn't sleep on that interminable ride, but reclined so my incision did not bear the weight of sitting up. I had a good view of the full moon as it rose, blazing huge in the night sky. I obsessed—I'd heard the stories of emergency rooms filled with traumas—why had I let him drive on a full-moon night, of all times? Please, I prayed, let the other people be truly unharmed. Please let the police treat Thom with dignity. What if he mouthed off, and they smacked him up against their cruiser, or berated him, or talked down to him?

When we finally arrived at the scene near the university, I was horrified how smashed up the car was—the whole front end, accordioned. Totaled. The other car, a sturdy Jeep, had a fair amount of rear-end damage. Thom sat on the curb, shrunken and shaking, bawling. I eased down onto the curb next to him, let my knee touch his.

"Are you all right?" I asked. He nodded, trying to calm himself without success.

"Rear-end accidents are common," I said. "This might have happened to anyone."

"Y-y-yeah, but stupid me, it happened to me," he said. "J-just when I got my freedom, I screwed it up." His sobs intensified. I sat quietly, resting my hand on his arm. After a few minutes, his sobs eased into shudders. I asked him how he had been treated.

"F-f-fine," he said. "Ev-everyone's been kind; the cops have been great, even the people from the other car."

"Good." I patted his arm—to soothe him or me, I wasn't sure. "Can you describe the accident?"

"I-I-I started the car up after I had something to eat—realized how dark it had gotten—and I guess 'cause it was cold out, the w-window all of a sudden fogged up." He put his forehead in his hands. "I-I-I couldn't find the defroster knob. C-couldn't see out the windshield at all. The light must have turned red. Then I sm-sm-smashed into them." His tears started again, silent, shoulders rocking. He dashed them away with his good hand. His eyes had gone flat; they sucked light now. No more radiating glow like they had when he took the keys from my hand. The flickering street lamps turned his skin sallow, almost green. His cheeks looked hollowed and sunken, as though he had dropped fifteen pounds in one devastating afternoon.

I desperately wished I could rewind this section of life, reel it back in and mete it out differently, in smaller, more manageable portions.

I wished I'd been strong enough to bear the brunt of his displeasure and say, "No way, not such a long drive, not on a full-moon day, not in an unfamiliar town."

On the drive home, and for many months to come, he relived each traumatic moment with me again and again. "Wh-what should I-I have done differently?" he asked.

"Somehow we overlooked discussing the windshield fogging up," I said. "Your driving teacher missed that, too. I guess it would have been best to warm up the car and put the defroster on before starting to drive. But that's twenty-twenty hindsight."

We talked about each step, how he might have problem-solved. He posed fresh driving nightmare-scenarios, and asked how I would handle them. I didn't always have answers.

After the accident, he was as tense a passenger as I had been when he was learning to drive. At even a touch of the brakes he would stop breathing and white-knuckle the dashboard.

Then one day, he caught a ride to town, arrived home with a bus schedule, and set about learning how to decode it. I grieved as he taught himself about the public transportation system—sorrowed for his loss of autonomy. But I never let on, and Thom didn't mention the idea of driving again. I could have fought for him, pushed him to regain his courage, and stretch again for freedom. I didn't have the guts. On a heart level, I was convinced if he went free, the boogeyman world would gobble him up and spit him out. I couldn't bear it.

## Educational Surprise—June, 1994

One early evening, I stood in the large communal kitchen in the lodge stirring a huge wok of sautéed vegetables, helping to prepare dinner—tonight for twenty. Dianne was sitting at a table at the far end of the room, near the internal mailboxes, sorting through her mail.

Thom clumped in and said hello to Dianne. He rustled in his mailbox, and pulled out a small newspaper article. He glanced at it, then did a double take and read it more carefully. When he looked up, he waved the paper in the air. "A-anyone know who p-put this in my mailbox?"

"What is it?" I asked.

"I-i-it's about a new high school starting up in Eugene this September." He squinted at the paper again. "R-r-read this! They're expanding the W-W-Waldorf school. It sounds really cool."

Curious, I wiped my hands on my apron and walked over to him. He passed me the torn piece of newspaper. When I glanced up, his eyes were bright and alive.

"Th-th-this's where I want to finish high school," he said. "W-we've got to check into it. M-maybe Grandma can help."

"After the Excel program, I don't know if I'd have the nerve to ask her again. Even though it was a great success, it did cost a bundle."

"Y-yeah, but you know Grandma," he said, grinning. "F-for education, sh-she'll go for it."

In September, Thom started his Waldorf schooling.

"What's it like?" I queried.

"I-I really like the math. F-f-for once in my life, I-I'm just one of the r-r-regular guys. W-we're all treated with respect. My class is tiny—six. S-some of the kids are cool." He paused. "W-we do this weird movement stuff called 'Eurythmics.'" He stumbled on the word. "N-no, that's not it. 'Eurythmy,' that's the name. They b-built a whole room with a special, super smooth hardwood floor for it. N-n-no shoes are allowed. Th-they even got *me* to participate."

For the next nine months, Owen or I drove my son the twenty miles each way to school. Thom delighted in the new friendships he was making. We bought a home in central Eugene, and Thom moved in with Ray—who had relocated—to finish his final year. They lived only two miles from his school.

Thom got the role of the joker in the school's theater production of *A Curate Shakespeare As You Like It*. To see my son—who had hidden behind massive hair and deep frowns during his teenage years—hamming it up on stage, filled me with a fresh, hopeful joy.

# Chapter Fourteen

### Puzzle Pieces—April, 1995

I tapped my foot as I waited for the fax machine to spit out a personal recommendation for Vassar's Time-out grant application. Dr. Liebermann's letter—from a professional who knew me back when—could make a big difference. If I were awarded this $20,000 grant, I could take a year off and write, twelve months to dive as deeply as I needed into feelings and memories, to finally grapple with those painful decades of my life so I could move on. I grabbed the letter, smoothed the Thermofax paper, and scanned his opening paragraph.

"I first met Skye shortly after the delivery of her son, who was born with Tetralogy of Fallot, and subsequently sustained a stroke that left him further disabled."

"What!" My word came out as a bark and a scream. Owen materialized by my side. I poked repeatedly at the paper. "Liebermann says Thom had a stroke as an infant!"

"What?" His surprise echoed mine. "Let me see."

I thrust the paper toward him, and dropped into my desk chair. A chill settled in my bones. My world as a parent had often seemed like a puzzle made of pieces that did not fit into any coherent pattern. Now those pieces snapped into place.

At five weeks old, right after they imprisoned Thom like a lab animal in the plastic tube with his arms above his head for the chest X-ray, he had gone directly into his first heart catheterization. The cardiologist threaded the tube through a vein in his thigh all the way up into the chambers of his heart. It must have knocked a fleck of material loose, and because of the defect between the lower chambers of his heart, it was able to travel directly to his brain instead of being filtered out by the lungs.

My God, a stroke. Thom *did* have a stroke—while bound to a cold metal table, no mother in sight, and when he was wide awake and in pain. It had occurred on September 12, 1974. I knew it—knew it in my heart, my cells, in my corpuscles.

He had come home from that hospital stay a different child—impossibly irritable. Instead of a cheerful baby blinking at the bright morning light, he shocked awake as though demons had converged upon him. He'd screamed and fought his baths when, just twelve days before, he had splashed and cooed in the water. He must have experienced his movement and freedom torn away in an instant, in this "cerebral accident" that hyper-sensitized the left side of his body. He hadn't been an unusually sober baby; after the devastating changes of the stroke he had suffered infant depression, for heaven's sake. A common stroke side effect. I had mistakenly thought his distress was from the overall hospital stay—being so sick, being handled by strangers.

I stared at Owen, my hand clamped at my throat. "How could I have been so blind?" I whispered. I didn't know what to do with my anguish. "How could I have bought the story that my child had cerebral palsy from birth?" I shook my head. This visible disability—this measure the world uses so readily to pass judgment on him—was not a fluke of nature, but happened at the hands of a doctor: a doctor whose goal was to help him, but who instead caused irreparable physical and emotional damage.

"Call Liebermann," Owen said. "Call him—right now. You need answers."

I picked up the telephone. My hands were quivering, but I still remembered the phone number I had called for help hundreds of times two decades before.

"Yes. We were quite sure he suffered a stroke." Dr. Liebermann sounded surprised by my question. "Certainly either I, or the cardiologist, talked with you about this."

"Never," I said. "You never said a word. Not once. That I would remember."

"I'm sure it's in his records," he said.

We quickly reached an impasse. At the end of the conversation, I smacked the receiver down, shortcutting the last syllable of his "goodbye."

That night, Owen and I talked for a long time. When he fell asleep, I lay awake far into the night, tossing, smushing my pillow into ever more unsatisfying shapes. I could not quiet my mind. I chewed for hours on the idea of suing the doctors, but by the time I fell into a pre-dawn sleep, I knew I could not sustain the energy for litigation. Either way, Thom's treatment would have been the same. Brain injury is brain injury. Intentional or not, there had been an error of omission—it didn't seem like grounds for suing. Thom might well take his lead from me; I had to look for the highest good. Blame could only harm us both.

But with an undeniable inner trembling—fear for what I would learn, and desire to know every facet of the details—I hungered for the facts. The next day, I placed calls to request all of my son's medical records. I had not done this before; it had never occurred to me his records might reflect new information. If I had been told about the stroke, it would have been noted in his chart. I needed to know if I had been in denial—a dispirited, exhausted mother, struggling to understand a morass of unfamiliar medical verbiage—or if these doctors had violated my trust.

The many physicians' offices—pediatrician, cardiologist, orthopedist, and the hospitals where his surgeries were performed—were reluctant to fulfill my request. Thom's cardiology file alone was almost two inches thick. But I insisted; having his records was my right. Even if they were filled with advanced medical terminology, I had to decipher the truth from them. I sent each office the required written requests with money in advance for the copy expenses. But I knew before I ever received them—and painstakingly read every familiar, disheartening word of his medical history—I would not find what Dr. Liebermann had said he was sure was there.

What I found was different information: a description of myself as an "over-involved, over-anxious mother." Stroke: never mentioned. Double sucker-punch.

Perhaps, if the catheterization had not been performed, Thom would have had a luckier fate. Twenty-twenty hindsight can only stir up "what-ifs." I suspect the heart specialist didn't tell me because he was afraid of a lawsuit. He probably rationalized he was protecting me for my own good. I wonder if Dr. Liebermann stood with the cardiologist in collegial solidarity. Today, the medical literature tells me, with the technology now available, and because of the risk of stroke, they operate on this particular heart defect immediately after birth, avoiding the threat of stroke by closing the hole between the ventricles.

Next, I had to break the news to Thom and Ray. I dreaded a confrontation, but they had rights as well. I called them and set up a date for the weekend. They arrived together on Saturday morning.

"Wh-what's going on?" Thom asked.

"I have some … news," I said. The how-tos and what-ifs ran circles inside my head and heart. Sharing this information was important for all of us, but it must not devolve into focusing blame. Thom needed to figure out his own response to this revelation. Then, perhaps, the healing that truth can bring could take root—for all of us, but most of all, for Thom. He bears the lasting burdens.

I took them into a secluded room, asked them to sit on the floor with me, and lit a candle which I put in the center of our little circle. Our friend Elena joined us. When I read Dr. Liebermann's letter out loud, my voice shook a bit at the start. I could sense rage roiling up in Ray. He would condemn the doctors. My glance commanded him to stay quiet. Then I read on in a steady voice.

For an agonizing amount of time—minutes—Thom stared at the candle without saying anything. Finally he spoke. "Th-this doesn't change anything," he said, "and it changes absolutely everything."

"Right," I said, with a long sigh. "It's subtle, and it does change everything, for all of us. It changes your whole life story." He chewed on his lip, and nodded. Nothing else needed saying.

One fact remains: I was not told the truth. Because of this experience, I am a different woman with doctors today. I do not accept what they say at face value. I ask difficult and embarrassing questions. Doctors work for me.

The next morning, Thom showed up on our doorstep with scissors and handed them to me. "I want you to cut my hair," he said. His mass of thick, wiry ringlets came below his shoulders and his bangs usually hung over his face as well.

Startled, I stared at him. We were in for change, all right. "I'm not the one for this task," I said, surprised by my own boundary-setting. Thom was blasting into a new phase, and at his age, his mother shouldn't be the one to push the button. I had the faith—in this moment—my refusal would not block his way. I have learned a lot about my faith over the decades. Like breath, like the tides, it flushes and recedes and rolls in again. I can trust that in its own time, it will return.

Taken aback, he eyed me. "H-haven't you always wanted me to cut it?" he asked.

"It's true, I don't like it covering your handsome face," I said. But I loved his thick dark waves, the texture so springy, it could hold its own in any fray. His hair had been his teenage rebellion, an obvious way to stand out beyond his physical disabilities. I had allowed him that, never insisted he cut it. It had seemed a safe way to rebel. "You sure you want to? Where will you hide?"

"S-such a mom," he retorted, and took the scissors back.

Next I knew, he was sitting backward on a chair in our dining room, a magenta towel snugged around his neck. Elena wielded the scissors. She glanced up, gave me a knowing smile, and winked. Owen looked on too, his arm draped over my shoulder. He most likely sensed I needed a touch of comfort during this abrupt change.

"Where do I start, Thom?" Elena asked.

"H-here, under here, where it won't show," he said, lifting the heavy curls from the nape of his neck.

"Do you want a mirror so you can watch?" she asked.

He pressed his eyes shut. "No way. T-too scary. Just don't cut me! I-I can't bear the sight of blood."

Elective surgery, I thought. Bloodless. And for once, Thom was in charge. Hallelujah!

"I'll be careful," she said. The scissors gnawed through the wiry hair until the points met and snapped. The first long ringlet dropped. Three heads dipped toward the floor, three sets of eyeballs peered at the lock. But not Thom's. I held my breath, gauging his reaction. He kept his eyes closed. Tears sat suspended on the rims of my eyes. He was surer of himself now; he could let the hair go.

"Keep going?" Elena asked.

Thom nodded.

I turned to Owen, amazed Thom had not one moment's hesitation. Owen's eyebrows reflected his own surprise.

"Now where?" Elena asked.

"Here." Thom held up his long bangs. I took a breath. He really meant to go through with this. He was crossing a new threshold, stepping into his own life. Late, but in his own perfect timing.

"You're sure?" She tilted her head uncertainly.

"G-go for it," he said. "One-half inch everywhere except right here—" he grabbed one hank at the back of his head. "I-I want a tail."

Lock after lock dropped to the floor. The pile grew as he shed his past. With each snip he seemed to come forward, out of the cave of protection his hair had provided the last four years.

"Now, try those electric clippers," he said. A soft buzzing began. Finally Elena stopped. He dusted his head forward and backward with his hand, then surveyed the large, fluffy mound of hair on the floor.

"S-save it, Mom—for the birds. I w-want them to weave it into their nests next spring."

His hair—a symbol of those awful teenage years—and he wanted it to soften nests and warm baby birds. Wonderful.

He lifted his face up. "Now. The mirror."

I handed it to him, and he peered at himself. I was not sure what he saw, but I saw a boy revealed now as a man. In that moment, I felt my age. His bright smile, the glow in his eyes, transformed me. My throat ached for the future obstacles that would inevitably challenge my son, and again and again call upon his courage and my faith.

My throat ached, and my heart lifted—for him, and for me, and for Owen—irrevocably bound together by grit, by gratitude, and by love.

# Epilogue—2015

A year ago, Hawk and I reconnected over lunch. We mused about our history and the decades since. I am struck by what a steady husband and good father he is. At the time we came together in 1979, we were unclear about what we wanted and who we were. Perhaps the most important gift we gave each other—through the challenges and disintegration of our marriage—was to answer those questions. He also provided valuable feedback about our time together that enlarged my perspective.

Thom struggles daily with severe chronic pain. Fifteen years ago, the medical establishment labeled it fibromyalgia; now it's identified as central pain syndrome. He also suffers constant spasms, mainly in his left arm. His bone-on-bone left shoulder jerks with every spasm, adding acute, local pain. Because the stroke left that side of his body weakened, he is not a candidate for a shoulder replacement. UCSF refused to operate on the shoulder at all—they sent him home and told him to live with it. We found an orthopedic surgeon in Sonoma County who specializes in shoulders. He performed arthroscopic surgery on Thom's shoulder in December, and removed tooth-sized bone fragments from the joint. This has reduced his acute orthopedic pain about 75 percent.

A new medical subspecialty is taking form—Adult Congenital Cardiology. In 2001, the need was identified, but the subspecialty wasn't created until late 2012. This specialty is so very new, there is not yet a countrywide standard of care—although it is coming soon. The first certification examination will be held on October 20, 2015.

A significant number of children who underwent heart surgeries such as Thom's are suffering complications in mid-life—some life-threatening—that require surgical intervention. It is imperative that these adults, who are the first generation born with these heart defects to survive—due to the invention of those ground-breaking surgeries—be followed properly by doctors trained in this new sub-specialty.

Although it turns out that Thom's heart is functioning well, we discovered the broad range of how cardiologists approach his follow-up care. Specialists who are supposedly adult congenital cardiologists at one well-respected institution on the West Coast thought Thom could be overseen every two years with only an electrocardiogram. They accepted his chest x-ray from a different cardiologist taken the year before. The doctor spent a mere ten minutes examining him.

At the University of California, San Francisco, where Thom is a patient now, he receives an extensive echocardiogram in addition to an electrocardiogram and chest x-ray every year. The cardiologist queries him carefully as well. When Thom finally admitted to having irregular heartbeats, they sent him home with a monitor to wear for a week to make sure the irregularities were benign.

If you, or someone you know, underwent surgery as an infant or young child for a heart defect, it is important to be examined regularly by a certified adult congenital cardiologist, or a team committed to certification in the near future.

Please spread the word. You could save a life.

## About the Author

Skye Blaine writes short essays, memoir, fiction, and poetry, developing themes of aging, coming of age, disability, and most of all, the process of unlearning—the heart of the matter. In 2003, she received an MFA in Creative Writing from Antioch University. This memoir, now titled *Bound to Love*, won first prize in the Pacific Northwest Writers Association literary contest in 2005.

She has had personal essays published in five anthologies, and in national magazines: "In Context" (now known as "Yes!" magazine) and "Catalyst." Other personal essays have been published in the "Register-Guard" newspaper, and the "Eugene Weekly." Skye also presented radio essays on KRML 1410 AM in Carmel, CA.

Her first novel, *Call Her Home*, is due out in 2016.

She can be reached at skye@skyeblaine.com, and welcomes comments.

Thank you for taking time to read *Bound to Love*. If you enjoyed it, please consider telling your friends and posting a short review on Amazon and/or Goodreads. Word-of-mouth referrals are an author's best friend, and I appreciate them deeply.

## Colophon

This book is set in Minion Pro, 12 point.

Minion is a serif typeface designed by Robert Slimbach in 1990 for Adobe Systems and inspired by late Renaissance-era type.

…

As the name suggests, it is particularly intended as a font for body text in a classical style, neutral and practical while also slightly condensed to save space. Slimbach described the design as having "a simplified structure and moderate proportions." (Wikipedia)

www.ingramcontent.com/pod-product-compliance
Lightning Source LLC
Chambersburg PA
CBHW050629300426
44112CB00012B/1725